To Henry

A man who shares my passion for WWII history.

[signature]

キング

A Tomb Called Iwo Jima

Firsthand Accounts from
Japanese Survivors

Dan King

A Tomb Called Iwo Jima

Copyright © 2014 by Dan King.

First Published July 21, 2014 by Pacific Press

All rights reserved. With the exception of quoting brief passages for the purposes of review, no part of this publication may be reproduced without prior written authorization of the author. The information in this book is true and complete to the best of our knowledge.

To contact the author, or order signed copies please visit www.historicalconsulting.com

Or write to: Dan King
                P.O. Box 14872
                Irvine, Ca. 92623

ISBN-13: 978-1500343385
ISBN-10: 1500343382

Edited by Linda Ryan
Cover Design by Alexander Mukai Jr.
Illustrations and Photo layout by Rusty Shackleford
Promotional Video by Jocelyne Leger, narrated by Roger Wyatt
Japanese calligraphy by Satoru Ogawa
Back cover photos by author and Adam Surrey
Poem on back cover by Saburō Kojima. He penned it in 1944, a year prior to his kamikaze mission to Iwo Jima. It reads, "*If I become a shield for the Emperor, I will have no regrets even should I become a rotting corpse lying in a field or floating on the sea.*"

Proudly printed in the United States of America
CreateSpace
North Charleston, SC

Dedication

To Bradd Smith, a man who shares my passion for Pacific War history.

To the late Virginia King, the person from whom I obtained my sense of humor, curious nature, and respect for other people and cultures.

To my wonderful daughter Cindy, whose high-voltage smile can light up the darkest night. Always remember, "*ai rabyutte.*"

I never met a man I didn't like.
—Will Rogers

Acknowledgments

Special thanks to:

Nobuhiro Nakamura – A Japanese naval historian who has been generous with his time, energy and support.

MGySgt John "Oni Gunso" Edwards (USMC-ret) and LtCol Gary Meyers (USMC-ret) - For valuable advice, editing support and technical review.

I acknowledge the following for their assistance with information and photographs:

- Teruko Abe
- James Atwater
- Steve Baer
- David Coleman
- James Crawford (Col., US Army)
- Ray Elliot
- Scott Freund (SFR Productions)
- Bonnie Haynes
- Bruce Hirt
- Sachio Kageyama
- Diane Kuebler
- Christopher Marks
- Harue Masuda
- Takashi Matsuda
- Jim McGee
- Tom McLeod
- James C. McNaughton, PhD
- Yoko Nagasaka-Myers
- Ron "00 Witch" Nichols
- Dale Quillen
- Sheila Quinlan
- Junko Sakashita
- Yukie Sasa
- Katsuhiko Shirakata
- Shoko Seina Shiraishi
- LtGen Lawrence Snowden
- Tom Stanton
- Mark Steinhauer
- Mark Stevens
- Kōji Takaki
- Hiroshi Ujita
- The late Jirō Yoshida
- Bill Zieman

Legend Flyers:
Bob Hammer, Mike Anderson, Ben Johnson, Nick Cirelli, Paul Ferrara, Jon Anderson, and Chris Stuart.

Military Historical Tours:
Col. Warren Wiedhahn (USMC-ret), LtCol. John Powell (US Army-ret), and Anne Swenson. (www.miltours.com)

Dan King

The following people's contributions are greatly appreciated:
Martin T. Bennett, Spencer Chen, Phil Corless, Bob Dupre, John Eckhardt, John Edwards, Tony Evans, Cindy Good, Vicki Hawkins, Jareth Holub, Wilson Horde, William Jayne, Dustin King, Michael Kinkaid (in memory of father Charles Kinkaid), Cindy King, Dr. Crystal Koerbles, Diane Kuebler, Doug Lister, Matt Marsala, Josh Martinez, Josh Melnychuk, Doug Meny, Masashi Nagadoi, Patrick "Padi" New, Ron Nichols (in memory of Major General E. M. Nichols Jr.), David Ojerholm, Vickie Prosser, Stirling Rasmussen, Ginger Crick Reeves, Jim Richard, Terry Ricks, Sydney Rodriguez, Mark Stevens, Bradd Smith, Michael Sweeney, Steve Tilley, Randy Van Dyken, Pete Winer.

Japanese and American combatants in alphabetical order:

Tsuruji Akikusa -
   Navy radioman, *Nanpō Shotō* Naval Air Group
Yoshinobu Hakuta -
   Captain, commander Independent 314th Infantry Battalion
Genichi Hattori -
   1st Lt, Executive Officer, Independent 10th Anti-Tank Battalion
Genji Hattori -
   Army Captain, Genichi Hattori's younger brother
Rinosuke Ichimaru -
   Rear Admiral, commander of 27th Naval Air Flotilla
Shūji Ishii -
   Corporal, Army medic, 2nd Mixed Brigade Field Hospital
Shoji Kageyama -
   Seaman 1/C, Navy radioman, Akikusa's friend
Shōichi Kawai
   Sergeant, Army Radioman, Independent Mixed 17th Infantry Regiment Communications Unit
Saburō Kojima -
   Chief Petty Officer, Navy Kamikaze, 601st Naval Air Group
Yasuo Kumakura -
   Seaman 1/C, Navy radioman, Akikusa's friend

A Tomb Called Iwo Jima

Tadamichi Kuribayashi -
   General, commander of 109th Division
John McKenzie -
   Boatswain's Mate 3/c, USS *Darke,* USN
Edward Mervich -
   Corporal, US Army 147th Regimental Combat Team
Haruji Mita -
   Seaman 1/c, aircraft maintenance, 301st Naval Air Group
Tadashi Mita -
   Akikusa's childhood friend
Isamu Miyazaki -
   Warrant Officer, Zero pilot with the 252nd Naval Air Group
Yasuhiko Murai -
   1st Lieutenant, Independent 314th Infantry Battalion
Masayoshi Nemoto -
   Ensign, navigator, plane captain of a Betty bomber, K704th Squadron
Shinjirō Nishi -
   Corporal, Army maintenance, 23rd Sentai Army Air Group
Takeichi Nishi -
   LtCol, 26th Tank Regimental commander, Olympic medalist "Baron Nishi"
Satoru Ōmagari -
   Lieutenant (jg), Navy aircraft maintenance, *Nanpō Shotō* Naval Air Group
Ivan Prall -
   Sgt, US Army combat correspondent, Seventh Air Force
Saburō Sakai -
   Chief Petty Officer, Zero pilot, Yokosuka Naval Air Group
Sadasue Senda -
   MajGen, commander of the Army's 2nd Mixed Brigade
James Short -
   Lieutenant, platoon commander, 5th Tank Battalion, USMC
Lawrence Snowden -
   Captain, company commander, F/2/23 USMC
Kinpei Teraoka -
   Vice Admiral, commander of the Third Air Fleet

Minoru Tada -
   Ensign, Navy anti-aircraft battery commander in *Keibitai* unit

Kazuo Tsunoda -
   Chief Petty Officer, Zero pilot, 252nd Naval Air Group

Tsunezō Wachi -
   Navy Commander, head of the Iwo Jima *Keibitai* land defense unit

Hershel "Woody" Williams -
   Corporal, USMC, Flamethrower operator, 1st Battalion, 21st Regiment, Third Marine Division, Medal of Honor recipient

Iwao Yamada -
   PO1/C, Navy radioman aboard a Betty bomber, K704th Squadron

Jerry Yellin -
   Captain, US Army P-51 pilot, 78th Fighter Squadron, 21st Fighter Group

Haruo Yoshino -
   Ensign, plane captain of Type-97 torpedo bomber, submarine patrols

A Tomb Called Iwo Jima

Author's Comments:

While much has been written on the battle of Iwo Jima from the American perspective, there has been very little published in English to share what the Japanese veterans experienced. I believe this is largely due to three factors: the complex nature of the Japanese written language; the high cost of traveling to Japan to interview WWII veterans; and the general reluctance of former POWs to speak about their experiences.

The battle of Iwo Jima continues to inspire generations of Americans, and has sent hundreds of thousands of young men and women to Marine Corps enlistment centers. While the battle of Iwo Jima was primarily a Marine Corps battle, the US Navy, US Army, Coast Guard, and Seabees all contributed to the effort and deserve recognition.

This book is a compilation of my interviews with Japanese survivors of the battle, and the family members of those who died during the battle or since. I promised to tell their stories with no political correctness or modern day revisionism. I added historical references and context to help illustrate their extraordinary eyewitness accounts.

I interviewed the following eight Japanese veterans and examined their photographs, flight logs and correspondence from WWII:

1. Tsuruji Akikusa, Petty Officer 2/c, Radioman, Navy *Nanpō Shotō Kōkūtai* (South Seas Naval Air Group)

2. Satoru Ōmagari, Lieutenant junior grade, Aircraft Maintenance, Navy *Nanpō Shotō Kōkūtai*

3. Shinjirō Nishi, Corporal, Army Aircraft Maintenance, 23rd Sentai, (Oscar fighter squadron)

4. Iwao Yamada, Petty Officer 1/c, Navy bomber radioman, K704th Squadron

5. Saburō Sakai, Warrant Officer (later Ensign), Zero pilot, Yokosuka Naval Air Group

6. Isamu Miyazaki, Warrant Officer (later Ensign), Zero pilot, 252nd Naval Air Group

7. Hikōji Nozaki, Airman 1/c, Navy bomber crewman, K704th Squadron

8. Haruo Yoshino, Warrant Officer (later Ensign), Type-97 Navy torpedo bomber navigator, Tateyama Naval Air Group

I read the following veterans' published Japanese-language memoirs:
9. Shūji Ishii, Sergeant, Army medic, 2nd Mixed Brigade Field Hospital
10. Haruji Mita, Seaman 1/c, aircraft maintenance, 301st Naval Air Group
11. Minoru Toda, Ensign, anti-aircraft battery commander, Navy *Keibitai*
12. Shōichi Kawai, Corporal, Army Independent Mixed 17th Infantry Regiment Communications Unit
13. Torao Miyazaki, Corporal, Army 312th Infantry Battalion

I spoke directly with the following veterans' relatives regarding their own memories as well as reading the correspondence that they received during the war:
14. Teruko Abe, widow of Corporal Tadashi Abe, Army Independent 20th Mortar Battalion.
15. Rosa Chikako Ogawa, daughter of Navy Captain Tsunezō Wachi, *Keibitai* commander.
16. Gentarō Hattori, nephew of Army 1st Lt Genichi Hattori, Independent 10th Anti-tank Battalion.
17. Harue Masuda, sister of Chief Petty Officer (later Ensign) Saburō Kojima, 601st Naval Air Group.
18. Yoshikazu Higuchi, son of PFC Mitsuru Higuchi, Army 2nd Mortar Battalion.

During my multiple visits to Iwo Jima I was honored to meet the late General Tadamichi Kuribayashi's son, the late Tarō Kuribayashi, and the General's grandson Yoshitaka Shindō, who is an elected official in Japan. In addition, I met the son of Baron Takeichi Nishi, Yasunori Nishi, who temporarily inherited his father's title of Baron until it was abolished by US occupation forces. Yasunori Nishi recently held the position of Chairman of the Iwo Jima Association of Japan. Yasunori Nishi shared with me an emotional experience he had when he first visited the LA Memorial Coliseum where his father earned his gold medal in the equestrian jumping event in the 1932 Olympics.

Since 2002, I have visited the island of Iwo Jima many times as a volunteer Japanese language interpreter for the Iwo Jima Association of America. Every time I set foot on the island I get goose bumps and a feeling of being watched

A Tomb Called Iwo Jima

by unseen eyes. It is with feelings of great reverence for the American and Japanese dead, and their bereaved families, that I have undertaken this eight-year project to document the Japanese side of the story.

I have done my best to tell their stories in a chronological manner that best follows the battle. If there are any errors or omissions they are mine. I welcome questions, suggestions or general comments.

Contents

Part 1: Navy Radioman Tsuruji Akikusa

Return to Iwo Jima	1
Ships on the Horizon	3
The Dream of Flight	7
War in China	11
You're in the Navy Now	13
Communications Training	20

Part 2: Preparing Iwo Jima for War

Iwo Jima and the Spy	24
Ensign Minoru Tada	27
The Gods of War	31
Akikusa's False Start	35
Corporal Abe Marries His Future Widow	40
The Medic	44
Hattori's Letters from Iwo Jima	46
Akikusa Runs the Gauntlet	50
The Bunker	58
Working Underground	63
Ensign Satoru Ōmagari	67
More Letters from Iwo Jima	73
A House Divided	74
Care Packages and the Rocket Men	78
Corporal Nishi and the Oscars	80
The Attack on Saipan	88
Bad News	90
Kuribayashi's Oath of Combat	95
The Last Flight Out	100
Prelude to Invasion	106

Maps & Illustrations
Photos

Part 3: Invasion

The Americans Arrive	112
The Marines are Landing	116

The Kamikaze	123
The Flag	124
The Return of the Bettys	125
Akikusa and the Tank	129
Underwater Kamikaze	130
Akikusa Wounded	130
The Imperial Mum	136
Even the Dead are Called to Fight	145
Kuribayashi's Farewell Message	148
The Olympian	150
The Doctor's Dilemma	157
The Final Days	157
The Seabees	160

Part 4: The Holdouts

The Field Hospital Surrenders	162
The Naval Construction Battalion Bunker	163
The *Nanpō* Bunker	165
Surprise in the Tunnel	168
The Great Escape	171
Scrounging for Food	174
Calls to Surrender	177
Captured	181
100 Bullets	181
Saved by a Dog	183
The Anguish of Surrender	184
Life in the USA	188
Homeward Bound and Beyond	197

Epilogue	206
Appendix	
I: Casualties	207
II: Records from the 147th Infantry, US Army	208
III: Mopping Up	212
IV: Surrender Leaflet	214
V: Japanese Military Ranks	214
About the Author	216
End Notes	218

A TOMB CALLED IWO JIMA

PART 1
Navy Radioman Tsuruji Akikusa

Return to Iwo Jima

The calendar read Wednesday, September 10, 2008. A small passenger jet circled the volcanic summit of a little island located in the Ogasawara Island chain. There was a special passenger on board, a bespectacled 81-year-old Japanese man who had spent ten months living on, or more accurately living *inside* the island. From the moment the American jet took off from US Naval Air Facility Atsugi in Japan, Tsuruji Akikusa's heart was flooded with painful memories. The WWII naval radioman sat silent for the duration of the three-hour flight. The island is an active Japanese Maritime Self Defense Force (JMSDF) military installation and not a tourist attraction. However, Akikusa was no tourist; "The Japanese Navy sent me the first time, but it was the US Army that brought me back, and I am forever grateful for this opportunity to come back," he said.

The trip began with an idea from the US Army's Public Affairs Officer in Japan, Major (later Colonel) James Crawford III, who first learned about Akikusa from Takashi Matsuda, one of the Japanese civilian employees at the base. For years, Akikusa wanted to return to Iwo Jima to make peace with the past. For personal reasons, he chose not to join any veteran associations. As a result, despite being one of the few surviving veterans of the battle, he was not permitted to participate in the annual pilgrimage.[1] Major Crawford was determined to help Mr. Akikusa get back to Iwo Jima. Akikusa's dream became a reality thanks to political juice from a patriotic member of the Japanese Diet, and the energetic support of US Army Brigadier General Francis Wiercinski.

Akikusa, Major Crawford, Mr. Matsuda and a small contingent of US Army personnel and civilian cameraman flew on General Francis Wiercinski's jet to Iwo Jima. As the plane approached the island, the pilot banked so the passengers could get a better look. Akikusa pressed his face against the window as the plane soared over Mount Suribachi and the black sand invasion beaches.

The jet landed on the paved runway that lies on top of the WWII-era Motoyama Airfield. The engines whined down to reveal a reverent silence that flooded the cabin. The door slowly opened to reveal a sun-drenched airfield with paved roads, buildings, hangars, a fire station, and a traffic control tower bearing the name Iwo Jima in both English and Japanese script.* Although Akikusa recognized the familiar odor of sulfur, gone were the smells of gunpowder and the ghastly stench of rotting corpses. A heavy sigh rushed from his lips as he stepped down onto the tarmac. The vast tunnel system he lived in during the battle was directly beneath his feet. Despite ongoing recovery efforts by the Japanese Government, thousands of soldiers and sailors are sealed in caves and tunnels across the island.

Although once the center of activity for tens of thousands of men, the island is quiet except for JMSDF supply flights and visits by US Navy fighters from Atsugi that use the runway for landing practice. In addition to several hundred JMSDF personnel, the island is home to friendly feral cats, turkeys of unknown origin, songbirds, East African land snails, scorpions and centipedes.

Akikusa's group traveled in a minivan to Rear-Admiral Rinosuke Ichimaru's HQ bunker. They entered the tunnel and were guided to the Admiral's living quarters, which still contained his wooden chair and a steel bed frame. The underground bunker still had smashed furniture and shelves, empty sake and beer bottles, blue enameled metal dishes marked with anchors, gas masks, canteens and various rusted detritus covered in a layer of dust.

They then drove to the top of Mount Suribachi where Akikusa paid his respects by saying a prayer and placing an American and Japanese flag pin at the base of the Marine Corps monument. Akikusa walked to the edge of the volcano to peer down at the invasion beaches and said of the US Marines, "They were very brave men."

"Old Glory" no longer flies on Mount Suribachi, instead, there is a Japanese flag. Near the Japanese flag is a pole with fish-shaped streamers called *koi nobori* that flutter softly atop the dormant volcano. These windsocks are flown to commemorate "Boys Day" (*Tango no Sekku* or *Kodomo no Hi*). For centuries, Japanese parents have flown these koi fish streamers in hopes that their sons would grow up resilient and strong. There is a black fish flag to represent the father, and a red fish banner to represent the mother. Below

---

* On June 18, 2007, the Japanese Government changed the name from Iwo Jima to the pre-war pronunciation of "Iō Tō" (Ee-oh-toh). The English on the control tower was repainted to "Iwo To" sometime after Akikusa's 2008 visit.

these two fish are normally smaller blue or green fish that represent the son(s). However, on Iwo Jima, only the parent carp streamers fly to signify that their sons are gone. This flagpole acknowledges the broken hearts of 20,000 sets of parents whose prayers for a safe return went unanswered.

After leaving the summit of Mount Suribachi, the group drove down to the black sand beaches where so many Americans paid the ultimate sacrifice. Akikusa walked to the water's edge and explained what he had seen the day that the Marines landed.

Returning to the airfield, Akikusa was immersed in a surreal fog as the van passed dozens of stone markers engraved with the names of Japanese units that were sealed below. The markers more accurately could be described as tombstones. In fact, the entire island could be called a tomb.

Akikusa searched for an entrance to Captain Samaji Inoue's *Nanpō Shotō* Naval Air Group command bunker, but so much had changed since 1945. With the help of one of the JMSDF officers stationed on the island, Akikusa found the northern entrance to the bunker that was overgrown with thorn bushes and not visible from the road. Akikusa looked back over his shoulder to get his bearings, choked back thick tears and said, "This is it. Kumakura killed himself down in there." Akikusa pressed his hands together and softly chanted a Buddhist prayer to deliver an overdue message to his friend's soul.

Major James Crawford and the Japanese officer stomped their way down through the thorny undergrowth to create a path for Akikusa. As they neared the cave entrance Major Crawford exclaimed, "Holy cow, it's hot down there." Without pausing, Akikusa asked, "It hooks left, doesn't it?" Major Crawford peered in and confirmed that it did. Akikusa walked past him into the dark tunnel, alone.

A floodgate opened to reveal suppressed memories that transported Akikusa back in time. He was the only one on the island who could still hear the echoes of gunfire, explosions, and piercing screams from a battle that ended over a half-century ago.

Ships on the Horizon

The calendar read Wednesday, January 24, 1945. Just before dawn, radioman Tsuruji Akikusa pressed his eye against a narrow three-foot long hollow tube that ran through to the outside wall of his concrete bunker. The small opening was originally one of several passageways for communication wires, but pre-invasion shelling had stripped them away. The hollowed out wire passages made excellent observation ports because they enabled the Japanese to safely monitor the invasion beaches below Tamana-yama.* Inside the dark bunker, Akikusa scratched at his pesky head lice and peered though the small observation hole out into the bright sunlight. His uniform was home to vermin, and reeked with the pungent odor that comes from living like an animal. Baths were a distant memory as water was too precious to waste on hygiene.

There were similar observation posts at other sites across the island: Mount. Suribachi; the Funami-dai Command Center at the northern tip of Chidori Airfield (Motoyama Airfield No. 1); and Nidan-Iwa (Hill 382 or Radar Hill). Akikusa's spot was perhaps one of the best seats in the house, offering an unobstructed vista of the entire southern half of the island.

A few weeks prior, the island's supreme commander, Lieutenant General Tadamichi Kuribayashi, had distributed mimeographed copies of his handwritten oath that read, "We must kill ten of the enemy before giving up our own lives."† Akikusa wasn't sure how he was going to fulfill the first part of Kuribayashi's command since he was never issued a weapon, but it was only a matter of time before the enemy handled the second part.

Akikusa pressed his face against the opening of the observation tube; the brisk ocean air felt good against his sweaty face. He could see the waves in the pre-dawn haze hitting the beaches functioning as a luminescent signpost for the enemy on where to land. However, there was no doubt as to where the Americans would attempt to breach the island's defenses. As the darkness slowly retreated, he fixed his eyes on the constellation of US invasion ships carpeting the dark surface of the water. Akikusa noted the numbers and types of ships that revealed themselves. The seemingly endless armada stretched far out over the horizon. The only sound was the morning breeze whispering into the observation tube. A shiver ran down Akikusa's spine, an involuntary convulsion that brought cooling relief from the heat of the crowded tunnel. Akikusa had a box seat right above the long black sandy beach on which a

---

* The locals named this area "Tamana-yama" for the large Momotamana trees (*Terminalia catappa*) that once flourished on the island.

† 我等は敵十人を倒さざれば死すとも死せず。(Original Japanese)

tsunami of US Marines would soon come rolling. He peered intently through the small opening and wondered, *What are they waiting for?*

His friend Yasuo Kumakura sat down next to him, his presence noted by a telltale grunt and stale tobacco-breath. While maintaining his gaze at the ships, Akikusa asked, "Hey Kuma, you know what today is?" Without waiting for a reply from Kumakura, Akikusa said, "It's January 24th, our 179th day here."

Kumakura snorted, "Why keep track? We aren't ever going home." The distant peak of Mount Suribachi was gently bathed in the soft glow of the rising sun.

"Keep your chin up, we'll make it home someday," Akikusa's reassuring words were more for himself than for Kumakura.

The Americans routinely pounded the tiny island from the air and sea for months, and had stepped up their efforts in the past few weeks. *Why don't they get it over with?* That morning, Akikusa craned his neck to get a better view of the enemy ships. As he counted, his outlook took on a grayer hue that matched the color of the ships offshore. *There are a lot more of them today.*

Staring through his over sized peephole, Akikusa was startled by a dark orange flash from the sea. On its heels was a thunderclap rumbling over the beach and terraces; it was mixed with a Doppler scream and a boom. The shell slammed silently into the rocky soil near the airfield. At a distance, the sights and sounds of battle didn't match up like in the movies. The impact launched a dirty column of sand, rocks and razor-sharp iron hundreds of feet into the air. The explosion sent an invisible shockwave of concussive air against the peephole. A cloud of brownish-black smoke shrouded the ship that fired the opening shot. Several other cruisers joined in to create a booming cacophony.[*] The impacts tossed truckloads of dirt into the air like a cat tearing feathers off a bird. For the next several hours the ground beneath, around, and above the Japanese defenders trembled as the shelling continued. The caves and tunnels were buttoned up tight with rocks and sandbags, yet the pungent odor of gunpowder steadily seeped in through the ventilation shafts.

Rocks and boulders showered down only to be heaved up into the sky again. The thundering sound reminded Akikusa of a summer typhoon back

---

[*] USN Task Group 94.9, the heavy cruisers *USS Chester* (CA-27), *Pensacola* (CA-24) and *Salt Lake City* (CA-25), and nine destroyers.

home when his family would gather inside and listen to the storm. He wondered how his parents would react when they received the telegram that no parent every wants to get.

The US sailors and marines on the ships must have cheered as Iwo Jima disappeared beneath the smoky barrage that methodically swept the southern part of the island. Even though the US Navy impressed itself by hurling useless debris high into the sky, the maelstrom engulfing the island had little affect on the defenders. And despite months of bombing, the Japanese fortifications were growing in number. The following is from a WWII US intelligence report.

"Aerial photos taken during early 1945 revealed that the number of field fortifications, pillboxes, and covered artillery positions increased despite air bombardment… A study of these changes resulted in a sharp upward revision in estimate of enemy strength on Iwo…. Photographic coverage of Iwo Jima on 24 January 1945, indicates that damage to installations resulting from bombing strikes between 3 December 1944, and 24 January 1945, was, on the whole, negligible. These strikes have apparently not prevented the enemy from improving his defensive position and, as of 24 January 1945, his installations of all categories had notably increased in number. The island is now far more heavily defended by gun positions and field fortifications than it was on 15 October 1944, when initial heavy bombing strikes were initiated."[2]

At noon, the shelling stopped but resumed after what Akikusa assumed was a lunch break for the US blue jackets, leading him to ponder, *Does the enemy observe banker's hours?* As the wind gradually cleared the smoke, the acrid odor of gunpowder continued to drift down into the caves and tunnels through the air vents. During the day's shelling and aerial bombing, the stoic defenders offered no rebuttal. There were strict orders to hold fire until the command was given; it would come in the form of the familiar "attack" bugle call.

As evening fell, the US ships stayed in their positions. The other radiomen around Akikusa talked about an enemy landing occurring under cover of darkness. "That's what we would do," said one sailor. There was tension in the caves. A petty officer tried to reassure his men, "The 'Blue Eyes' won't come tonight because of their inability to see in the dark."

The evening passed into night and there was still no sign of a landing. The ocean was eerily dark and silent. From the absence of light and sound, one could not imagine that there were hundreds of ships and tens of thousands of Americans so close to the island. The ships were under blackout conditions, but here and there a ghostly trace of light escaped one of the ships. It reminded Akikusa of the fireflies in the rice paddies back home.

His friend Shōji Kageyama leaned over and whispered, "We are supposed to hold out until our fleet arrives, right? Well, where are *our* ships?" The same question crossed the minds of the nearly 22,000 defenders that were burrowed deep inside the island.

The Dream of Flight

The author interviewed Tsuruji Akikusa in 2008, and then corresponded until they met again in 2012. During the 2012 trip to Japan, Akikusa invited Major Jim Crawford, Takashi Matsuda and the author to visit a Japanese traditional hot springs for the weekend. Following two days of luxurious soaking in piping hot baths and dining on sumptuous food wearing cotton *yukata* robes, Akikusa drove the group to his country home to see his old photos and WWII-era documents.

Akikusa's home was large with a nicely tailored Japanese-style garden. After removing their shoes in the foyer, the group was escorted into a room covered in *tatami* straw mats and took seats on the floor around a short-legged table. The Iwo Jima veteran served hot green tea and small confections to the guests who admired the various paintings and antiques that filled the room. In one corner was the family *Butsudan* Buddhist altar where Akikusa has prayed every morning and night for decades. He prays for the souls of his departed family, and for the spirits of his dead comrades that he left behind on Iwo Jima. Akikusa shared tales about his childhood, and of his father and famous uncles. Accompanying his stories came the old family photo albums.

Akikusa was the oldest child, born to humble farming parents Kōhei and Masu Akikusa who named him Tsuruji, which means "The Next Crane." The red-crowned Japanese Crane is a sacred bird, and is seen as the bearer of good fortune and long life in both Japan and China. Tsuruji Akikusa would become living proof of that ancient belief.

At the time of Akikusa's birth on January 7, 1927, the village of

Yabegawa (current day Ashikaga City in Tochigi Prefecture) was a speck of a berg, with 52 households and a population of 323 souls. It was named after the small river that ran through the village. Yabegawa had no automobiles or indoor plumbing, but did have electricity. The nearest telephone was at the Kameya family's *sake* store, and it was an open party line shared by others. Although Akikusa's home didn't have a telephone, it was one of only three households with a radio.

The village consisted of farms anchored around a modest Shintō shrine and a Buddhist temple situated on opposite ends of the little town. The religious centers were not in competition, but worked in harmony to attend to the needs of the residents who adhere to both the Shintō and Buddhist faiths, which is a uniquely Japanese situation. The Japanese are not a religiously zealous tribe; they don't proselytize nor do they attend weekly services. They won't argue over religion and hold no concern for what beliefs others hold; it is, after all, a private matter. One is married by a Shintō priest, and ushered into the afterlife by rhythmic mantras falling from the lips of a Buddhist priest. Japanese think there is no hypocrisy in placing both Shintō and Buddhist icons in their homes.

The aging veteran drove the author around the small farming town. The first stop was the town's Shintō shrine, *Sugahara Jinja*, home to the deity *Tenjinsama* that guards the village. It was here that Akikusa and his family would offer prayers for good fortune. At the entrance to the courtyard stand a pair of five-foot-tall granite monoliths, their edges rounded by over 100 years of wind and rain. One is engraved with the faded inscription, "Victory Commemorative Russo-Japan War;" while the other bears the barely legible names of a dozen men who gave their lives in the conflict. "My grandfather fought in that war," Akikusa said.

The quiet courtyard is solemnly guarded by a few ancient leafy nutmeg trees, which provide tranquil shade for infrequent visitors. The shrine also boasts an old gnarled plum tree that shares its fragrant pink cloud of blossoms with anyone who visits in the spring. Akikusa pointed to an empty corner of the property and explained that there once stood a grand cedar tree that burst high into the heavens; during the war it sported a rising sun flag. The tree is gone now, and so are the patriotic flags that adorned the shrines and homes across the land; they were quickly tucked away after the war.

Akikusa undoubtedly sees the shrine through the eyes of a fifteen-year-old boy about to enlist in the Navy, pleading to the deity for a safe return. In his mind he can still see the ancient cedar tree standing proud with the national flag flapping high above the throngs of well-wishers who gathered to say prayers for their sons, brothers and fathers that were going off to war. Akikusa looked up and sighed, "It's a shame they cut it down, it was a beautiful old tree."

Behind the shrine still stands the Kameya family *sake* store that has been in business for three generations. Akikusa remarked with a smile, "I would go on errands to buy *sake* for my father there. Sometimes I got candy, too."

After leaving the *Sugahara Jinja* shrine, Akikusa guided his guests to the Buddhist temple. It is of the *Shingonshū* sect, which pays homage to Japan's beloved Prince Shōtoku, one of the earliest members of the Imperial family. The temple's 400-square-yard courtyard was the perfect spot for young Akikusa and his friends to play sandlot baseball. The girls jumped rope, singing their chants in high-pitched voices that the boys tried to ignore. There was one girl who had caught Akikusa's eye, a button-nosed girl named Ayako. They were classmates through elementary school and middle school and held an unspoken innocent fondness for each other; stealing smiles and glances in class. The pair trekked side by side on the four-mile one-way journey to school. "Back then we walked to school rain or shine. It made us tough," Akikusa said as he led the way into the temple grounds.

Akikusa walked under a stone gate entrance and turned left to point out at a large flat heavy stone that seemed out of place. "See this? We used to play marbles on it," he said. He knelt down deftly as if he were a much younger man. "See these divots on top of the slab?" he asked. "We gouged them out by pounding on it like this," he said as he demonstrated by picking up a fist-sized rock and began hammering on the large stone. "We rolled marbles across the face of the stone and played different games," he said as he mimed the action. He was a nine-year-old boy once again.

There were rows of graves behind the temple, some of which had witnessed centuries of mourners. Akikusa said, "My parents and most of the Akikusa clan are buried here."[*] However, empty are the graves of his uncle

---

[*] The dead are not buried but are cremated in Japan. Family members share a plot with the cremated remains placed in ceramic urns in a chamber under the headstone.

Sergeant Hideo Aoki who died in Burma, his cousin Sergeant Yūzō Akikusa of the *Mitō* Regiment Combat Engineers who died in the Philippines, and his uncle Lieutenant General Shun Akikusa, head of the *Kantō* Army Intelligence Division who died in a Soviet gulag. Like tens of thousands of other soldiers and sailors, their remains were never recovered.

One large headstone stood out, a polished black granite memorial stone that bore the inscription "China Incident and Pacific War, Honorable Dead Memorial." Akikusa pointed to the fourteen names engraved on the face of the memorial, eight of which bore his surname. After the war, Tsuruji Akikusa took it upon himself to erect a proper memorial for the war dead that came from Yabegawa. He felt it was the least he could do for coming back alive. His withered finger gently rubbed each name as he read them aloud with reverence, "This was my cousin who died in China. This one died at Guadalcanal. And this one was a naval pilot, shot down a few days before the war ended." He knew them all. His finger rested on the name of an eighteen-year-old named Tadashi Mita, and he choked up for a moment. "We grew up together. He was my best friend in the world," he whispered. Then, as if speaking to himself, he glanced around and said, "We played right here in the courtyard as kids."

In different times, the temple's wide courtyard was the gathering place for the summer *Obon Matsuri* festival. During the month-long *Obon* season, the Japanese welcome home the spirits of their departed loved ones. It is a time to tend family graves, and offer prayers and food to the spirits at the household Buddhist altar.

There was a special night for ritualized folk dancing and merriment at the festival. Young Akikusa looked forward to this annual event. Everyone gathered, wearing their light summer *yukata* robes to dance around a platform where musicians performed. The people moved in a large circle dancing in unison to booming drums, shrill fifes, strumming *shamisen* (three string banjo) and a tinny bell. Each song had its own repetitive dance choreographed from generations past. Some dances were slow and dignified, others lively depicting farm life or ancient folklore. Everyone moved together as one to the cheery music under the paper lanterns fitted with electric lights.

To a youngster, *Obon Matsuri* meant bright happy music, special summer foods, soda pop, games and staying up late telling ghost stories.

Upon leaving the temple, the Iwo Jima veteran drove his guests a short distance to the 110-year-old house where he was born. The two-story clapboard wooden home is a weathered but sturdy structure with original hand-blown window glass marked with small imperfections. Akikusa said, "My grandfather built this house by hand. My father was born in the house, and so was I. Back then people were born in their own homes, you know." The house is set down a sixty-foot-long gravel driveway with an entrance marked by an eighteen-inch-high stone marker. To the left is a rustic horse stable with walls made of mud and straw. The simple barn has stood more than 110 years with only a few loose antique shingles to show its age. Hanging from the thick, hand-hewn rafters are woven straw pads and various relics of the farming days, now covered with rust and a heavy layer of dust. The stable has become a storage area cluttered with odd farm implements whose functions are now a mystery to the younger generation.

"We used to dry the rice harvest in this area," Akikusa said with a sweeping motion of his hand over an area of the yard overgrown with bushes and sapling trees. "My mother had a vegetable garden over there," he said as he pointed to another area. To the right of the stable is a long forgotten pigpen. It has a roof and old walls that are leaning askew. Akikusa pointed to another empty part of the property and added, "There was a big tree over there, and we had chickens over there."

After the war, Akikusa was unable to carry on the tradition of farming due to his injuries, so the house and farm went to his younger brother. "My little brother passed away, so his widow lives here alone," he said. The grandkids moved to the city, so the family's farming days are over. Upon walking back down the gravel path to leave Akikusa's birthplace, the author asked about the stone marker at the entrance, to which Akikusa replied, "Our horse died while I was in the service. Grandma loved it so much that she gave it a funeral and buried it." The weathered granite marker bears a simple, faint Japanese inscription, "Our Dear Horse."

After a healthy dose of reminiscing, Akikusa decided it was time to pay a visit to Yabegawa Elementary School where he had attended his own funeral back in January 1946.

War in China

In July 1937, Japanese newspapers heralded the "Marco Polo Bridge

Incident," a clash between Japanese and Chinese troops at Lugao Bridge south of Beijing. It would ignite the fuse on the smoldering powder keg in China. Ten-year-old Tsuruji Akikusa recalled the neighbors' jubilation at hearing the news. At school, the students proudly shared stories of relatives serving in the military.

On Sunday, August 15, 1937, while the Akikusa family was visiting the temple to offer their *obon* respects, the Japanese had undertook their first overseas bombing of the Chinese mainland. One of Akikusa's uncles, Petty Officer 2/c Yoshinori Aoki (later Ensign), was with the Kisarazu Naval Air Group, which was one of the units that carried out that attack. PO 2/c Aoki was in one of twenty Type-96 "Nell" bombers that left Omura Air Base (near Nagasaki) to bomb a pair of Chinese airfields outside the capital of Nanking. Japanese newspapers heralded the naval air crews as heroes.

However, Tsuruji Akikusa's enthusiasm towards the war was soon dampened when a recall notice arrived addressed to his forty-two-year-old father, Army Reserve Corporal Kōhei Akikusa. The family patriarch was to report for duty on September 10, 1937. The war, known as "The China Incident," was barely two months old when the Akikusa family gathered to share *sake* cups filled with water in a traditional parting toast called *mizu sakazuki*.* Young Akikusa bid a painful farewell to his father at the train station the next day.

When the author asked Akikusa how he felt seeing his father go off to war, Akikusa looked down at his folded hands and said nothing. A few years later, he and his father's roles would be reversed.

While his father was away in China, the young Akikusa promised to study hard and take care of his younger siblings. Akikusa's military indoctrination began in middle school. Each school day started with the students bowing to a portrait of Emperor Hirohito that hung in the classroom. "Army officers taught us military etiquette, the duties of a soldier, and devotion to the Emperor," said Akikusa. "We learned how to march with a rifle. We knew how to disassemble and clean it, too."

After what felt like an eternity, Akikusa's father returned from China on

---

* The custom mimicked the ancient *seppuku* custom of swallowing a bit of water before the deed.

February 10, 1939. He brought home a scrap album documenting the dates and locations of his service on the continent. There were photos of his war buddies and temples, dried pressed flowers, various foreign cigarette labels and other keepsakes, too. One photo showed Akikusa's father sitting at a desk, and behind him tacked to the wall were sheets of paper with *kanji* ideograms scrawled by a child's hand. "He displayed the letters we sent him," said Akikusa with a smile.

Although his father was now home, his father's brother, army Major Shun Akikusa was still in Manchuria. After Major Shun Akikusa graduated from *Rikugun Shikan Gakkō* (West Point Academy of Japan) he first served in the 1st Imperial Guard Regiment. The Army then sent him to Tōkyō Foreign Language College to study Russian before dispatching him as a spy to Harbin, Manchuria, which was a cosmopolitan, multi-cultural city with beautiful European-style brick buildings, factories, stores and foreign consulates.

Major Shun Akikusa's job in Harbin was to coordinate with the German Embassy to conduct espionage activities against Russia. In 1938, Major Shun Akikusa was deeply involved in the development of the Army's "Nakano Intelligence (spy) School" and became its first commandant. He was eventually promoted to Lieutenant General in 1943, and made chief of the entire army intelligence service in Manchuria with over a dozen branches.[3] This was akin to being named head of the Nazi Abwehr or the American Office of Strategic Services (OSS). When the war ended, LtGen Shun Akikusa surrendered to the Russians and is buried outside the Soviet gulag where he died in 1949.[*]

You're in the Navy Now

On Dec 8, 1941, radios across the Japanese Empire crackled with news of the surprise attack on Pearl Harbor. Radio announcers boasted that Japan would deliver all of Asia from the oppression of the West in what was termed the "Great East Asia Co-Prosperity Sphere" of Japanese influence. The Japanese were touting a new world order; the battle cry was "Asia for the Asians."

News of the attack on Hawaii was followed by reports of stunning victories

---

[*] A famous graduate of the Nakano Intelligence School was 2nd Lt Hirō Onoda, who held out in the Philippines until 1974. He later wrote the book My Thirty Year War.

at Manila, Sumatra and Singapore. Akikusa recalled, "It seemed like our forces were unstoppable." His airman uncle, Petty Officer 2/c Yoshinori Aoki, was now with the Takao Air Group in Taiwan. Hours after the Pearl Harbor attack, Mitsubishi G4M Type-1 "Betty" twin-engine bombers from Aoki's Takao Naval Air Group were among the hundreds of Japanese navy and army aircraft that attacked the Philippines. American aircraft under the command of General Douglas MacArthur's US Army Forces in the Far East were largely destroyed on the ground.

The Japanese Empire was caught up in a rose-colored victor's frenzy. Eager army and navy recruiters slapped up posters in cities, towns and villages across Japan. The Navy's snazzy recruiting posters depicted a dashing young *Yokaren* aviation cadet in flight gear. Akikusa admired the idealistic posters and told his chums, "As soon as I am old enough I'm going to be an airman like my uncle." Akikusa was the eldest son, so he was expected to inherit the farm and care of his parents in their old age. But he wanted adventure, he wanted to fly.

The Navy's *Yokaren* (Youth Aviation Course) provided the equivalent of a high school education while training young men, ages sixteen to twenty, to become pilots, radiomen, navigators, and aerial gunners. Most of Japan's naval pilots and aircrews were graduates of the *Yokaren* program.

In early February 1942, shortly before graduating from Yabegawa Middle School, Akikusa begged his father for permission to visit the Navy recruiter to take the first of two qualification exams for *Yokaren*. His father did his best to talk him out of it and warned, "Pilots have a short lifespan." His father was unable to squelch his dreams of flight; so young Akikusa secretly borrowed his father's ink-chop seal to forge the consent form.

Shortly after covertly taking the test, Akikusa received a card from Yokosuka Naval Base with instructions to report for a second round of testing to commence on February 23, 1942. Akikusa's father quickly figured out what his son had done, but was unable to get things straightened out in time. His son would have to show up or risk legal consequences from the Navy. Akikusa expected to pass the exams, graduate from middle school and be off to *Yokaren* to earn his wings in April 1942. He had it all figured out.

For this weeklong secondary battery of tests, Akikusa was excused from school to travel to Yokosuka Naval Base. On the fourth day of the *Yokaren* exams, Akikusa was called into the head flight instructor's office. Akikusa stood in the doorway and bowed a salute, he feared he was about to be sent home for an infraction of some kind. The instructor gestured for him to sit down to a dish of sweet bean cakes. After a brief, friendly chat, the youngster was excused without explanation.

Akikusa performed well on the tests so was confident that once the paperwork cleared, he would be given orders to report to the *Yokaren* campus at Tsuchiura Naval Base in neighboring Ibaraki prefecture.

A few weeks later, Tsuruji Akikusa graduated from Yabegawa National Middle School on March 30, 1942. A few of his classmates went off to further their education, but most started working full time as farmers, laborers, apprentices, etc. While he waited for the Navy to call him up, Akikusa decided to get a temporary job. It would look bad if an able-bodied young man wasn't working to contribute to the family. His friend, Tadashi Mita, worked at Nakajima Aircraft Company's Dōnryū Kōjō Aircraft Institute, and encouraged Akikusa to apply to the company's Youth Engineering School. He and Tadashi Mita rode their bicycles to the facility where Akikusa earned a small sum as he studied the rudiments of aircraft construction, world history, geography, mathematics, English, and general engineering. Japanese manufacturers such as Hitachi, Mitsubishi, Mitsui and others organized similar schools for students who would otherwise not be able to continue their formal education past middle school. It was also a form of three-year trade school for future employees.

Akikusa's days at the Nakajima Aircraft Institute ended prematurely that summer when an official letter from the Navy arrived in mid-August. He opened it front of his parents and was shocked to read, "Report to Yokosuka Navy Base Recruit Training Depot No. 2 on September 1, 1943." This meant that he wouldn't be going to flight school but serving as a regular sailor. He was confident that he had passed the *Yokaren* aviation entrance exams, so what had gone wrong? Akikusa's father revealed that the kindly officer who offered Akikusa sweet bean cakes in his office was an old family friend. Akikusa's father had pulled a few strings to sabotage his son's chances of getting into the *Yokaren* flight program.

However, Akikusa had inadvertently volunteered for the Navy by applying for the *Yokaren* Course *and then* selecting the communications course as a secondary choice. Akikusa was off to start a new life in the Navy, but it would not be in the "flying navy" as he had hoped.

At hearing the news, a neighbor remarked, "Be thankful, you aren't going into the flight program, the flyboys never come home." Perhaps so, but Akikusa secretly resented his father for dashing his dreams of flight.

As the date of his departure approached, the Akikusa clan gathered for a farewell party. They signed a Japanese flag (*yosegaki*) for him and conducted a farewell toast with water. This time it was the son who was going off to war. The following morning, neighbors and friends assembled to see him off. The fifteen-year-old wore his *yosegaki* signed flag tied over his shoulder like a sash. Carrying little paper flags, the group walked to the shrine to pray for a safe return. Representatives from the various patriotic societies within the village lined up to shake his hand. As the group sang military songs, Akikusa mounted the family horse that was festooned for the special occasion. A rousing three cheers from the crowd startled his steed, and caused Akikusa's chest to swell with pride. With his family in tow, Akikusa slowly rode out of the village like an ancient warrior. The elderly folks dropped back at the bridge over Yabegawa River and and waved their farewells. The rest continued to the train station where they gave him another round of cheers under a cloud of fluttering hand-held paper flags.

Akikusa dismounted, handed the reins back to his cousin and looked into the eyes of his mother. She wasn't smiling like the others; she was holding her little paper flag still. Akikusa said that as the train pulled away, "Images of my family's faces flashed through my mind like a revolving lantern."

Akikusa arrived for duty at the newly opened Yokosuka 2nd *Kaiheidan* Recruit Training Depot at Owada Bay, in Takeyama. The calendar read Tuesday, September 1, 1942. As a Seaman 4th Class Recruit, Akikusa was assigned to the 5th Squad (*han*) of the 26th Platoon (*buntai*) commanded by Lieutenant (jg) Kikuchi. All of the boys in his platoon were volunteers. Akikusa's serial number was "*Yoko Shi Sui* 49367" (横志水49367). *Yoko* stood for Yokosuka Navy Base, *Shi* meant volunteer, and *Sui* is short for seaman. His personal ID number was 49367. He was proud to write this information on the white labels that were sewn into all of his clothing and his Donald Duck–style cap. The flat cap came with a special tally that read "2nd Yokosuka Kaiheidan" embroidered in yellow thread. Once the sailors advanced to their various secondary specialization schools, they would get a new ribbon with the name of that school or base. They would get a third cap tally once they received their final posting to a base or ship. Each time they were transferred they would receive a new cap ribbon. Later that year, Akikusa's dream of collecting cap tallies was dashed when, as a cost reduction measure, the Navy announced a single-tally system that simply read, "Great Imperial Japanese Navy."

But the D.I.s were helpful and accommodating, almost like big brothers, as they instructed the recruits on how to properly wear their new uniforms. Akikusa recalled how difficult it was to adjust his *jonbera* shoulder flap.* That night he was filled with pride as he heard the bugle call "Taps" for the first time as a navy man.[4]

On the morning of his second day in the Navy, Akikusa was awakened by a bugle call, a shrill boatswain's whistle and the command, "All hands awake!" Even as the last few notes of Reveille were bouncing off the barracks walls, Akikusa and the other recruits were doing their best to quickly roll and stow their canvas hammocks above their open-ended wooden wall lockers. The recruits needed to get into the habit of rolling the hammocks tightly to reduce storage space aboard ship. Prior to battle, the tightly wrapped hammocks were hung outside ships' bridges to absorb shrapnel, and could also be cut free to serve as rafts in the event of a sinking.

Like a hungry wolf, one of the D.I.s slowly circled the ranks of nervous recruits while screaming at them to pack their hammocks faster. *What happened to the kindness from yesterday?* With an air of disgust the D.I.s inspected the teenager's fumbling efforts to stow their hammocks and settle their gear.

After the recruits were dressed and standing at attention, a D.I. examined each uniform as if it were a rare gemstone. The D.I. stopped behind one boy and shouted, "You! One step forward!" The recruit leapt out of line and came to attention like a dart hitting a board. The D.I. demanded to know why his cap tally was misaligned. The squad stood motionless as the man growled, "You are all soft and lazy. You need a good dose of military spirit." Another D.I. produced a longer version of a wooden police baton and said, "This is what

---

* *Jonbera*, the Japanese pronunciation of "John Bull," the nickname for British sailors. The Japanese patterned their navy after the British Royal Navy.

we call 'the club to instill military spirit.'"* Akikusa had never heard of such a thing. *What was he going to do with that club?* The man ordered the boys to spread their legs, bend over and raise their hands in the air. The club wielder lined up behind the initial cap tally offender and delivered a sharp punishing blow down on his buttocks. Akikusa heard a sickeningly dull 'whack' as the instructor beat each recruit, working his way towards Akikusa who was frozen with fear. *No one told me about this. Are they allowed to do this?* The answer was a hard blow to his backside causing pain to shoot up the base of his spine making him see stars. Blood rushed to his head creating a swelling sound in his ears that nearly drowned out the ranting of the petty officer's parade-deck level voice.

For the next two months it was bedlam as the D.I.s screamed, shouted, and rousted the recruits. The recruits' movements were controlled by the sound of boatswain's pipes, bugle calls, barked orders and roundhouse *ōfuku binta* slaps to the face. Walking was not allowed; all movement was done in squad formation at double-time. The basic training was designed to harden the boys and drive the milk of human kindness from their hearts.

Akikusa recalls always being hungry during boot camp, "They fed us low-grade brown rice, watery *miso* soup, small portions of fish, vegetables and pickled vegetables." Instructors were not stingy with roundhouse slaps or howdy-do greetings with a leather slipper (worn while in the barracks), punches in the face, or doses of the club. None dared to write home about the corporal punishment because their mail was censored by Lt (jg) Kikuchi. This ensured that cards and letters would contain nothing that would worry the recruits' parents. The boys' mothers might be fooled, but their fathers, uncles and grandfathers knew the score as most had already served in the military.

There was little time for self-pity because each 17-hour day was packed with classes, group calisthenics, rowing, group swimming in the bay, endless homework, and laundry. The teenagers studied naval history, military etiquette, warships, basic flag signals, and English. The recruits learned to shoot rifles

---

* *Gunjin Seishin Chūnyūbō* was not a standardized club, but could be seen in various lengths and widths. The club usually had the inscription either written or carved into it. The important aspect was that it was a hard wooden bat-like object used to inflict maximum pain and humiliation with minimum physical injury. Every Japanese Navy veteran has his own story to tell about this wooden instrument.

and pistols, and practiced the martial arts of *Jūdō* or *Kendō*. There was even a martial art developed for honing bayonet-fighting skills called *Juken-jitsu*.

The D.I.s were creative in their methods of punishing the teenage boys whose only pleasures were their sparse meals. One morning, a Drill Instructor burst into the barracks, bellowing for the recruits to re-pack their hammocks. "This is sloppy work! Wrap those ropes tighter this time, and do it faster!" The action was repeated several times, with the boys handing their large canvas cocoons to each other in bucket-brigade fashion until they dripped with sweat. They unwrapped and re-slung them, climbed in, and started the process again. After meeting the D.I.'s approval the man told them, "Too bad you tykes fooled around so much with your racks, now we don't have time for breakfast." The recruits' eyes welled up with tears of frustration as the Drill Instructor rubbed salt into their emotional wounds by shouting, "Stow that! Sailors don't cry!"

In addition to physical training, the recruits' hearts were worked over, too. They were taught a set of five key principles within the 1882 *Gunjin Chokuyū* (Imperial Rescript). It was set to paper shortly after the samurai class was abolished during the Meiji Restoration of 1868. The Imperial instructions consisted of 2,700 *kanji* ideograms that governed the serviceman's life, thoughts and actions.[5] The following five paraphrased lines were aimed at teaching proper conduct. Each line is labeled as "No. 1" since all of the principles are equally important. Note: *gunjin* means "military man" and applies to both army and navy personnel.

1. The *gunjin* is Loyal (*Chūsetsu*)
1. The *gunjin* is Polite (*Reigi*)
1. The *gunjin* is Brave (*Buyū*)
1. The *gunjin* is Trustworthy (*Shingi*)
1. The *gunjin* is Thrifty (*Shisso*)

The recruits learned the precepts by rote by chanting in unison while marching in place, holding their booklets out at arm's length. One particular message was pounded into their heads; *never become a Prisoner-of-War*. It was a crime that would bring shame on their units, their families and their hometowns.

Section two; Chapter eight of the Imperial Rescript was entitled, "Value

Your Family Honor":

"*He who knows (and thus seeks to avoid) shame is strong. Be vigilant, ever mindful of your family herald crest, making the utmost effort, even unto death, to avoid suffering the shameful crime of soiling your name by being taken alive as a prisoner.*" (Author's translation from actual WWII Japanese military booklet.)

The Japanese military was so thorough in the indoctrination of troops that major battles in the Pacific accounted for no more than a dozen prisoners among thousands killed. For example, during the Burma campaign, British Commonwealth and American forces killed 17,166 Japanese while capturing only 142, most of who were incapacitated by wounds, malnutrition or disease.[6] In the Guadalcanal campaign from January 1 – February 15, 1943, the US XIV Corps captured only eighty-four Japanese in such poor health that almost half were unable to walk.[7] For the first two years of the Pacific War, Allied forces took only 604 Japanese POWs.[8]

Communications Training

Akikusa graduated from boot camp on October 31, 1942, with the rank of Seaman Third Class (Sea 3/c), with orders to report to Yokosuka *Tsūshin Gakkō* for nine months of training.[9] Akikusa found himself in the 64th Cycle of the Navy's Basic Electronic Communication Course.[10]

The instructors at Yokosuka Communications School created an environment of rivalry and fierce competition among the young trainees who were evaluated on their performance. The men were graded on a curve, with no two students in the same *buntai* receiving the same score.

There were classes on radio operation, the mechanics of short and long wave communication, the effects of atmosphere, sending and receiving Morse code, decoding, and other related topics. During Morse code training, instructors reinforced the seriousness of their jobs as radiomen with a sterning warning, "One mistake in sending or receiving a message could cost the lives of hundreds of men."

The boys were tested on their speed and accuracy. Akikusa said that coded messages were much harder than in-the-clear messages. With an open message he could guess the meaning of a word even if he missed a single character. With coded messages, the letters and numbers were meaningless until later decoded by a second man.

To keep their bodies fit there was volleyball, baseball, *sumo* wrestling and running.

Into the second month of training, the recruits were given permission to enjoy Sundays away from the base in the homes of volunteer-citizens that were referred to as *kurabu* (Club) or *geshuku*. The households that hosted the students usually had a son or husband in the navy, and were eager to do their part for the war effort. The woman of the household was old enough to be their mother and was referred to as "Auntie." Smoking and consumption of alcohol were forbidden.

Half of the communication school's students would stay on base, and the other half would leave for the day until 5:00 p.m. On Sunday morning, the men would first head to the ever-crowded *Shuho* (Navy Exchange) to spend their meager pay on stationery, snacks, sweets and clear lemon soda curiously called "cider" though there wasn't a touch of apple used in its creation. Prior to taking their brief shore leave, the trainees received a *bentō* lunch, carried in a rectangle-shaped aluminum box, so as not to burden the supportive families. The students moved in their ten-man squads as they exited the front gate, nervously hoping their shore leave wouldn't be retracted by the shrill sound of an Instructor's police whistle.

Once inside the cozy Japanese home, Akikusa said that it was wonderful to lie on tatami straw matting with its sweet grassy fragrance. During their Sunday time off, the boys would read the newspaper, take naps, listen to records, play chess or write letters. "Those Sunday afternoons were wonderful. No one yelled at us, or beat us all day," Akikusa said. As the curfew time drew near, Auntie would have to wake some of the boys who resembled pampered house cats stretched out on the *tatami* floor. "It's time. I've brought you some green tea," she would say while placing a tray on the floor.

With strong cups of hot green tea sipped, and gratitude expressed, the future radiomen hurried back to the base. With each step, their bodies grew taut in anticipation of the beatings and deprivation that was waiting. And they didn't have to wait long. One Sunday afternoon, as Akikusa's squad returned to the base, he saw one of the other squads lined up for a beating. The beatings spread like a virus to the other squads who were often punished without ever knowing why. An instructor would enter the barracks and dramatically remove his coat and wristwatch, pull on a pair of white heavy cotton work gloves and grip the club firmly, as if preparing to chop down a tree. The trainees knew what was coming and quickly lined up for their "instillation of military spirit." Akikusa said, "It was cruel and inhumane. Our backsides would be tender for days. Sitting down on the wooden seats during class was so painful it was hard to focus on our lessons."

As the months passed, the beatings became less severe and more infrequent. Akikusa grew accustomed to navy life and performed well in all of his classes. The future radiomen took several field trips to places of historical or religious significance. One such place was the battleship *Mikasa*, the flagship of Admiral Heihachirō Tōgō during the Russo-Japan War (1904-05). Another memorable field trip was to Nara's Kinugasa Park to view the 2,000 or so cherry trees that were in full bloom. The Navy told the young sailors that they too, were cherry blossoms, which were the most beautiful when they fluttered to the ground in their peak of perfection.

With graduation from Yokosuka Communication School fast approaching, the boys spent all of their limited free time studying. No one wanted to be recycled into another training cycle. Prior to completing the course, the future radiomen participated in the customary march through Tōkyō to pay their respects, and receive blessings, at the major military shrines; Meiji Jingu; Miyashiro, and Yasukuni Shrine where the souls of the nation's war dead were said to reside. The march was intended to show the men that they were part of a bigger picture. It was also meant to show respect for those who had come before them. The radiomen were told that someday their souls too, would be enshrined at Yasukuni.

On July 22, 1943, Akikusa joined his graduating class of 728 radiomen and proudly sewed a small round proficiency patch onto his left sleeve. It was a five-petal yellow cherry blossom on a circular dark blue background. The newly minted radiomen posed for a graduation photo.

Akikusa was ordered to report for duty at Yokosuka's Mutsuai Communications Unit. He would be going with Shōji Kageyama, a fellow graduate from the Yokosuka Communications School. Akikusa felt relieved to be going with a classmate.[11] They had been in different training squads, so they took this opportunity to get to know each other and quickly became friends.

The Mutsuai Communication Unit was situated in a beautiful landscape, with new buildings nestled inside a patchwork of green farms. Akikusa's happiest memory of his time with the Mutsuai Communication Unit was the Japanese version of a USO show came to perform for the radiomen.* The entertainers were from Shōchiku Studios in Ōfuna, Kamakura. On a warm Sunday morning, the ringing of "The Visitor Bell" announced the anticipated arrival of the performers. A throng of sailors rushed to welcome the patriotic actors, musicians, singers and comedians who wanted to do their part of the war effort.

Following the obligatory formal speech by the unit commander, there were dramatic performances, dances, and comedic sketches that left cheeks aching with laughter, and hands sore from clapping. Some of the costumes and irreverent skits were inappropriate for a military installation, and the radiomen ate it up. There was an intermission for lunch, where the sailors got to share a meal with the performers.

At one point in the afternoon portion of the show, the entertainers invited audience participation, which brought out rousing cheers from the crowd. The radiomen, who were from all over Japan, regaled each other with songs performed in their local dialects. The highlight of the audience participation was the dance by a stern chief petty officer named Akimoto. He came on stage wearing geisha make up, and brought down the house with roars of laughter for his dance performance in drag.

The following week, Akikusa and his friend Kageyama enjoyed a Sunday pass, which they decided to use to visit Shōchiku Studios for a tour. However, when they arrived at the studio's main gate they learned that tours were by reservation only. The pair explained that they were from the Mutsuai Communication Unit and were then treated like VIPs.

Shōchiku Studios was in the middle of filming two propaganda movies, *Kaigun* (The Navy) and *Fuchinkan Gōchin* (Sink the Unsinkable Warship). It was a wonderful experience for a country boy. "We saw 'Hollywood magic' and met a couple of beautiful actresses, too," said Akikusa. He wrote home about the experience knowing his parents would be happy for him.

On November 1, 1943, Akikusa was promoted to the rank of Senior Seaman. He sewed his new rank patch on to his right sleeve; carefully checking several times to ensure it was straight and level.

---

* *Ian geidan* 慰安芸団 (Troops Entertainers).

PART 2
Preparing Iwo Jima for War

Iwo Jima and the Spy

Tsunezō Wachi graduated from the *Kaigun Heigakkō* Naval Academy, located in Etajima, in 1922. He enjoyed a twenty-three year career that began as a midshipman on the cruiser *Izumi*. During his early carrier Wachi attended Gunnery School, Torpedo School and Communication School. Wachi served on several ships; *Nagara*, *Asama*, *Tama*, *Naka*, the destroyer *Yunagi* and the battleships *Fuso* and *Mutsu*. There were lesser assignments such as the river gunboat *Atami* in China, the oil tanker *Sata* and the icebreaker *Odomori*.

In 1924, Wachi was the communications officer aboard the light cruiser *Tama* for the annual midshipmen overseas cruise to the USA. It was on this trip that Japan returned the body of US Ambassador Edgar A. Bancroft, who had died of natural causes, to San Pedro, California.

In 1926, Wachi was handpicked for the prestigious Naval College, and then studied Spanish at the Tōkyō Foreign Language College.* To fulfill their foreign language requirement the officers could also choose to study English, German, French, Russian or Mandarin. Wachi discovered a lifelong fascination with horses during a summer break with the neighboring 1st Cavalry Regiment. Wachi later worked at the Naval Staff Bureau, then commanded a special 25-man intelligence-gathering unit disguised as a communication school in Saitama. This unit grew to include 1,000 men who were recruited for their communication, decoding and language skills. The unit was involved in breaking foreign military codes and designing cryptology. During his career, Wachi was dispatched overseas to various places such as China, Manchuria, Shanghai, Mexico, Columbia, the Philippines and Singapore.

Tsunezō Wachi was hard working, intelligent, well-connected, and knee-deep in Japan's intelligence gathering activities. While serving as a Naval Attaché for the Japanese Embassies in Mexico and Columbia, he engaged in espionage against the United States. In particular, in Mexico City he was an assistant attaché with the covert mission of spying and decoding US naval

---

* The same language school where LtGen Shun Akikusa studied Russian

messages. Wachi had a staff of three naval personnel who worked undercover as civilians. One of Wachi's radioman stated that Wachi gathered information from a retired US Army colonel who supplied information on US ships passing through the Panama Canal.[12] Other information was garnished from a Nazi spy operating in Buenos Aires. In his memoirs, Wachi explained that he chose to codename his operation with the letter "L", because "L" came before "M", and "M" stood for Mexico.[13]

On December 7, 1941, Wachi's intelligence team intercepted the famous message, "Air Raid Pearl Harbor. This Is No Drill." Within days, Wachi's spies were able to procure a detailed accounting of US losses, which he forwarded to Tōkyō. As a result of a US-Mexico treaty, Mexican authorities deported the Japanese diplomats, who traveled to New York for repatriation along with Ambassador *Kichisaburō Nomura*. The Japanese diplomats, military men, businessmen and their families left New York on June 18, 1942, aboard the Swedish vessel *Gripsholm*. It made a stop in Rio de Janeiro to pick up more Japanese citizens, and then rounded the Horn of Africa for Lourenço Marques (Maputo) in Mozambique.[14] Wachi and the others traveled on to Singapore aboard the Japanese transport vessel *Asama Maru*. From Singapore, Wachi flew back to Japan on August 26, 1942, with military attaché Commander Ichirō Yokoyama.*

Upon reporting for duty, Commander Tsunezō Wachi was dispatched on a fact-sharing mission to Kwajalein, Truk Lagoon and the Marshall Islands to disseminate information about the US Navy to the various naval commands. Wachi remarked in his memoirs that, at the time, he believed the Allies would counterattack through the Philippines only. The information from his spy network made him confident that bases in the Central Pacific, such as Iwo Jima, would largely be ignored by the Allies.

In 1943, Wachi returned to his intelligence-gathering job with a special communications unit in Saitama. However, he felt the Navy no longer acted on his reports but viewed them passively as "curious news." Wachi wanted to get into the war so he requested a transfer. In February of 1944, his disappointing assignment was to a backwater island called Iwo Jima.[15]

---

* Ichirō Yokoyama was later promoted to Rear Admiral in May 1945, and was part of the Japanese surrender party aboard the USS *Missouri* on September 2, 1945.

Due to new concerns over a possible American counterattack through the Central Pacific, Imperial General Headquarters organized the defense of Iwo Jima. Vice-Admiral Chūichi Nagumo, who headed the newly formed Central Pacific Fleet, placed Commander Tsunezō Wachi in charge of the *Iwo Jima Keibitai* naval guard Force of 1,362 men that would be joining Wachi from Chichi Jima. The *Keibitai* had several responsibilities: defend the airfields; build machine gun bunkers and artillery casemate bunkers; and man the anti-aircraft batteries. The transport plane carrying Commander Wachi departed Kisarazu Navy Air Base for Iwo Jima on March 16, 1944.

At the same time, the Army's 109th Division was organized under Saipan-based General Hideyoshi Obata's 31st Army. With the intention of strengthening Iwo Jima, General Obata ordered 56-year-old Colonel Kanehiko Atsuchi* to transfer 4,883 men from Chichi Jima to Iwo Jima on March 20-23.[16] In May, MajGen Makoto Ōsuga's 2nd Mixed Brigade from Chichi Jima joined the roster. The Army and Navy were both transferring units to strengthen the defenses of Iwo Jima.

When Commander Wachi arrived in March 1944, Iwo Jima was home to about 1,000 civilians. One of those residents was a young boy named Shōzō Ishina. Prior to the war, the civilians led a slow, peaceful life. Supply ships arrived from Tōkyō every three months bringing mail, newspapers, bureaucrats, visitors, rice, etc. The Ishina family ran a small hotel called "Taiheikan Inn" where bureaucrats, students, ichthyologists and biologists would stay during their visits. The family also farmed sugar cane, coca plants and lemon grass. The pre-war inhabitants were a tight knit community with an organized baseball program, and a tennis team complete with uniforms. Ishina's parents were one of the few households with a radio; it was connected to a tall antenna in the yard to receive broadcasts from Tōkyō.

Commander Wachi's first task was to harden Iwo Jima against air attack and invasion. For starters, the Navy supplied 150 of the 25 mm twin-mount AA machine guns, twenty-eight 5-inch naval AA guns, and a handful of 6-inch naval rifles to be placed in concrete casemates.[17] Wachi followed standard operating procedure and placed the guns for a shoreline defense. He admitted

---

* Sometimes seen spelled Atsuji, but the pronunciation of his family name is Atsuchi.

he lacked experience in regards to defensive fortifications, and that such an important job was more suited to an engineer. In the end, it wouldn't matter so much where the guns were placed, since he still believed that the Allies would bypass Iwo Jima.

Soon after Commander Tsunezō Wachi arrived, the Thirty First Army commander, General Hideyoshi Obata, paid Wachi a visit. During the inspection tour, Wachi remarked to General Obata, "It would make my job easier if I had a horse."[18] To Wachi's surprise, a week later General Obata sent a supply ship from Guam that carried an unexpected cargo: three horses with saddles and tack; an ample supply of grain and feed; and two enlisted men who were assigned as groomers. Wachi picked a horse for himself, and assigned the other two steeds and their caretakers to a Colonel Watanabe and a Major Oka. One of Wachi's sailors had been raised with horses so became Wachi's attendant. The animals were alive as of mid-July 1944, but their ultimate fate is uncertain.[19]

In April 1944, the Japanese continued to send men to Iwo Jima. One of them was Private Kiichi Abe, a tunnel engineer who said, "Life on Iwo Jima wasn't bad in the beginning. We had control of the air and seas so it was a pleasant, peaceful place."[20]

Ensign Minoru Tada

Another April arrival to the island was Ensign Minoru Tada, a naval reservist and recent graduate of Chūo University in Tōkyō. After attending a lecture by a naval recruiter at the school, he decided to become a pilot so joined the Navy's *Yobigakusei* program, which was similar to the American ROTC (Reserve Officer Training Corps). According to records from the Japanese Navy Department (*Kaigunshō*), on July 30, 1943, at schools all across the Empire of Japan, over 50,000 applicants took the admission examination, and only 9,800 were accepted. Minoru Tada was happy to be admitted into the program but was disappointed at not being given his first choice of aviation. On October 1, 1943, Tada, along with 1,400 other cadets, went to the Tateyama Artillery School as members of the training program's 3rd cycle.

Following their basic training, the cadets were asked to choose between seventeen different schools for their specialty training which included: navigation; sea mines; anti-submarine warfare; special naval landing force

(SNLF); gunnery; shore-based artillery; anti-aircraft gunnery; electronic communications; and special-communications (intercepting and decoding enemy messages). Their test scores and evaluations played a key part in determining which special school they would be assigned.

Minoru Tada's advanced training would be in anti-aircraft gunnery training at Tateyama Artillery School. Two days prior to completing the course, the 129 members of his anti-aircraft gunnery class assembled to receive their various assignments from Lieutenant Commander Gōtarō Ogawa. The combat postings were on the front lines; Yap Island, Truk Lagoon, First Fleet, Saipan, Andaman Island (Indonesia), and others. There were two men going to an unfamiliar island called Iwo Jima; Minoru Tada (anti-aircraft), and Masaya Ide (naval landing force).

After dismissing the group, Commander Ogawa told Minoru Tada, "You are being sent to Iwo Jima because you've been sick lately."[21] Tada was disappointed to learn he was going to the Ogasawara Islands, technically part of the city of Tōkyō, which were considered a backwoods posting where nothing important would happen.

On April 1, 1944, Minoru Tada graduated from the Tateyama Artillery School with the rank of ensign and given a three-day pass to visit his family. Wrapped inside a piece of white paper, he left behind at his parents' home a lock of hair and his fingernail clippings; they were to be used at his funeral in the event he never returned.

On April 16, 1944, Ensigns Minoru Tada and Masaya Ide boarded the newly-built transport *Kumanosan Maru* at Yokosuka Harbor and headed for Chichi Jima.*

Chichi Jima had calm water bays, but due to the rugged terrain the defenders could only carve out a pitifully small fighter airstrip down by the water. Its southern neighbor Iwo Jima had no calm water bays but boasted two airfields. Prior to the war, supply vessels could unload at Iwo Jima in calm weather using the wooden jetties, but aggressive American submarine patrols and carrier-based aircraft attacks made it too dangerous to tie up at Iwo Jima. As a result, supply ships first entered one of Chichi Jima's calm water ports,

---

* *Kumanosan Maru* was later sunk on June 24, 1944, by the submarine *SS Grouper*. The name is sometimes misspelled in English as "*Kumanoyama Maru*."

usually Futami Bay, to unload vehicles, troops and supplies; some of which were kept for Chichi Jima's own defensive needs. The remainder was loaded onto smaller vessels for the final 150-mile leg of the hazardous journey to Iwo Jima.

Ensigns Tada and Ide spent over a week on Chichi Jima before finally making their way to Iwo Jima at noon on April 26, 1944. They were greeted by Commander Tsunezō Wachi who drove them to the *Keibitai* Headquarters building and introduced the newcomers to the other officers. Ensign Masaya Ide would become the Executive Officer to a physician, naval captain Dr. Masa Inaoka. Ensign Minoru Tada would take command of an anti-aircraft battery in the southern part of the island. Dr. Inaoka sternly warned the pair of freshmen to drink only boiled water saying, "We already have too many amoebic diarrhea patients on this island, and we don't need any more."[22] Commander Wachi and Dr. Inaoka treated the pair of ensigns to a belt of *sake* rice wine before sending them out to meet the men under the command.

A crusty old warrant officer drove Ensign Tada to Chidori Airfield, which was named after the *chidori*, a bird that appears to run drunkenly along the water's edge as it searches for food. Chidori Airfield was also called "The Lower Airfield" by the defenders. The Americans would call it "Motoyama No. 1." Chidori Airfield had three runways. The warrant officer pointed to a grouping of damaged and bullet-ridden aircraft that were lined up to one side of runway no. 2 and said, "Ensign Tada, your anti-aircraft battery is over there, next to those wrecks." Near the aircraft wrecks were ten Type-96 25 mm twin-mount anti-aircraft machine cannons.

The man continued, "We use them as bait for the enemy strafing attacks." Ensign Tada felt that his guns were in a terrible spot, and what was even worse, was that they were sitting above ground protected by only a wall of sandbags.[23] This battery of anti-aircraft guns was known as *Minami Kaigan Kijūhōdai* (Southern Coast Machine Cannon Battery).

Ensign Tada said he was not permitted to relocate the guns, so he ordered his men to construct pits in which to lower them. He responded to their silent expressions of disbelief with the admonition, "It will help you live longer and kill more of the enemy."[24] Due to the sandy nature of the terrain, the pit walls were constructed from wooden ammo crates and 55-gallon fuel drums filled with rocks. It took three days to construct the waist-deep gun pits, but Ensign

Tada knew it was the right decision.

There was yet another larger problem facing Ensign Tada, although his men had dug small air raid shelters for themselves, they were still living above ground in wooden barracks and old civilian homes. He put in a written request for cement and rebar to build solid bunkers, but the limited supplies were being used to build defensive positions for other units. The idea hit Ensign Tada to re-purpose some of the wrecked bombers and transport aircraft by burying them halfway in the sand and covering them with large stones held in place with concrete.* After getting permission from the *Nanpō Shotō* Naval Air Group Liaison officer, Ensign Tada set his men to work breaking up the first of many aircraft. Several days later, Commander Wachi came by riding on his horse to conduct a routine inspection. The normally stern Commander Wachi chuckled in approval of Tada's resourcefulness saying, "Good job. These aircraft are serving the country twice."

Ensign Tada was later tasked with helping unload a shipment of Type-3 14 cm (5.5 inch) naval rifles that were destined for the area around Mount Suribachi. The naval rifles had been removed from old WW1-era cruisers and bore the manufacture date of 1914. "What are we supposed to do with these old relics?" Tada asked rhetorically. It took a great amount of effort to place the guns near Mount Suribachi where they would have their concrete casemates built around them.

In his memoirs, Commander Wachi noted that the reinforcements arriving from Japan were primarily draftees, teenage volunteers, or aging re-treads that were past their prime. Most of the battalions were so-called "Independent" units, which was a euphemism for "slapped together." These independent units were formed from a core of experienced soldiers, but the bulk of the men were older reservists, draftees and "90-Day Wonder" college student officers like Ensign Minoru Tada.

In order to boost morale, Wachi ordered a military parade to commemorate the Emperor's birthday on April 29, 1944. Wachi's men stopped working on the defenses to form up for a horseback review by Commander Wachi with all the pomp and circumstance they could muster.

On May 27, to commemorate "Navy Day" Wachi ordered Ensign Tada

---

* Several of these bunkers still stand.

and other battery commanders to conduct a test firing of all anti-aircraft guns at 3:00 a.m.

The Gods of War

On May 22, 1944, Japanese Imperial General Headquarters (IGHQ) re-organized the 109th Division under the leadership of General Tadamichi Kuribayashi. The General and his adjutant First Lieutenant Masayoshi Fujita arrived on Iwo Jima on June 8, 1944. Kuribayashi took control of the island and folded Colonel Atsuchi into his command staff. Tunnel engineer Kiichi Abe said that Kuribayashi stepped up the pace of construction to seven days a week in around-the-clock shifts. Abe claimed the unhappy tunnel engineers were exhausted by Kuribayashi's frantic work pace.[25]

In the beginning, Kuribayashi stayed at the Ishina family's Taiheikan Inn. According to Shōzō Ishina, Kuribayashi and his adjutant Lieutenant Fujita spent the daylight hours out inspecting the troops, and then returned for dinner. This is confirmed by the memoirs of Ensign Minoru Tada, Major Horie Yoshitaka and 1st Lt Yasuhiko Murai that all state Kuribayashi and most of the personnel were living above ground in civilian buildings in the summer of 1944.

One day, Shōzō's mother asked Lieutenant Fujita if her son could watch the planes coming in to land. A day or two later, Fuijta drove the family to Chidori Airfield where young Shōzō was thrilled to see aircraft landing up close.

One of the planes witnessed by the youngster might have been one that was carrying Chief Petty Officer Haruo Yoshino (later Ensign). CPO Yoshino was the plane captain and navigator of a Type-97 torpedo bomber. At the end of April 1944, his crew was dispatched from Tateyama Naval Air Group to Iwo Jima to conduct convoy escort and submarine patrol duties. Yoshino was a well-seasoned veteran of many campaigns; Pearl Harbor, Midway, and Santa Cruz. During the Pearl Harbor attack, Haruo Yoshino flew from the deck of the carrier *Kaga* to strike the battleship USS *Oklahoma*. During the battle of Midway, Yoshino was one of the seven search planes sent out to find the US carriers. He survived the sinking of the *Kaga*, and later fought from the carrier *Shōkaku* in the battle of Santa Cruz. Due to the shortage of available carriers, Haruo Yoshino was transferred to the land-based Tateyama Naval Air Group.

On Iwo Jima, Yoshino lived in a tent at the mouth of a cave close to Chidori Airfield. He and his crew would be driven to their plane each morning to fly patrols in a cat-and-mouse game with American submarines. The subs only surfaced at night, but since Yoshino's plane was not equipped with radar he could only operate during the day. Lookouts stationed across the island would send reports of nighttime submarine sightings to Captain Samaji Inoue's *Nanpō* Naval Air Group. "We got reports with detailed information on the location of enemy-subs and launched before dawn, but could never catch one on the surface," said Yoshino.[26]

On June 15, 1944, the US Marine 2nd and 4th Divisions landed on the island of Saipan. At this same time on Iwo Jima, Ensign Minoru Tada and his battery of anti-aircraft guns were banging away at American carrier planes from Task Groups 58.1 and 58.4, which were sent to neutralize the airfields on Chichi Jima and Iwo Jima. In addition to the strafing Hellcats, the Helldivers and Avengers dropped 500-pound bombs, fragmentation and cluster bombs.

Ensign Tada wrote that in the middle of the attack, the gunnery officer for gun No. 1, was screaming and bashing his gunner's helmets with his pointer stick, "Idiots! Keep firing!" The left and right trackers of the No. 1 gun had taken their feet off the pedals, and tossed their hands in the air shouting "Banzai! Banzai!" Ensign Tada looked up to see a burning Hellcat zooming overhead at the height of 150 feet. It splashed into the sea off the western beach.

Although the Japanese AA gunners managed to knock down a few American planes, the Japanese took it on the chin with the loss of twenty-eight aircraft. The American naval carrier pilots had a rough time as well with twenty-one combined losses over Iwo Jima and Chichi Jima (collectively referred to as "Bonin Islands").[27] Ensign Tada claimed that in that single day, his AA unit expended 4,270 rounds of ammunition, which was several times more than what was allotted per day. At that rate, he was worried that if the Americans didn't come soon there would be no ammunition remaining with which to repel the expected invasion.

Ensign Tada didn't know that Iwo Jima's AA gunners had caused damage to all of VT-32's TBF Avengers from the carrier USS *Langley*. Lieutenant David Marks was flying one of the single-engine bombers that day. He dropped his payload diagonally across the northern end of Motoyama Airfield. Although they were all able to make it back to the carrier, some of the planes carried dead and wounded crewmen. This attack signaled the start of 249 days of aerial and naval bombardment that lead up to the February 19th invasion.[28]

Haruo Yoshino and his crew were recalled briefly to Tateyama. He returned to Iwo Jima for anti-submarine duty in late July bringing with him several large *sake* bottles filled with fresh water, and dozens of cartons of cigarettes for the aircraft maintenance crews.

On June 18th, planes began to arrive from the amalgamated *Hachiman Kūshū Butai* (Hachiman Air Raid Unit). Ensign Minoru Tada claimed that the unit had 112 aircraft, primarily Zeros, but also *Tenzan* B6N "Jill" torpedo-bombers and *Suisei* D4Y "Judy" dive-bombers from the following naval air groups: 252nd (Isamu Miyazaki, Kazuo Tsunoda); 301st (Iyōzō Fujita, Kunio Iwashita); Yokosuka (Ryōji Ohara, Tadashi Nakajima, Saburō Sakai); and Betty Bombers from the 752nd.[29]

Adorning the edge of the airfield were two long white banners whipping in the wind that announced their arrival; one bore a patriotic phrase made famous by the samurai Masashige Kusunoki, "*Hirihō Kenten*,"* and the other bore the name of the samurai god of war, "*Hachiman Daibōsatsu*." Ensign Tada said that the Bettys and Jills from the 752nd Naval Air Group were the first to arrive on June 18th. The following day began what would be known as "The Great Marianas Turkey Shoot" in the Mariana Islands.

According to Ensign Minoru Tada, bad weather in Japan meant that the Zeros from the 252nd Naval Air Group didn't arrive until June 21st. On June 24th, overwhelming US naval air forces devastated Iwo Jima's "flying navy."

Ensign Tada was directing his anti-aircraft guns that day when he saw a bomb falling straight at him. He was momentarily knocked unconscious and woke up to the sound of a voice calling his name from far away. He was half-buried in a pile of rocks and rubble, and bleeding from several shrapnel wounds. Tada saw a large piece of shrapnel sticking out of his boot, and then passed out. His men took him to the navy field hospital in the north near Admiral Ichimaru's command bunker. Due to the surge of wounded men, Ensign Tada was placed in a tent outside where he was examined by a naval lieutenant named Dr. Toshio Yoshino who said, "Don't worry, its not fatal. But

---

* *Hiriho Kenten* means, "Injustice cannot defeat Principle, Principle cannot defeat Law, Law cannot defeat Power, Power cannot defeat Heaven."

I am sending you back home." Ensign Tada told the doctor that he wished to stay on the island, but the doctor ignored him and moved to the next patient.

The following day, a messenger from Commander Tsunezō Wachi arrived to inform Ensign Tada that he would be medically evacuated. Tada was happy to be going home but felt that he would be a called a coward for leaving. He wrote a note and stuck it in his pocket that read, "Report: I wish to remain on the island with the *Keibitai* unit. I have no dependents whose future I would worry about. (signed) Ensign Minoru Tada."[30]

Several days later, Ensign Tada heard the sound of hoof beats. Commander Wachi had ridden his horse to the navy field hospital to check on several of his junior officers. Commander Wachi said to Tada, "A submarine will be here in a couple of days to take out the wounded. I am sending you back so you can recuperate." Ensign Tada reached into his breast pocket and handed his note to Wachi who examined it, nodded, folded the note and said, "Understood."

On July 13, 1944, Commander Wachi arrived on his horse again to deliver an order to Ensign Tada, "You are hereby ordered to board the *Tonegawa Maru* tomorrow morning. You will report to Yokosuka Naval Hospital immediately. You will remain under my command in the *Keibitai*, so must return as soon as you are able." Ensign Tada felt that the words, "remain under my command" helped him save face. He was still assigned to Iwo Jima so he wasn't running away.

The following day, the *Tonegawa Maru* and her cargo of wounded men were flushed from Iwo Jima by air raid sirens and red warning flares from the control tower. They barely beat the arrival of B-24 bombers from Saipan. Ensign Minoru Tada said that he was taken to Chichi Jima, transferred to the destroyer *Hatsuharu* and then taken to Yokosuka on July 19th. He would not return to Iwo Jima until long after the war.

The large-scale aerial battles and naval barrage of July 3 – 4 were the final nails in the coffin for the naval air arm on Iwo Jima. The author met with several Japanese aviators to hear about their experiences on Iwo Jima including Saburō Sakai, Isamu Miyazaki, and Haruo Yoshino. They were united in their statements that their losses were due to four primary factors: imbalance in numbers of aircraft; rugged Grumman F6F Hellcat fighters piloted by aggressive pilots; lack of replacements; and naval barrages that targeted the airfields.

"In the skies over Iwo Jima, every day there was more of them and fewer of us," said Isamu Miyazaki.

Saburō Sakai told the author during a 1994 home interview that he admired how the Americans constantly improved their aircraft and pilot training, and learned from their mistakes. Sakai said he knew the war was lost when Saipan fell, but there was no option but to fly and try to stay alive. It wasn't about how many planes he shot down, but about keeping his wingmen alive.

Due to the combined effects of aerial and naval bombardments, the *Hachiman Butai* Unit was left with no serviceable planes so the pilots and aircrews were evacuated to mainland Japan via transport planes and re-organized under the Third Air Fleet. Imperial General Headquarters then re-classified Iwo Jima as a frontline air base to be used as a refueling and staging area for reconnaissance missions and anti-shipping attacks under the command of Rear-Admiral Rinosuke Ichimaru. The Admiral would have his headquarters on Iwo Jima and have control over several naval air groups that were stationed in mainland Japan: 752nd (Bettys from Kisarazu); 252nd (Zeros and Jills from Tateyama); 301st (Zeros from Tateyama); 801st (Flying Boat "Emilys" from Yokohama); and 1023rd ("Tabbys" from Kisarazu).

On July 13th, Ensign Kazuo Tsunoda and the some twenty Zero pilots, many of whom were raw replacements, were reorganized into the new 252nd Naval Air Group and sent back to Iwo Jima. Ensign Tsunoda was a seasoned mustang that had seen combat in China, Guadalcanal and Rabaul, and had served aboard the carrier *Sōryū* during the battle of Midway with fellow mustang and Zero ace pilot Kaname Harada. Tsunoda had also been a flight instructor, and had flown in the Marshall Islands campaign with ace Isamu Miyazaki in the 252nd Naval Air Group.

Akikusa's False Start

While Iwo Jima's aircraft were taking a pasting, back in Japan radiomen Akikusa and Kageyama were granted a three-day shore leave. Akikusa returned home to see his grandmother sitting on the veranda busy with her usual handiwork. She heard his footsteps and looked up, "Why are you back so soon? Oh no, did they kick you out?" He showed her his shore leave and she quickly ordered a neighborhood child to go out into the fields to share the news. Once inside the house, Akikusa learned that his younger brother had joined the Navy and was at a naval communication school. His younger sister Iku was still in Tientsin China, working as an army nurse.

Soon, neighbors and friends gathered to pepper Akikusa with questions about the war, especially about Saipan, but he had no answers. He recalled, "I was just a lowly seaman who didn't know anything." He learned from *them* about the battles with the British at Imphal, Burma, and the fall of Tarawa. They told him that the US Navy was running amok in the southern seas, and that Saipan was in danger of falling to the enemy. The Japanese Government had control over the only radio broadcast company, known as NHK.* The magazines and newspapers claimed that hundreds of enemy airplanes had been shot down, and dozens of enemy warships were sent to the bottom of the ocean. *Could it be true?*

If Akikusa's parents had misgivings about the war they were careful with whom they shared them. Akikusa said, "People back then had to be mindful of what they said in public. The Special Higher Police could pick you up for questioning at any time." The Special Higher Police, or *Tokubetsu Kōtō Keisatsu* (*Tokkō*), was the civilian counterpart to the military's *Kempeitai*, and roughly equivalent to the F.B.I. in terms of combining both criminal investigation and counter-espionage functions. It has also been compared to the Nazi Gestapo. The *Tokkō* gathered information from a nationwide network of patriotic citizens who, as part of the *Tonarigumi* system (neighborhood watch), submitted reports and rumors of unpatriotic conversations or actions within their neighborhoods. Even in the tiny burg of Yabegawa, people knew to keep their heads down and their mouths shut.

That night, Akikusa had a hard time getting to sleep. One of the neighbors' comments spun around in his head, "They never grant sailors 'special shore leave' unless they are going into heavy combat." He tried to put it out of his mind as he slid under his mosquito netting and sprawled down on his soft *futon* bed. *Ah, there was nothing like it.* In the darkness, he realized how much he missed the sound of the frogs croaking in the rice fields.

Akikusa's special shore leave passed all too quickly. On his way out of

---

* *Nippon Hōsō Kyōkai* (NHK) had both AM and FM stations, as well as overseas broadcasts aimed at Japanese living in Hawaii and the west coast of North America with a program known as "Radio Tokyo."

the village, walked across the Yabegawa bridge and came to a rice paddy. He paused to take it all in one more time. He glanced down at his feet and saw a tadpole swimming in the shallow water of the rice paddy and said to the little creature, "I am coming back home, no matter what. Even if I return looking like you with no arms or legs."

When Akikusa returned to the barracks at the Mutsuai Communications Unit, he nodded a greeting to Kageyama who said, "They're throwing us a farewell party tonight. We are to report to Yokosuka Communications Unit tomorrow for transfer to a unit called *Nanpō Kantai Shirei-bu* (Southern Area Fleet Headquarters)."

That evening, June 18th, the petty officers gathered for a send-off complete with handshakes, speeches and words of advice. Akikusa produced a wooden box filled with his mother's homemade sweet bean *manjū* cakes. Akikusa handed a *manjū* cake to a warrant officer and jokingly begged to know where he and Kageyama were heading. The older man replied, "No one knows where the Southern Area Fleet Headquarters is located, or whether it's with a fleet or a land-based unit. It doesn't matter because you must do your duty and sacrifice yourself in the execution of that duty if need be." The man took a bite of the *manjū* cake and savored the nostalgic home-style flavor. He swallowed and said with a confident smile, "Don't worry, you've trained on the best equipment the Navy has to offer. If you ever have questions just contact us. We never forget our shipmates." And with that, he popped the rest of the *manjū* cake into his mouth and gave Akikusa a reassuring slap on the back.

The appearance of beer made the farewell party come alive as military *gunka* songs erupted amid the sounds of clinking glasses and laughter. After several hours, the party ended with the somber funeral procession-like rendition of *Umi Yukaba*. The song was a way to wind down any party and remind the men of their destiny to "die as a rotting corpse either in a field, or floating on the waves." The tipsy radiomen stumbled back to their barracks, slung their hammocks and rolled into their racks.

It's said that, "Morning comes silently on little cat feet." Perhaps, but not so for a pair of hung-over teenagers. Reveille brought an unfamiliar stomachache for Akikusa. The pair of friends went about their morning routine and then reported to the parade deck. Following the unemotional prattle of an officer's well-worn farewell speech, over 100 radiomen formed parallel lines and waved their caps in the traditional *bōfure* salute to Kageyama and Akikusa as they walked out the front gate. The duo turned back, came to attention, and saluted their comrades who responded with a roaring chorus of banzai cheers. The pair headed to the train station to catch the local to Yokosuka Naval Base.

When Akikusa and Kageyama presented their written orders at Yokosuka, they were met with, "Wait here." The duty officer returned with four younger sailors and said, "The six of you will report to *Kanoya Kōkūtai*." He pointed to Akikusa, "You are in charge of this six-man dispatch unit. There are others at Kanoya waiting for you, so hurry." It would be a long journey to the southern tip of Japan, and Akikusa felt better knowing he was not alone.

Akikusa and Kageyama opted for window seats on the right side of the train so they could catch views of Mt. Fuji. The trains didn't run all night, so the men made their overnight stop in Kōbe. They hefted their sea bags for the ten-minute walk to the grave of Masashige Kusunoki (1294-1336), located inside Minatogawa Jinja Shrine. They entered the main gate, and headed to the right to pay their respects at Kusunoki's grave. Kusunoki was a 14th-century samurai who gained fame for his support of the Emperor Go-Daigo during a one-sided, losing battle at Minatogawa River in 1336. This battle gave birth to his phrase, "But that I had seven lives to give to the Emperor."[*] The Japanese military used the Kusunoki family crest of a mum floating on water, called *Kikusui*, as a symbol of devotion and self-sacrifice. The Navy adopted Minatogawa Jinja as their patron shrine.

Later the next day, Akikusa was awakened from his catnap by the train conductor's nasally announcement, "End of the line, Kanoya Station, end of the line."[31] The men exited the station and boarded a bus for Kanoya Navy Air Base. When they reported for duty they were told that they had missed their assigned transport flight to the southern combat zone. There were more men needing transport than there were available planes, so the six men would have to wait. *Hurry up and wait.* The radiomen slung their sea bags over their shoulders and moved to a transitional barracks to cool their heels.

The next morning, the entire base was called to formation for a send-off for ten Zero fighter pilots heading south to the front lines. "The pilots looked heroic and splendid in their flight gear," said Akikusa. A twinge of jealousy

---

[*] *Shichishō Hōkoku* (七生報國).

struck him as he noted the aviators were his age. The base commander climbed a short set of wooden steps to a podium to address the pilots. The aircraft ground crews cranked up the engines, which banged and coughed to life. Exhaust fumes spilled across the field. The officer's voice was sharp and loud so he didn't need a microphone to be heard over the radial engines. He bellowed out inspirational words in military fashion, and ended with, "It is your duty to protect our nation even with your lives." The pilots saluted and double-timed it to their waiting aircraft that seemed to be purring in the morning sun. Akikusa felt a chill of pride run down his spine as the Zeros took off and circled the airfield. The shiny new aircraft came in low over the hangars to a sea of waving caps.

Akikusa noted that the general atmosphere at Kanoya wasn't as strict as Yokosuka, and there were no beatings. The group of radiomen waited for several more days with no word on their transport plane. They were issued day-passes, which they used to visit the shops in town to spend their money on sweets and snacks. "I won't need money where I'm going," they would announce to the shop girls with an air of bravado. With no transport aircraft either coming or going, the radiomen eventually received instructions, "You will leave for Yokosuka and await further orders."

What? That's stupid. We just came from there, thought Akikusa. The following morning on the bus back to the train station, Kageyama suggested, "Let's sit on the seaward side of the train on the way north to get a different view." As the train chugged north through various cites and towns, groups of passengers got on and off, bringing with them muted conversations of the war. Akikusa overheard that American B-29 bombers had raided northern Kyūshū. The Kanoya Navy Base commander's grave words to the Zero pilots became crystal clear, "It is your duty to protect our nation with your lives."

The radiomen made it back to Yokosuka where they were once again issued three-day shore leave passes. Akikusa found himself back home among his family. On that last evening of his second furlough, he sat cross-legged on the floor at the dinner table with his father and grandfather while his mother worked in the kitchen preparing her son's favorite dishes. His grandfather turned to him and said with a frown, "This is your second shore leave so they must be sending you someplace awful." Old people tend to speak their minds too freely, even in Japan. Akikusa hoped his mother hadn't heard the off-putting observation.

After dinner, he went for a nostalgic twilight last-look at his small neighborhood. When he returned, he patted the family horse on the neck and felt comforted by the familiar musky odor. His grandmother stepped up to him with a solemn expression and said, "You have to come back alive because flowers don't grow in graveyards. Do you understand?"

Akikusa nodded, "Don't worry Grandma, I promise."

Corporal Abe Marries His Future Widow

In April 1938, twenty-year-old Tadashi Abe was drafted into the Army's 78th Regiment's Anti-Aircraft unit. It was stationed in Korea, which since the turn of the century was a Japanese colony.* In 1940, Abe was injured in a training accident and treated at the army hospital in Seoul. There he met his future bride, a nurse named Teruko Kageyama. It was the quintessential 'Florence Nightingale Syndrome.' The pair began a heated courtship that boiled into a marriage proposal.

PFC Tadashi Abe's future bride, Teruko Kageyama, was born and raised in current day North Korea. Teruko Kageyama's father had served in the Japanese Army during the Russo-Japan War of 1905, and after his discharge decided to make his home on the Japanese-occupied peninsula working as a policeman. Teruko's father encouraged her to become a nurse due to the horrors he witnessed on the frontlines. As a result, Teruko went to nursing school at age sixteen, and then joined the International Red Cross. In April 1939, Teruko Kageyama was drafted and served in various army hospitals in Korea and China.

PFC Tadashi Abe completed his tour of duty, and was discharged into the Army Reserves. He landed a steady job as an office manager at a transport company in Seoul. And like Teruko's father, he decided to make a life for himself on the Korean Peninsula. He married his nurse-bride Teruko Kageyama in Seoul, on April 1, 1941.

Teruko's brother, Petty Officer 3/c Kiyoshi Kageyama, was a ship's engineer serving aboard the heavy cruiser *Chōkai*. In November 1941, PO 3/c Kageyama was transferred to the 4th Fleet's special transport *Kinryū*, an armed

---

* The Japanese Army's 78th Regiment was formed in Pusan, Korea in 1916.

merchantman. Shortly after the Pearl Harbor raid, Teruko received word that her brother Kiyoshi was killed in the invasion of Wake Island on December 23rd. After the two unsuccessful landing attempts at Wake Atoll on December 8th and 11th, the Japanese Navy needed more troops to send ashore. PO3/c Kiyoshi Kageyama and many of his "non-essential" shipmates were deputized into the 2nd Maizuru Naval Landing Force. Although not formally trained or equipped as a Japanese Marine he went ashore and became one of several hundred Japanese sailors killed by the US Marine Defense Battalion.*

In May 1942, Teruko bore her husband a daughter that they named Yoshiko. Things were going well for the young family until March 1944, when an ominous postcard arrived from the Army Reserve Center. Teruko was pregnant with their second daughter, Michiko, when Tadashi Abe was recalled to active duty. PFC Tadashi Abe was promoted to Corporal and assigned to First Lieutenant Shigeo Nishiyama's 1st Company, Independent 20th Mortar Battalion. Teruko said her worried goodbyes as her husband and the other soldiers embarked on a transport vessel at Pusan, Korea, on July 1, 1944.

Corporal Tadashi Abe's unit later boarded a transport ship in Yokosuka as part of Escort Convoy No. 3710, which left Yokosuka on July 10, 1944.

Out on his first war patrol, Lieutenant Commander Albert Becker took his submarine, USS *Cobia* (SS-245), north to the sea-lane between the Ogasawara Islands and the main island of Honshu. On the morning of July 13th, the USS *Cobia* stalked Corporal Abe's Escort Convoy No. 3710, and sank the transport *Daiji Maru*. She was packed to the gills with supplies: 960 tons of cement; 420 tons of coal; 200 tons of ammunition and supplies; plus troops from the 204th Naval Construction Unit, many of which were *gunzoku* civilians, and over half of whom would die.[32]

One of the survivors of the sinking of *Daiji Maru* was twenty-six-year-old Corporal Shōichi Kawai, a radioman with the newly formed Independent Mixed 17th Infantry Regiment Communications Unit. Corporal Kawai was a reservist who had previously served a tour of duty with the 41st Infantry Regiment as a machine gunner before becoming a radioman.

---

* The author spent a week on Wake Atoll in 2003 with six American combat veterans to film the Emmy-nominated documentary, "Wake Island: The Alamo of the Pacific."

Kawai had seen plenty of action: Peking and Southern China; Indochina (Vietnam); then under General Tomoyuki Yamashita in Malaysia at Kuala Lumpur and Singapore; Panay and Mindanao in the Philippines. Corporal Kawai had fought against Chinese, British, Indian, French and American forces before being discharged in December 1942. Kawaii was a newly married man when he was recalled for duty on March 17, 1944, and sent to a radio refresher course. "Many of us radiomen had served together," he wrote. Their ages ranged from twenty-six to thirty-five-years-old, and all of them were married. After a few months of re-training, the group of fifty radiomen, commanded by First Lieutenant Kōtarō Inada, said goodbye to their wives and children and headed north from their home base in Hiroshima to Yokohama Harbor. They were equipped with four Model-94, Mark-3 field radio sets, which would be put to good use once they reached their final destination, which was rumored to be one of the Izu islands south of Tōkyō. The radiomen reached Yokohama and spent three days billeted in an elementary school waiting for supplies to be loaded aboard their transport ship *Daiji Maru*.

While waiting for *Daiji Maru* to complete the loading process, Corporal Kawai saw tanks lined up at the wharf, "They were not the small tankettes that we used in China, but mostly the larger newer models," he wrote. He said that didn't know it at the time, but these belonged to LtCol Takeichi Nishi's 26th Tank Regiment.* Nishi's twenty-eight tanks were originally slated to join the defense of the Mariana Islands, but it was evident that the US Marines would reach Saipan first, so the tanks were to be transported to Iwo Jima on the deck of the transport *Nisshu Maru*.

On the morning of the sinking, radioman Corporal Shōichi Kawai recalled hearing the mess call followed by a large explosion. The deck shuddered under the blare of a klaxon horn. Kawai followed instructions to remove his *jika tabi* rubber shoes, wrap-up leggings, leather belt with bayonet, musette bag, canteen, and trousers. He donned his life jacket as he had done during the drill, and then hung his accouterments over his neck. "No one panicked as we waited for instructions," he wrote. He would leave his transport pack with hobnail boots and helmet behind. A voice came over the loudspeaker stating that the vessel had been struck amidships by a torpedo. Kawai heard a second

---

*   Takeichi Nishi was posthumously promoted to Colonel.

explosion. The seasoned veterans waited for fifteen minutes for the order to abandon ship, all the while the ship slipped lower into the sea. The escort destroyer *Hatsukaze* raced about dropping depth charges that sent geysers of water high in to the air with a loud whapping sound.

By now, all of the troops had crowded their way to the main deck making it difficult to even turn around.

There was a huge hole in the side of the ship beneath where Kawaii was standing. "I was afraid that if I jumped into the water I would get sucked back into the ship and drown," wrote Kawai. Due to the mass of troops on deck he couldn't move away from the torpedo hole. Once the order was given, he had no choice but to go over the rail like a disciplined lemming. He grabbed onto something floating by, but soon became exhausted and let go of everything that was hanging around his neck except his canteen.

Corporal Shōichi Kawai was fished out of the water at around 3:00 p.m., but 389 soldiers and sailors would not be so lucky. Corporal Kawai, Corporal Tadashi Abe (in a different ship), and the other nervous men of Escort Convoy 3710 arrived at Chichi Jima later that afternoon. Corporal Kawaii would remain on Chichi Jima for the time being.

However, under cover of darkness, Corporal Tadashi Abe (20th Mortar Battalion) and PFC Mitsuru Higuchi (2nd Mortar Battalion) left for Iwo Jima in smaller ships, landing on July 14, 1944.[33] Once on Iwo Jima, Abe and Higuchi came under the control of Colonel Chosaku Kaidō's Brigade Artillery Group. Corporal Abe was assigned to the Southern Defensive Zone, and PFC Higuchi was assigned to the Mount Suribachi Defensive Zone.

On July 18th, USS *Cobia* struck again sinking two supply ships near Chichi Jima: *Unkai Maru No. 10*; and *Nisshu Maru*, which was carrying Olympic gold medalist "Baron" Takeichi Nishi's 26th Tank Regiment, the Independent 26th Mortar Battalion, and part of the Independent Mixed 17th Regiment. Although 95% of the troops aboard *Nisshu Maru* were rescued, the Japanese lost valuable equipment: Baron Nishi's tanks; a shipment of Type-98 spigot mortars; anti-aircraft guns; Type-96 150 mm mortars; and a large supply of ammunition, cement and building material.[34] The following month, Baron Nishi took some of his men back to Tōkyō for replacement tanks.[35]

Lieutenant Commander Albert L. Becker received the Navy Cross for his actions in harassing Japanese shipping during the summer of 1944.[36]

First Lieutenant Kōtarō Inada, Corporal Shōichi Kawai, and the fifty-man radio unit were all reunited and fitted with new gear on Chichi Jima, but had no assigned duties, so spent several weeks living in commandeered civilian homes. They witnessed several air raids until August 23, 1944, when Lieutenant Kōtarō Inada told his men that he was leading them to Iwo Jima the next day. The radiomen knew that food was in short supply on Iwo Jima so took matters into their own hands. Risking severe punishment, that night they snuck into a storage cave near the wireless station at Yoakeyama and stole several boxes of canned rations. Corporal Kawai wrote that theft of food was the primary crime committed in the army, and that the *Kempeitai* was on the alert but seldom able to catch the culprits.

At midnight on August 24, 1944, Corporal Kawai and the other radiomen shipped out for Iwo Jima under complete darkness hoping, and praying, to evade further entanglement with US submarines.

The army radiomen finally came ashore on Iwo JIma the following afternoon in small wooden Daihatsu boats that were lowered from their mother ship; they hit the beaches much like the US Marines would. Lieutenant Inada, Corporal Kawai, and the other army radiomen were divided among the Division and Brigade headquarters. Corporal Kawai was instructed to take three men and position them in a wooden civilian home located near a rock face that was 900 feet east of Kuribayashi's Division Headquarters. Kawai's four-man squad was issued pickaxes and shovels with orders to carve out a U-shaped tunnel in the face of the cliff. They completed their excavation work on their new home in the end of September and were issued a radio to begin the work for which they had been trained.

Due to the heat inside the tunnel, the radiomen were usually dressed in nothing but loincloth underwear and combat caps. As a result, soldiers across the island resorted to sewing their rank insignia to their caps making it easier to distinguish ranks inside the dimly lit caves and tunnels. They only wore their uniforms when an officer, or the *Kempeitai,* made the rounds.

The Medic

Prior to the war, Shūji Ishii was employed as a photographer for the *Mainichi Shinbun*, a major newspaper in Tōkyō. Ishii was drafted into the army in May 1944, leaving behind a wife and two children. After minimal training as a medic, he made the journey to Iwo Jima disembarking on the western shore on July 27, 1944.[37] PFC Shūji Ishii was trucked to a point near Tachikawa Point and billeted in a wooden building. He was placed in Captain Kazuyoshi Morimoto's 2nd Mixed Brigade Field Hospital. As a medic, PFC Ishii was under the direct control of an army doctor, Captain Iwao Noguchi, who was the chief physician in charge of 160 medics, orderlies, doctors, pharmacists, and clerks. Upon arrival, PFC Ishii was immediately put to work digging tunnels so the hospital could be transferred underground. Ishii stated that they used pickaxes and digging bars to carve out three feet of tunnel per day, unless they were using dynamite in which they could achieve six feet of tunnel per day. Hauling the dirt up to the surface was backbreaking work that left Ishii and the others covered in a thick crust of sweat and dirt. Since he was issued a sparse ½ liter of water per day, it was only during rare rainstorms that he could rinse himself clean.

Ishii explained that the 2nd Mixed Brigade Field Hospital was eventually comprised of three underground levels and two major bunker complexes: Bunker No.1 contained the Headquarters cave, the pharmacy cave, the galley cave, and the clerical cave; Bunker No.2 consisted of several external medicine caves and the surgery facilities.

Ishii said that long before the US Marines landed, the Japanese were constantly under siege by various diseases. Poor hygiene, unsanitary and insufficient numbers of latrines, and blowflies led to constant outbreaks of amoebic dysentery. As a result, everyone experienced dysentery, some worse than others. There were not enough latrines to handle the high volume of dysentery cases so men were relieving themselves where possible. There was no toilet paper so the men used leaves, and pages torn from newspapers and magazines, which they discarded on the ground. There was naturally no water for washing one's hands. Ishii claimed that Iwo Jima was a sanitation nightmare.

Ishii's said the Japanese military simply sent too many people to the island and couldn't take care of them. The US Navy blockade meant there were insufficient amounts of food, medicine, water and general supplies available to handle the thousands of men who were suffering from malnutrition, dehydration, exhaustion and dysentery. The doctors and medics were running low on medicine and bandages, but there was one item that they had an adequate stockpile for when the Americans landed; hand grenades, the cure-all for their patients' maladies.

Hattori's Letters from Iwo Jima

In 2011, Rex Butler, a WWII memorabilia collector, bought a collection of war relics at a flea market that once belonged to a US Marine who fought on Iwo Jima. Butler was able to track down the next-of-kin of the Marine to return some of the more personal belongings.

In the grouping were a Japanese postcard and a letter. The postcard was to First Lieutenant Genichi Hattori from his younger brother. The letter was from Mrs. Kurie Hattori to her son Genichi Hattori. In one paragraph of the letter, she referred to Chikako, Lieutenant Hattori's three-year-old daughter, who was "lying fast asleep on her mother's lap." Hattori's mother also wrote of B-29 raids that were destroying cities across Japan. The missive was written, "at night using a shrouded black-out lamp." Another line of the faded letter reads, "Chikako is happily pointing to a photo of you in uniform on horseback."*

The author was privileged to be involved in helping return the letter to Chikako who said that it became a connection not only to her father, but to her departed mother, and grandmother as well.

Genichi Hattori was born on February 3, 1916, in Sakurai City, Nara. He was at the top of his class in both elementary and middle school. In 1934, Hattori graduated from Nara Prefecture's Forestry Trade School in order to follow in his father's footsteps as president of the *Kigen* Lumber Corporation. His father's untimely illness thrust Genichi into the role of becoming the 6th generation of the Hattori clan to manage the forests of Nara. The sacred forests yielded solid, straight lumber sought after for centuries to build temples. Hattori's family had been of the samurai class loyal to the Toda *Daimyō* in the historic battle of *Sekigahara* in 1601. The Hattori family tree had proud, deep roots.

Two years after graduation, in December 1936, twenty-year-old Genichi Hattori was drafted into the 4th Imperial Guard Regiment. He proved himself

---

* Lieutenant Genichi Hattori's widow, Sawako, remarried in 1948 taking the surname Yoshikawa. Her second husband treated little Chikako as his own. Sawako passed away in 1993, but Chikako is alive and well with a family of her own.

a leader and was accepted into the Officers Candidate School. In July 1938, Hattori received a field commission to 2nd Lieutenant and was dispatched to the Manchurian-Russian border. Hattori wrote to his parents often, frequently including photos.

Because Hattori was a field-commissioned officer, and not a product of the Officer Academy, he was not considered a career man so was discharged after his tour of duty ended in May, 1941. He left active duty for the Army Reserves and returned to Nara Prefecture to work in the forest industry. In June 1941, through an arranged marriage, Genichi married Sawako Kawai. In February 1943, the couple was blessed with a baby girl named Chikako. Hattori was elected to the position of Secretary to Nara Prefecture's Minister of Forestry, and had a promising business and political future ahead of him.

Things changed dramatically when the Army sent a recall notice in June 1944. Hattori was given a promotion to First Lieutenant and assigned to the Headquarter section of the "22nd Osaka Unit," a shore battery that guarded the entrance to nearby Osaka Bay. Hattori wouldn't be going overseas, so would be able to make occasional trips to visit his wife and daughter. He had a younger brother named Genji who was also recalled to active duty.*

When Lieutenant Genichi Hattori arrived in Osaka, he learned there was a unit in desperate need of an Executive Officer to replace one that had been hospitalized with appendicitis. The unit was shipping out immediately so there was no time to go through normal channels to request a replacement. Lieutenant Genichi Hattori was re-assigned to Major Haruhiko Matsushita's 10th Independent Anti-Tank Battalion. The unit promptly boarded a transport ship in Osaka Bay and headed for Yokosuka with 303 officers and men.

Once the ship pulled into Yokosuka, Lieutenant Hattori was granted a brief shore leave so he hired a car to take him to visit his younger brother, who was the commander of a coastal artillery guarding the Navy's Kisarazu Air Base. The younger Hattori wrote in his memoirs that the brothers spent three painfully short hours together before the older brother shipped out for parts unknown. The younger brother promised to write once a week, and send care packages twice a month.[38]

From the beginning of his ocean journey to Iwo Jima, Lieutenant Genichi

---

* Gen-ICHI is the older brother, and Gen-JI is the younger brother.

Hattori penned letters to his parents, wife and younger brother. Judging from the total of forty-four pieces of correspondence the Hattori family received, roughly one-third of their letters, cards and care packages sent to and from Iwo Jima reached their recipients. A unique aspect is that Lieutenant Genichi Hattori was the Executive Officer of his battalion, which made him the censor for outgoing mail. He censored his own postcards and letters by affixing his *hankō* seal in the military censor's box on each card and letter that he wrote. In turn, since the younger brother was the commander of the shore battery at Kisarazu, he too, could write without going through a censor. The brothers could, and did, write freely to each other.

On June 28, 1944, Lieutenant Genichi Hattori's Independent 10th Anti-Tank Battalion boarded the converted passenger liner *Noto Maru* and joined a convoy bound for Iwo Jima via Chichi Jima.[39]

Another army officer that was on board *Noto Maru* was Second Lieutenant Yasuhiko Murai. According to Lieutenant Murai, the deck of the *Noto Maru* was covered with pallets of freshly cut bamboo poles that had were tied to act as rafts in case the ship was torpedoed.[40] Lieutenant Murai was one of twenty-five instructors that were plucked from the Infantry School and sent to Iwo Jima on three days notice. The energetic junior officers from the Infantry School were needed to function as troop handlers to deal with the large number of inexperienced draftees that were coming to Iwo Jima. Half of the Infantry School officers would travel to Iwo Jima by sea, like Murai, and the other half would fly to Iwo Jima in a pair of army *Hiryū* "Peggy" bombers. Lieutenant Murai had with him an attendant who carried his footlocker, in which was packed Murai's father's American-made Colt pistol with 25 rounds of ammunition, a sword in a plain wooden sheath, some amulet charms, and the 1,000 stitch belt that his father had worn during the previous war.

The convoy to Chichi Jima was part of the *I-go Yusen Sakusen* plan to transport men and materials to the Ogasawara Islands. The *Noto Maru* traveled along with the destroyers *Hatakaze* and *Shiokaze*, and the anti-submarine escort ship *Kaibōkan* No. 4. Due to aggressive American submarine patrols, the convoy was under the watchful eye of three Aichi E13A "Jake" seaplanes, and eight Nakajima A6M2-N "Rufe" floatplane fighters from Chichi Jima that conducted air combat patrols.[41] The ships safely reached Chichi Jima's Futami Bay on July 1, 1944.

Part 2: Preparing Iwo Jima for War   49

An SBT landing craft came alongside the *Noto Maru* to transfer Lt Yasuhiko Murai, the Infantry School officers, and part of the 145th Infantry Regiment south to Iwo Jima. Lieutenant Yasuhiko Murai's landing craft was packed to the gills as it grounded up on the sand at Iwo Jima's East Boat Basin area at 1:30 a.m. The men unloaded their equipment in the darkness as trucks arrived to cart their gear away from the beach. The drivers were in a rush to get the men and equipment dispersed before dawn. There were no bunkers yet for the 145th Infantry to occupy so they had to dig their own. Murai noted the elementary school (*Taishō Kokumin Gakkō*), the Taiheikan Inn, and several wooden homes in the immediate area. The remainder of the regiment would be shuttled over from Chichi Jima in the coming weeks in various Daihatsu landing craft and other small boats as they became available.

The next afternoon, a pair of Peggy bombers flew in carrying the remaining junior officers from the Infantry School. The twenty-five junior officers, led by Captain Kenjirō Nagata, walked to the Ishina family's Taiheikan Inn to report to General Kuribayashi who welcomed the young officers. After they were issued their assignments, Kuribayashi explained the importance of the island in Japan's overall security plan. Lt Murai and three others were assigned to Captain Yoshinobu Hakuta's Independent 314th Battalion in the Eastern Defensive Zone.*

Army Captain Kenjirō Nagata was assigned to the Independent 312th Infantry Battalion in the Suribachi Defense Zone. One of his enlisted men was Corporal Torao Miyazaki, a thirty-five-year-old schoolteacher, who would leave behind two young sons and an infant daughter.[42]

Lieutenant Hattori and the 10th Independent Anti-Tank battalion stayed on Chichi Jima for roughly two weeks before landing on Iwo Jima on July 15th. They were also placed in the Suribachi Defensive Zone under Major General Makoto Ōsuga's 2nd Mixed Brigade.† Lieutenant Hattori positioned his 47 mm anti-tank guns in two lines of bunkers to defend Suribachi's northeastern plain (Green Beach area), an area in the path of Captain Dave Severance's E

---

*   Captain Yoshinobu Hakuta was posthumously promoted to Major. In English, his last name sometimes appears as Hakata, or Hakuda, but "Hakuta" is the correct spelling confirmed with the Japanese Iwo Jima Association.

†   Some books claim this unit arrived on July 20th, but 1st Lt Hattori's handwritten letter claims he arrived on July 15, 1944.

Company, 2nd Battalion, 28th Marine Regiment (E/2/28). Captain Severance's Marines would be immortalized by photographers Joe Rosenthal and Sergeant William Genaust for something they did with a flag and a piece of Japanese irrigation pipe.[43]

Akikusa Runs the Gauntlet

Naval radioman Akikusa was promoted to Leading Seaman on May 1, 1944, and was proudly wearing his new rank insignia on his right sleeve.

After his second shore leave, Akikusa bid farewell to his parents and returned to the transit barracks at Yokosuka Naval Base where he, Kageyama, and fifteen others, waited for further orders. Several hours passed without any word, so the men unpacked and settled in. There was always plenty of waiting in any navy. It was here in the barracks that Akikusa made friends with another farm boy, Yasuo Kumakura. Akikusa described Kumakura as "strong and stocky with thick bushy eyebrows, like caterpillars, and hairy arms that made him look older than he was." Kumakura liked to smoke a traditional Japanese *kiseru* pipe. He would take a cigarette and break it into pieces, then place the sections standing vertical in the tiny brass bowl and chain smoke with great satisfaction. Kumakura talked with his hands and used the skinny pipe when making dramatic points.

Shortly before dinner, a blast from a police whistle pierced the air as a petty officer wearing a red duty armband exploded into their quarters, "Outside now!" They formed up to get the word that they were shipping out that night, but to where they did not know.

The naval radiomen would be embarking on the *Enjū Maru*, a 5,374-ton Canadian Merchant Marine vessel, originally known in 1919 as *SS Canadian Miller*, which once carried cargoes of canned salmon.[44] She later sailed under a Greek flag, then Panama colors, and finally under the flag of the Rising Sun. As the men stood on the dock, Yasuo Kumakura said, "My first chance to go out to sea and it's not even on a proper naval vessel."

Under a din of police whistles and shouts, Akikusa watched seemingly endless numbers of soldiers trudge up the steep gangway, heavy-laden in cloth-covered steel helmets, carrying rifles and transport packs on their backs. They disappeared into the ship's hold as if being devoured. When Akikusa's boarding group number was called the trio of radiomen; Akikusa, Kageyama and Kumakura, joined the others in shuffling below decks, and were met with the blended odors of fuel oil, diesel exhaust, grease, rust, freshly assembled wooden crates, and sweat. A trip by troop transport in a convoy is a remarkable experience. Akikusa came to Iwo Jima that way.

After several hours of waiting, Akikusa felt the deep rumble of the idling engines; the vibrations passed through the floor and into the humid summer air. The ship's steam whistles announced their departure. Akikusa almost expected a grand sendoff like in the newsreels, but there were no streamers or bands playing martial music. *Things aren't often what we expect them to be.* Once the ship was underway, the radio boys came topside to witness the lights of Tōkyō Bay slowly slip away. The enlisted men were allowed to move freely on deck, except for a small portion that was set aside for officers.

No one could, or would, tell them where they were going, or how long it would take to get there. As the night fell, the young men searched the sky for the North Star to track their movements. The guiding star appeared on the starboard and then on the port side, telling Akikusa that they were moving in a zigzag pattern to avoid enemy submarines. In the dim moonlight he could see the faint wakes of other vessels but couldn't make out details due to blackout conditions. One of the vessels drew close; it looked to Akikusa like a stubby tugboat with a long rear deck, "That must be an escort destroyer," he noted to Kageyama. The sight of the warship was comforting. Soon, the North Star settled in one place, telling them they were heading south. The ocean was rough that night and the boat steadily rocked up and down through the inky darkness. "We must be headed to the Ogasawara Islands, don't you think?" asked Kageyama. Akikusa couldn't reply because he was too seasick. Akikusa was embarrassed, *what kind of sailor gets seasick?* Kumakura suggested he stare at the stars, maybe that would help. The young men looked up at the Milky Way studded with billions of tiny dots of light. "It was incredible, truly spectacular," recalled Akikusa.*

In his state of nausea it seemed that an eternity had slipped beneath the hull of the ship. Akikusa heard the cheery bugle tune of "mess call" but waved off the idea of eating; his mouth was dry and tasted of bile. His friends Kageyama

---

* The author took the 28-hour ferry from Tokyo to Chichi Jima and can attest to this breathtaking wonder.

and Kumakura went down to the galley, leaving Akikusa clinging to the windy railing like a bird on a wire. He was trying to suck in as much fresh, cool, sea air as possible.

The dawn revealed to Akikusa that they were part of a convoy, but he still didn't know the destination. In June and July 1944, US submarines were fattening their kill tallies with Japanese transport vessels culled north of the Ogasawara Islands. The *Enjū Maru* was one of six vessels being escorted to Chichi Jima in convoy number 3729, which was part of operation "*I-go Sakusen Yusō*."[45] Sailing alongside the *Enjū Maru* were the transports *Shōgen Maru*, *Tonegawa Maru*, *Ryūkō Maru*, *Hokkai Maru* and *Unkai Maru No. 7*. From the deck of his flagship *Matsu*, Rear-Admiral Ichimatsu Takahashi commanded the 2nd *Gōei Sendan* escort destroyer squadron, which included *Hatakaze*, and three sub chasers: *Kaibōkan* 4, 12 and 51. Providing air cover for the convoy were aircraft from the aircraft carrier *Zuihō*'s 931st Naval Air Group.[46] The *Zuihō* had her own dedicated group of escort destroyers; *Yamagumo*, *Nowaki*, *Akatsuki* and *Hatsutsuki*.[47]

The lookouts were at their posts with binoculars, straining for signs of enemy submarines. The *Enjū Maru*'s crew had good reason to be nervous because an American submarine had damaged their ship six months earlier in these same waters.*

Kumakura returned from chow call with two rice balls that he handed to Akikusa saying, "Here, you should eat something." Feeling grateful, yet unsure of himself, Akikusa gingerly took a small bite, and then another, carefully chewing. The second bite uncovered a familiar tiny, dark pink, salted plum that which helped ease his sour stomach.

The day passed without incident as they observed the color of the sea gradually change from green to bluish hues. Silvery flying fish popped out of the water for a brief moment, their gossamer fins giving them sufficient glide time to earn their nickname.

Shortly before sunrise on the following day, Akikusa noted the ocean had changed to a stunning blue color. The escort destroyers were no longer visible. A wave of panic came over him as a klaxon horn blared a staccato warning.

---

* US Submarine *Steelhead* (SS-280) damaged *Enju Maru* 110 miles from Chichi Jima on February 15, 1944. (Official Chronology of the US Navy in WWII)

A voice announced, "Battle Stations, Aircraft Alarm." There were two tiny dots far in the distance. The disembodied voice then bellowed, "Unidentified Aircraft. Distance, 10,000 meters." The crews manning the anti-aircraft guns trained their weapons on the incoming planes as the passengers dashed below decks for safety. Moments later one of the planes used a light to blink a simple coded message. A pair of Jake floatplanes from Chichi Jima's 901st Naval Air Group, assigned to escort duty, waggled their wings in a greeting and circled the convoy. Strict radio silence had prohibited the planes from identifying themselves prior to approaching the convoy.

Akikusa and the others returned topside to search the horizon. Ever so slowly, something appeared on the horizon like a giant green turtle poking its head out of the sea. "That must be Chichi Jima," said Kageyama. A feeling of relief came over Akikusa as the island grew in size. Dolphins cavorted in the shockingly clear water and surfed in the ship's bow wake as if to congratulate the *Enjū Maru* for running the gauntlet. As the ship pulled up to the dock in Futami Bay, a shrill boatswain's pipe came over the loudspeaker followed by a voice, "Prepare to disembark!" It was 3:00 p.m., on Saturday, July 28, 1944. As the troops moved towards the gangway Akikusa peered down into the amazingly clear water to see aquarium-like brightly-colored tropical fish darting among the coral. Akikusa and the others walked down the gangway to the sound of the boatswain's pipe. The island had a sandy beach, was lush and green, and its air was filled with the songs of birds echoing in hills. *This isn't so bad,* Akikusa told himself.

A navy signalman wearing the older round rating rank insignia met Akikusa and the other radiomen at the dock. The radiomen hefted their sea bags and followed the signalman inland up a well-worn path for about 500 yards. Continuing upward past some papaya, palm and pine trees, they arrived at a grouping of two-story wooden homes, one of which would serve as their barracks. The signalman provided an orientation on chow and bathing arrangements and the location of their assigned air raid shelter. The house to the right was the barracks for the naval accounting and storekeepers, and acted as a galley for the troops in the immediate area.

After the briefing, the newcomers were left to their own devices. Kumakura picked a few semi-ripe papayas, which they shared in a circle sitting on the ground. After a few bites of the rare fruit, Akikusa's empty stomach began to rumble. He had not eaten much during the voyage. Outside the galley building, a sailor banged on an empty pot hanging from a tree; the universally welcome sound for chow call meant sailors stationed at the different barracks had to "come and get it." The designated "food-fetchers," usually the junior man, took metal cans of rice and soup back to their squads. After dinner, the sun dipped towards the horizon, providing a colorful display of colors for the radiomen who were happily fed and rested. *I am going to like it here,* Akikusa thought. "After we ate, Kumakura showed off his talent for blowing perfect smoke rings with his little brass pipe," said Akikusa.

A few uneventful days passed with no work assignments for the radiomen. One day, the air raid sirens began to wail, growing louder, echoing through the trees and bouncing back from the cliffs across Futami Bay. Akikusa stood motionless, lulled into a sense of security by the peaceful atmosphere of Chichi Jima, until several men pushed past, which startled him into action. Akikusa scrambled for his designated underground shelter, barely squeezing in before cracking thunder filled the air. Akikusa didn't see any enemy ships or aircraft and had no idea what was happening. He felt movement behind him; "I forgot something, I'll be right back," shouted a man as he wriggled towards the entrance. Moments later, he returned with two rifles and a leather belt, heavy with cartridge pouches. The man shoved his way back into the shelter and shouted over the din, "They will be landing soon. We'll need these." Akikusa looked at the rifles and grew worried, *when will I get my rifle?* The ringing in Akikusa's ears nearly obscured the all-clear signal.

As the occupants emerged from the dark shelter, Akikusa noticed his friends hadn't been with him. The smell of cordite hung heavy in the air as he scanned a smoking pile of wreckage that was formerly their barracks. The galley building was destroyed, too. Bent pots, pans and utensils were scattered about as though an angry wife had caught her husband cheating. A voice shouted, "Aki, are you ok?" His heart leapt as his two friends emerged from the galley crew's shelter. The radiomen nervously laughed and shared their impressions of their first taste of war. They picked at the broken rubble of their billet, but found very little they could salvage from their personal gear. Everything was burnt, bent, or full of holes. Even Akikusa's good-luck flag was gone.

Chichi Jima functioned as a radio relay and communication center, so the destruction of the radio stations was an important goal of the US Navy. One of these raids occurred shortly after Akikusa left Chichi Jima. Lieutenant (jg) George H.W. Bush was a pilot with Torpedo Squadron Fifty-One (VT-51) aboard the aircraft carrier USS *San Jacinto* (CVL-30). He was assigned to bomb a radio transmission center on Mount Asahiyama. Bush's TBM Avenger was struck by anti-aircraft fire and he was forced to bail out. Although Lt (jg) Bush was rescued by the submarine USS *Finback* (SS-230), the fates of Radioman Second Class John Delaney, and Lieutenant (jg)William White, USNR, who substituted for Bush's regular gunner, are unknown.[*]

After Akikusa's billet was destroyed, the three friends decided to make the best of the situation and assembled a makeshift roof out of the wreckage. Akikusa's only possessions were his uniform and the navy–issued *tenugui* (thin white cotton towel printed with a large anchor) that was draped around his neck.

The following morning, after eating breakfast supplied by another unit, the trio went into the small town and were impressed by a large tunnel sporting massive steel doors. Kumakura said, "Too bad we weren't in there during the attack," the others grunted in agreement. The residents of Chichi Jima paid for the construction of the Ōmura Zuidō tunnel in 1936. It served as a corridor to connect the villages located on opposite sides of the island. The Japanese Navy later added huge steel doors, which transformed the tunnel into a massive air raid shelter suitable for trucks, small boats and thousands of men.

Akikusa and the others returned to the wreckage of their barracks and waited for orders. In the evening, a petty officer approached them and snapped, "Prepare to move out." He added the boilerplate follow-up command, "Don't forget your gear." That was easy; they no longer had any gear to forget.

That night, the trio walked to the bay and spotted a Type-2 SB(T) landing craft. It had a bow ramp, and was similar in appearance to American LSTs that were used to deliver vehicles, troops and supplies directly onto a beach.[†]

---

[*] The author visited Chichi Jima in 1992, and sent photos of the destroyed communications bunker to the President, who replied with a sincere handwritten letter of appreciation.

[†] The Japanese Type 2 SB(T) could carry fourteen tanks, 250 tons of cargo, or deliver 320 fully equipped troops directly to the water's edge. While American LSTs had a bow that would open like a French door, the Japanese version had a large bow ramp.

Akikusa recalled seeing light reflecting off several 20 mm anti-aircraft guns mounted on blisters on both sides of the bow; he thought they resembled his grandfather's barren *bonsai* trees in winter. The crew of army sailors (*senpaku hei*) was making preparations to get underway. As Akikusa walked up the ramp, the grumbling bass of the engines and vibrating deck caused him to worry, *I hope I don't get sick again.* Cloaked in darkness, the Japanese LST chugged out of the bay to the sound of the "Leaving Port" bugle call. A few officers on the dock held a farewell salute.

Without even thinking, Yasuo Kumakura reached into his pocket and produced his pipe, but his ritual was interrupted by an unseen voice, "No smoking." An embarrassed Kumakura shoved the slender pipe back into his pocket and cracked his knuckles in smoker's frustration. The passengers were instructed to keep their eyes peeled for enemy submarines. The running lights were off, and there were no other ships in sight. Akikusa willed himself not to get seasick again as the ship pushed on through the swells. Over the grumbling of the engine, an army sailor said to no one in particular, "Welcome to non-stop service to hell." The engine chugged through the night, as the propellers churned up a beautiful blue-and-white phosphorescent wake of plankton.

The hours stretched on until the pre-dawn hue revealed an upside-down funnel-shaped island on the horizon. The date was Sunday, July 30, 1944. Akikusa said that the island resembled the pipe Kumakura carried. From their western side approach, to the right was the bowl of the pipe and stretching out to the left was the stem. The defenders called the volcano "Pipe Mountain" (*paipu yama*). At that time Akikusa didn't yet know the name, official or unofficial, of the semi-dormant 554-foot volcano that would become the setting for one of the world's most famous photos.

As the boat drew close to shore an authoritative voice called out, "Get ready to move fast." They would be landing on the western side of the island on what the Americans named "Purple Beach 1." It was on the opposite side of the island where the US Marines would be landing in 205 days. Akikusa looked over the gunwale and could see waves hitting the black sands of the beach. Without fanfare, the boat lurched and stopped. Even before the tip of the ramp cleared eye-level, the boat's crew was shouting, "Get out!" The men at the front began to scurry down the ramp, but much too slowly for an NCO screaming at the top of his lungs. Soldiers and sailors struggled to carry boxes, crates, sea bags and other gear off the boat. There were trucks on the shore, and soldiers and sailors helping to unload the supplies.

As Akikusa moved forward towards the ramp, he saw sand jumping up like water on a hot griddle. *Enemy Aircraft!* There had been no air raid siren. He instinctively looked up but didn't see anything, and was bum-rushed down the ramp by troops behind him. He heard aircraft engines growling amidst the staccato sound of gunfire that was coming from all sides. It was every man for himself as he fell to the sand. Akikusa leaped to his feet and ran for cover towards the volcano to the right. He threw himself to the ground in front of a rocky terrace. But a surge of adrenaline kicked in and he scrambled up and over the terrace, and then another, all the while imagining a bullet tearing through his spine. *Please don't let me die,* he prayed. He spotted a clump of tall pampas grass and sprinted for its camouflaging leaves. He squirmed his body into the center mass and gulped for breath. He looked up to see an airplane trailing a stream of white dots of smoke.

Gunfire erupted from the volcanic mountain to his right; it was the echo of gunfire bouncing off the mountain from nearby anti-aircraft guns. He tightened into a ball and prayed, *Please hit me in the head, don't hit my arms or legs.* The pace of gunfire slowed down, and then stopped as the sound of aircraft engines faded away. Akikusa suddenly noticed the oppressive summer heat and his thirst. He had no rations, canteen or weapon. He scouted the grassy area but saw no one. *Did the others make it off the boat?* He had moved inland so couldn't see the beach below. Akikusa struggled with what to do; *Dare I return to the ship? No, what if the planes return and I get caught in the open?*

Looking for a better place to hide, he moved to a cluster of small trees and bushes. He was startled by a guttural voice that roared, "Hey! You! Get the hell away from here!" He looked closely, and spied a dirty, deeply tanned man in the bushes staring back through large wild eyes under the brim of a cloth-covered helmet. The man was part of a navy anti-aircraft gun emplacement artfully disguised halfway below ground. It was covered with camouflage netting and surrounded by bushes. Akikusa asked, "Excuse me, is the *Nanpō Shotō* Naval Air Group unit close by?" The man jabbed his arm through the netting and barked, "Get out of here!" Akikusa meekly shuffled away in the direction the angry stranger had pointed. *Welcome to Iwo Jima.*

The Bunker

Akikusa made his way past the edge of an airfield and met someone who helped him find the *Nanpō Shotō Shirei-bu* (Southern Area Islands Naval Air HQ) bunker complex. Captain Samaji Inoue's *Nanpō* bunker was located about a mile north of the beach on the Motoyama plain at Mount Tamana-yama. The *Nanpō* bunker was said to be one of the largest tunnel complexes on the island as it would eventually house 800 men. The bunker had enough food, water and ammo to hold out for three months. But it was still under construction so many of the troops were sleeping in civilian homes, warehouses, and in tents.

Akikusa was met by a group of men who happened to be coming out of the entrance; someone in the back shouted, "Hey, Akikusa! Is that you?" It was Kageyama, with Kumakura in tow. The men shoved each other playfully as they exchanged greetings of, "I thought you were dead!" They had been separated during the strafing attack and took different routes across the island, but ended up at the right spot.

"What a welcoming committee we had, eh?" said Kageyama with a wide smile.

One of the other men in the group was PO1/c Kazuo Yamaguchi, a slightly older man who was also an alumnus of Yokosuka Communication School. "Let me show you boys around," said Kazuo Yamaguchi who was the senior man in the huddle.

Akikusa followed Yamaguchi into the hand-dug cave; it was bigger inside than the humble opening led him to believe. The entrance was built at a 90-degree angle to defeat bomb blasts and flamethrowers. Akikusa coughed at the sour stench that came swimming towards him on a current of dry hot air. It burned his eyes, which were still trying to adjust from the glaring summer sun outside. The complex had multiple ventilation shafts and entrances, but was still uncomfortably hot. The men passed a stash of bamboo poles, rocks and sandbags (made from burlap rice bags) that were used to plug the tunnel entrance from the inside. There were alcoves for lookouts and entrance guards. Illumination came from electric lights, small kerosene lamps and hurricane lamps resting in carved-out shelves.

PO1/c Kazuo Yamaguchi said, "This is our designated entrance, there are many others, but this one is ours." Akikusa wondered how Yamaguchi could stand the smell. They moved down a tunnel and approached a side room where

Yamaguchi said softly, "This is where you'll be working." Inside the brightly lit anteroom sat a row of silent men wearing headphones, facing a bank of radio receivers. Akikusa recognized the Matsushita vacuum tube wireless key sets he trained with at Yokosuka. The room also had the familiar short, medium and long wave Kawasaki transmitters, making Akikusa feel somewhat at home.

Yamaguchi led the men further down the tunnel, "Here is where the officers gather for strategy meetings." Further into the bunker complex were the gasoline-powered generators for radios and lighting. The men passed the Communication Chief's quarters, and the food supply storage area with wooden crates stacked to the ceiling. Further inside the bunker was a two-part toilet area about fifteen feet wide. On first inspection, it appeared to be a dry pit, but the rancid stench told Akikusa that the liquid evaporated as fast as it was deposited. There was a separate pit for the other business. Beyond that was a carved stairway leading up to an observation port.

They also passed by the morgue pit. There were bodies in the bottom of hole, packed in like sardines, waiting to be cremated. The tunnels were constructed so that the offensive odors from the latrine and morgue were confined, but the smells managed to waft their way out to mingle with the living.

The sides of the tunnels were lined with 55-gallon drums filled with various liquids: water, kerosene, or fuel oil for the generators. Akikusa estimates there were 500 steel drums, which served double duty as lumpy bunks for the troops, although some of the officers had metal spring beds with mattresses. According to Akikusa, at its deepest point the *Nanpō* bunker was 90 feet underground with an average ceiling height of 7½ ft and a width of 10-15 feet. Some of the tunnels were 100 yards long resembling an ant farm. The digging, which the radiomen were excused from, was backbreaking work that required rocks, sand, and other material to be carried out by hand in flat woven bamboo baskets.

After the tour, Yamaguchi escorted the wide-eyed freshmen to the main entrance that was nearly as wide as a small bus. The barrels of fuel and water had been trucked in through there. It was an impressive bunker complex, indeed.

They all headed back out to their own entrance for some fresh air. Yamaguchi introduced two more radiomen, Tanaka and Yamazaki, who had also graduated from Yokosuka Communications School. It felt like a reunion.

The six men sat down to an ocean breeze on a patch of thick grass. Yamaguchi said, "We're classmates here. Don't hesitate to speak up. After all, we've eaten rice from the same pot. We'll help you adjust." Tanaka and Yamazaki nodded in unison. "Buck up, don't look so glum," Yamaguchi said as he produced a canteen from behind his back. "It's nearly full, too," Yamaguchi said as he handed the green canvas-covered aluminum canteen to Akikusa who unscrewed the silver cap; it banged against the canteen dangling from a short chain. Akikusa held the canteen with both hands and raised it to his lips but balked at the faint rotten-egg odor. He shot a questioning look at Yamaguchi, who smiled and nodded approvingly. Akikusa took a sip of the warm liquid that instantly reminded him of water from a hot springs bath.

Yamaguchi said, "And we can drink the whole thing." There would be a time in the future when Akikusa would give his right arm for a swig of that sulfur-tainted water. He passed the canteen to Kageyama, who made a face as he took a sip.

Water had always been a problem for the pre-war inhabitants of Iwo Jima. They used rain gutters and concrete catch basins to collect water. But when the island's population blossomed with the arrival of so many troops, the issue of water became a matter of grave concern. The Army brought in a special irrigation unit to dig wells with limited success. While the Japanese soldiers on Guadalcanal, and other islands, suffered from starvation, the unlucky souls on Iwo Jima were tortured by both hunger and thirst.

Yamaguchi unbuckled the flap of his musette bag to reveal a handful of rice balls and slices of pickled *daikon* radish wrapped in paper.* Large flies buzzed about as Yamaguchi transferred the rations to outstretched dirty hands. Akikusa nodded his head in silent appreciation, swatted away a fly, and bit into his rice ball. It too, had an odd taste. Seeing his expression, Yamaguchi said, "The rice tastes different because of the water. You'll get used to it." The lack of water was the first thing all the Japanese soldiers and sailors observed. "Look on the bright side," Yamaguchi said, "a lack of standing water means no

---

* The Japanese Navy version of the *zatsunō* shoulder bag (multi-purpose bag) has interior straps with buckles to secure the flap, while the Army version has interior ties. It resembles a WWII German breadbag (*Brotbeutel*).

mosquitoes, and that means no malaria."

As they consumed their rations, Yamaguchi shared the duty schedule and added an overview of the island. Yamaguchi then walked them to the farmer's house that would be their billet. There was an air raid shelter nearby. Yamaguchi pointed to some trees, "Those are octopus trees."* Akikusa could see where they got their name. "See the little green pineapple things? They are ready to eat when they turn orange. They are fibrous and tough to eat, but taste like chestnuts," Yamaguchi said. The locals pressed them for cooking oil, or fed them to their pigs.

Prior to the war, many of the locals worked at the sugar processing plant (*Tōkyō Seitō Kōjō*) or the sulfur refinery (*Iwo Kōzan Seirenshō*). The plants were under the control of Iwo Jima Industry Inc.[48] The rest of the inhabitants were fishermen or farmers who tended medicinal coca plants, sugar cane, lemon grass, bananas, pineapples, tomatoes and other crops. The residents couldn't grow their own rice because the climate was too dry, so they depended on supply ships for their staple food of rice.

Following the air raids in June 1944, the women and children were evacuated. An undetermined number of males between the ages of 16 and 40 were conscripted as *gunzoku* (civilian contract workers) and put to work farming and digging tunnels.

Akikusa, Kageyama and Kumakura settled in to their new home. However, the crews of the transport vessels that brought them were not so lucky. The empty *Enjū Maru* formed up with Transport Convoy No. 0408 and set sail for Japan on August 4. Since the carrier *Zuihō* and her complement of destroyers had returned to Japan ahead of the convoy, it had no air cover for the return trip. Iwo Jima's radar unit picked up an incoming formation of planes and warned the transports. The handful of surviving Zeros and search planes still on Iwo Jima were sent into the air, not to do battle, but to escape being destroyed on the ground.

The transports were spotted about twenty-five miles north of Mukō Jima by aircraft from RAdm Joseph J. "Jocko" Clark's Task Group 58.1; aircraft from the carriers USS *Bunker Hill* and USS *Lexington* caught the undefended convoy

---

* *Bonin pandanus* or "Octopus Tree" (*Tako no Ki*) has roots that stretch downward mid-air, resembling tentacles.

in open water. Naval gunfire from four light cruisers and seven destroyers, detached from RAdm Laurence T. DuBose's TG 58.1 and TG 58.3, sank the cargo ship *Ryūkō Maru* and RAdm Ichimatsu Takahashi's flagship *Matsu*. US aircraft sank the transports *Unkai Maru No.7*, *Enjū Maru*, *Tonegawa Maru* and *Shōgen Maru*. They damaged Coastal Defense Vessels CD-4 and CD-12, which escaped along with Sub Chaser No. 51 and the destroyer *Hatakaze*.

US naval gunfire and carrier planes combined to finish off Transport Convoy No. 0408 by sinking the cargo ship *Hokkai Maru*.[49] Also sunk, possibly by a US submarine, was the *Yayoi Maru*.

The following day on August 5, the Americans returned to Chichi Jima to deliver the *coup de grace* to Fast Transports No. 2, No. 4 and No. 104, and the cargo ship *Hinkō Maru*, which ran aground.* A dozen shuttle vessels were also lost in the two-day air raid. Although the transports were empty when they went down, the loss of their tonnage and trained crews was a hard blow to the Japanese who were desperate to reinforce Iwo Jima. The US Navy's surface and air forces racked up a juicy kill tally, but the real prize, the aircraft carrier *Zuihō*, had slipped through their fingers.[50]

After the fall of Saipan and the death of Admiral Chūichi Nagumo, Iwo Jima's *Keibitai* naval ground defense unit was transferred, on paper, from the Central Pacific Fleet to the Third Air Fleet. Commander Tsunezō Wachi would report to a new boss named Vice-Admiral Rinosuke Ichimaru who would be arriving in August. Commander Wachi was going to be dropped to the No. 2 position in the naval organization chart for Iwo Jima.

However, before Admiral Ichimaru arrived, there was a twist; another senior navy man would be coming to Iwo Jima; a pilot named Captain Samaji Inoue. In December 1941, Inoue had led the Taiwan-based 753rd Naval Air Group bombers to victory in the Philippines. In February 1944, Captain Inoue was assigned to the ground defense of Hainan Naval Air Group.† On July 10, 1944 Captain Samaji Inoue landed on Iwo Jima to take command of the Navy's *Nanpō Shotō Kaigun Kōkūtai* (Southern Area Islands Naval Air Group). Since *Nanpō* was an air group in name only, with no organic aircraft, Captain Inoue

---

* The author snorkeled on the wreck of the *Hinkō Maru*.

† Zero Pilot Toshimitsu Imaizumi cut his teeth with the Hainan Naval Air Group. See *The Last Zero Fighter*, chapter four.

was responsible for maintaining other units' aircraft that used Iwo Jima as a temporary air base or staging area. These were mostly bombers targeting the Marianas, and reconnaissance planes conducting anti-submarine patrols. Captain Inoue had an ample supply of maintenance personnel, radiomen, equipment, food supplies, bombs and other ordnance.

A problem soon arose because both Commander Wachi and Captain Inoue assumed that they were second-in-command of the island's naval forces. A rivalry began between Commander Tsunezō Wachi, the surface fleet man who had been Iwo's naval commander since March, and the newcomer Captain Inoue, the pilot who technically outranked Wachi but was a parallel in the organization chart. This new command structure became the source of friction.

As a result of the all-too-familiar lack of a clear direction that occurs in many organizations, a power struggle emerged between two men who didn't see eye-to-eye. One incident was Captain Inoue's annoyance with Commander Wachi's decision to release naval assets to the army without his permission. Wachi had granted a request from the 145th Infantry Regiment's commander to dismantle several wooden buildings, including the damaged elementary school. The lumber was used by the army to build shelves, tables and ammunition racks inside their tunnels. Captain Inoue learned about it after the fact and was angry that Wachi didn't come to him first. Commander Wachi didn't need to consult with Captain Inoue because the buildings, and all civilian property were under Wachi's jurisdiction as the *keibitai* commander.[51] Wachi was not intimidated by Inoue's complaints and stated that he wrote the following in a memo to Inoue, "Why don't you come out of your bunker once in a while and actually meet with the army commanders? With your poor attitude you can expect no further cooperation from me."[52] Wachi's insubordinate statement flew in the face of both Japanese naval tradition and social protocol.

Working Underground

Tsuruji Akikusa, who was assigned to Captain Inoue's unit, said the island was honeycombed with miles of tunnels blasted out with dynamite and scratched out of the earth with picks and shovels. However, solid rock formations and steam vents made it impossible to connect all of the bunkers. The units worked independently to construct their own fortifications, bunkers, air raid shelters and fighting positions.[53] As naval radiomen, Akikusa,

Kageyama and Kumakura, were spared from the backbreaking excavation work. Akikusa said the wireless operators' fingers were too important to risk damaging them with manual labor. The silent radio room was located several stories underground; the only sounds were the subdued metallic clacking of Morse keys, and the whisper of dull pencils scratching on logs called 'red books'. The wireless operators passed the coded messages to the decoders, who toiled in an adjoining area separated by a curtain of blankets to create a sense of normalcy. In one corner, a sailor stood watch over a bucket of water. The guard would dish out one cup of water per man, per shift. Akikusa wanted to plunge his head into the bucket and drink it dry. The small cup of water was just enough to prevent dehydration, but not enough to produce much sweat. "We radiomen didn't have individual canteens so we depended on that bucket," Akikusa said.

It was hot enough just being in the tunnels, but wearing a radio headset for six hours at a time was torture. His ears grew hot and moist under the rubber headset; a small bead of sweat would creep into an ear canal causing a itch; an itch that he didn't dare scratch for fear of missing a dot or a dash in an incoming message. It was brutal work, sitting in the hot, dry foul air listening intently for the next Morse code message.

Akikusa strained to jot down the dots and dashes that came racing through the receiver. There was pressure to get it right every time because a single missed syllable could mean disaster. There were three cardinal sins; dropped syllables, mistaken syllables, and extra symbols. "We had to listen hard for a specific symbol that marked the end of a message. It was harder at dawn and dusk when the radio waves were affected by atmospheric conditions," Akikusa said. "There was a feeling of relief when I heard the "end of message" symbol. I remember it well." To demonstrate to the author, Akikusa tapped out the code on the tabletop, "dot dot dot dash dot dash."

Both he and Kageyama were off duty one morning and decided to forgo sleep to explore the area. They exited the large main entrance and walked south down the long slope to the middle of the island. They walked past some bare papaya trees to the cheery tune of an *uguisu* bush warbler. In spite of the presence of so many men on the island, the little birds weren't afraid of humans. Akikusa said one could walk right up to the trusting little birds.

The pair of explorers passed a group of men digging an air raid shelter near a Chinese banyan tree. The laborers were coated with fine yellow dust, and paid no attention to the radiomen. The diggers hauled wicker baskets of soil and rocks from inside the dark hole. Akikusa counted himself lucky for being exempt from such tasks. The pair continued their stroll, passing under a *torii* gate that marked the path to the *Iwo Jima Jinja* Shinto shrine. The young men approached the shrine, bowed and reverently clapped twice to pay their respects. The shrine was used by the locals to celebrate the sugar cane harvest. The pair traveled further, crossing a forested area dotted with anti-aircraft emplacements and machine gun bunkers. They turned north and came upon a grassy plain that was to be the future Airfield No. 3. Akikusa said that it didn't even resemble an airfield. It was just a grassy flat plain with rocks and boulders here and there. Akikusa vividly remembered seeing a single wrecked aircraft, carefully camouflaged with nets and tree branches.

Friendly planes would occasionally fly in to reinforce the island, or use it as a staging point for attacks against the Marianas. It was common for Japanese planes to temporarily flee for safety when US bombers approached. Akikusa was on duty one day during one such incident. Akikusa received an urgent unencoded message tapped out by a friendly pilot who stated that he was running out of fuel and wanted permission to return. Akikusa scribbled down the message and presented it to the duty officer and waited for a reply to send. The pilot repeated his request for permission to return to Iwo Jima. The duty officer instructed Akikusa to tap the following response in the clear, "Permission Denied. Possible enemy activity. Seek out and crash dive into an enemy ship. End transmission." The pilot tapped a terse reply, "Please verify and report my death in battle." There were no further transmissions. "He probably flew around until he ran out of fuel and crashed into the sea. What a stupid waste of life. I often think about the pilot's final transmission," Akikusa said.

On August 13th, communication chief Lieutenant Yosaburō Takanō called Akikusa and Kageyama into his "office" which was a small carved out anteroom. He instructed them to head to the Tamana-yama Communications Unit bunker to deliver a personal letter and some supplies to the communications chief. The pair slung a heavy bag of uncooked rice over a bamboo pole and walked to the Tamana-yama Communications Unit to deliver the message and the supplies. They were delayed from immediately returning by B-24 bombers that blasted the airfields.⁵⁴ While waiting for the air raid to lift, Akikusa noted that the Tamana-yama Communications bunker was built like a fortress with 3-foot-thick reinforced concrete walls and a 3-foot-thick roof covered by two yards of rocks and sand. The floors were concrete instead of dirt, and men slept on thick mats instead of on the tops of steel drums. The best thing was that the galley served hot *miso* soup, steamed rice and vegetables.

After the all-clear signal, the pair reluctantly returned to their *Nanpō* HQ bunker. Shortly after this incident, Lieutenant Takano told them he was lending their services to the Tamana-yama Communications Unit for two weeks. To Akikusa, it meant hot food and a proper bunk on which to sleep; two things that the enlisted men cherished.

On August 15, 1944, Rear Admiral Rinosuke Ichimaru boarded a transport plane headed to the sulfurous island that would become his final resting place.⁵⁵ In order to coordinate and control Iwo Jima defenses, Japanese IGHQ sent him to command the island's Navy units. The Admiral was no political appointee, but a grizzled, hands-on leader who paid his dues in blood, sweat and engine oil. Ichimaru graduated from the Naval Academy located at Etajima in 1913, and spent four years serving at sea. He was an aviation trailblazer who in 1917 joined the Naval Aviation School's third graduating class.⁵⁶ In January 1925, Ichimaru became squadron commander at Kasumigaura Naval Air base. He was injured in a crash in May 1925 that nearly ended his career, suffering a broken leg and fractures to his face. After years of convalescing and several operations, Ichimaru returned to duty in 1929 as commander of the newly formed *Yokaren* aviation program. Ichimaru's Spartan-like discipline and demands for both physical and academic excellence earned him the moniker "Father of the *Yokaren*."

In the coming years, Ichimaru's career blossomed. In 1936, he was given command of the *Chinkai* Air Group, a reconnaissance and anti-submarine unit stationed in current day South Korea. Following this, he took over the Yokohama Naval Air Group, the Yokosuka Naval Training Base Naval Air Group, and then the Chichi Jima Naval Air Group. In November 1939, Ichimaru took the reins of the 13ᵗʰ Naval Air Group in China. Ichimaru raised eyebrows by often accompanying bombing missions over the continent. After his promotion to Rear Admiral, Ichimaru was given the 21ˢᵗ Air Flotilla, followed by a drastic change of scenery to New Ireland in New Guinea to lead the 13th Combined Air Fleet.

Ichimaru's final posting was to command the 27th Air Flotilla (*Kōkū Sentai*), a respectable sized organization with six Naval Air Groups that were spread out at Oita, Kisarazu, Katori and Iwo Jima.[57] In reality, it was a paper tiger with little in the way of serious offensive capabilities.

Akikusa and Kageyama moved again on September 1, 1944, from Tamanayama to Rear Admiral Rinosuke Ichimaru's Kitano Communications Unit bunker in the north. On September 15th, Akikusa received disheartening news over the wireless, the Americans had invaded Peleliu. It was clear that Iwo Jima was on the hit list, too. Akikusa told Kageyama, "The good news is that this bunker is in the perfect spot to survive the upcoming battle. If we can hold out here long enough, the Navy will sail in and destroy the US Fleet." They spent the next three months hunched over their radios deep inside the Kitano Communications Unit bunker in the north.

Ensign Satoru Ōmagari

Another officer who landed on Chidori Airfield on August 15, 1944, was Ensign Satoru Ōmagari. He was born June 1, 1922, in Fukushima Prefecture in the tiny farming town of Kodaka-chō. He was the third born to a family with seven children. Ōmagari's father died when he was twelve, so his grandfather, the town mayor, stepped in to help raise the four boys and three girls. His granduncle (a naval captain who fought in the Russo-Japan War) encouraged the boys to study hard. The oldest son graduated from a pharmacy college, served in the Army, and in 1941, opened his own pharmacy. The second son studied at prestigious Waseda University. Satoru Ōmagari studied engineering at Akita Mining College. The fourth son studied engineering at Tōhoku University.

The Pearl Harbor attack occurred while Ōmagari was a college student. "The war in Manchuria had been going on for several years, so I just figured we had opened another front in the Pacific," he said. He could have joined the military like hundreds of thousands of young men, but Ōmagari had no interest in wearing a uniform. He took advantage of his college deferment and thought, *with any luck the war would be over soon.*

In August 1943, the draft board sent Ōmagari a summons to appear for a physical exam. Ōmagari passed the medical exam with flying colors and was granted "A" draft status. Once he accepted his sheepskin, he faced being conscripted into the world's harshest army as a "two cent draftee," the nickname given to draftees who could be called up for the cost to send a pink-colored draft notice through the mail. The Japanese Army's reputation for brutalizing recruits meant he would be beaten and hazed by younger, less-educated men. The thought of this was disturbing to Ōmagari who came from a long line of educated men.

Just before graduation, a visitor came to the college; a naval officer who gave a lecture on the merits of the Navy's *Yobigakusei* ROTC program. Ōmagari qualified for the program in which the Navy accepted university, college or trade school enrollees (or recent graduates) and bestowed upon them the rank of Warrant Officer. After a period of training, the reservists would become ensigns with the right to wear the coveted *Kaigun Tanken* navy dagger that was said to attracts beautiful girls, and wards off evil spirits.* Ōmagari was instantly sold on the idea. If he had no choice but to serve in the military, it was better to volunteer to be a naval officer than risk being drafted into the Army as private.

After finishing their training, the reserve ensigns would return to their civilian jobs, or continue with their schooling until called for active duty. Traditionally, there only were two paths to becoming a naval officer; graduate from the Etajima Naval Academy, or work one's way up from the enlisted ranks as a "mustang." The first option was highly competitive, with only the brightest cadets able to gain admission; the second option required twenty years of hard work. The *Yobigakusai* ROTC program became the third option, and the fast track to a commission.

On September 10, 1943, about a month before graduating with his two-year degree in mining, Ōmagari passed the entrance exam for the *Yobigakusei* program's 7th cycle.

Upon graduation from Akita Mining College, Ōmagari went to Tsuchiura Naval Air Base for basic training. He thought it was a waste of time, because he had taken similar training in both high school and in college. The reservists took written and physical exams to determine if they were fit to become future

---

* "Oni yoke, onna yose" is the phrase in Japanese used to describe the alluring power of an officer wearing his naval dagger.

aviators. Roughly half of the cadets were classified as potential aviators, a category that encompassed pilots, navigators, gunners, flight engineers and wireless operators. The other half would be slated to study specialties such as "general seamanship," "surface navigation," "aviation maintenance," "communications," "accounting and administration," etc. Ōmagari's request for aviation maintenance was granted, so on October 1, 1943, he went to the Yokosuka Naval Base's Oppama Naval Air Group to study naval aviation maintenance. The 7th cycle reservists were each given the status of Warrant Officer and placed in 100-man companies, called *buntai*, and spent the mornings in classrooms, and had hands-on training in the afternoons. At Oppama Naval Base, Ōmagari was assigned to the 17th *Buntai*, which was a company of men dedicated to the Type-1, twin-engine, land-based Betty bomber.

Ōmagari was commissioned an ensign on May 30, 1944. "I purchased my navy dagger and was proud to wear it. I also felt a heavy weight of responsibility at being accountable for the lives of others," he said.[58] Upon completion of his courses at the Oppama Aviation Maintenance School on July 15, 1944, the head instructor asked the newly minted ensigns where they wished to be assigned. Ōmagari had studied mining so was familiar with natural resources and mining operations across the globe. He knew Japan couldn't win a war with the United States and felt that his fellow college-student-officers generally shared his viewpoint. The question was not *if* Japan would lose, but where he would be *when* Japan lost the war. Ōmagari said he preferred to be in the homelands when that happened, but knew if would have expressed that sentiment publicly he would be labeled a coward. Like all of the reservists Ōmagari responded, "I wish to go to the front lines, sir."

The next day, Ensign Ōmagari was among thirteen junior officers that received orders to report to the *Nanpō Shotō* Naval Air Group. Because of the south seas component to the name of the outfit, Ōmagari presumed it was located somewhere in the Philippine Islands. The group of thirteen reserve ensigns was told they would travel to their unknown destination via a transport ship carrying supplies and fresh conscripts. Meanwhile, their first act as officers was to issue uniforms to 300 inductees at Oppama Naval Base. "My first responsibility as an officer was that of a wet nurse," Ōmagari recalled.

Roughly a week later, *Nanpō Shotō* Naval Air Group commander Captain Inoue sent an urgent request through the chain of command. He needed more junior officers to manage the hundreds of enlisted men arriving by the boatload. As a result, seven of the thirteen 7th Cycle ensigns (four were from Ōmagari's own 17th *Buntai*) were ordered to Kisarazu Naval Air Base for immediate air transport to Iwo Jima. The remaining six ensigns would follow in September, as originally planned, on a transport ship.

In the early morning hours of Tuesday, August 15, 1944, Ōmagari hitched a ride in a Tabby transport plane courtesy of the 1023rd Naval Air Group. The Tabby was license-built version of the civilian Douglas DC-3 transport. There were several Tabbys heading to Iwo Jima that morning carrying water, food, ammunition, personnel and mail. In one of the accompanying planes rode Rear-Admiral Rinosuke Ichimaru and his staff. As the planes droned south towards Iwo Jima, Ōmagari was plagued with doubts: *would he be able to command older, more experienced men?*

After the C-47 lookalike Tabbys landed, Ensign Ōmagari and the other freshly minted junior officers were directed towards the air control shack to report for duty. Tired and feeling cramped from the long flight, the young ensigns walked across the field towards the control tower when they were attacked by an angry lieutenant who ordered them to line up. He demanded to know to which unit they were assigned, and it was Ōmagari who replied, "*Nanpō Shotō* Naval Air Group, maintenance section, sir." The officer then yelled at all them for their sloppy way of shuffling along. The lieutenant said, "This is a war zone, people die here. Since you don't seem to understand that, I will teach you a lesson." He then punched each of them in the face. The college boys later discovered that the lieutenant that "taught them a lesson" was Commander Wachi's Executive Officer Lieutenant Mineo Togiwa. The ensigns did their best not to become the subject of his attention in the future.

The ensigns were then handed over to the *Nanpō* Naval Air Group's Lieutenant (jg) Hideo Koshi of the 3rd Aircraft Maintenance Unit. Their new boss gave them a much warmer reception than they had gotten from the snarly Lieutenant Togiwa. Lieutenant Koshi assigned the shave tails to the position of special 200-man *buntai* commanders: Ensign Kenichi Yoshida was ordered to lead the 1st *Buntai*; Ensign Yutaka Nakamura took over the 2nd *Buntai*; and Ensign Satoru Ōmagari took the 3rd *Buntai*.

Ensign Ōmagari was escorted to his quarters located in a building about 100 yards from Captain Samaji Inoue's *Nanpō* HQ Bunker. He dropped off his gear and was taken to visit the main bunker. Ōmagari said, "It was a huge maze. It had a diesel-powered generator for lights and radios. In my smaller air raid shelter we used kerosene lamps and candles in hurricane lanterns." Even though he was an officer, Ōmagari slept on the ground when in his air raid shelter. "I had two white wool navy blankets, and a helmet for my pillow," he said.

Since Ensign Ōmagari had a degree in mine engineering, one might rightly assume his talents were put to good use supervising the construction of tunnels and air raid shelters. On the contrary, Ōmagari's primary function was to oversee aircraft maintenance. He stated that the following aircraft were operable when he touched down on August 15th; six Tenzan Jill torpedo bombers (752nd NAG), eleven Zero Fighters (252nd NAG) and two *Gekko* "Irving" Night Fighters (131st NAG). Since Iwo Jima no longer had a permanent air presence, planes would come and go, but this is what was on the airfield when Ōmagari landed.

Ōmagari's first operational task on Iwo Jima was to clear the airfield of wrecked aircraft. Looking every bit like slaves building the pyramids, Ensign Ōmagari's men used ropes to haul smashed aircraft hulks to the edges of the airfield. They hooked chains to a truck to drag heavier pieces off the flight line. "The transport aircraft engines were too big for our truck to drag away, so I submitted a request through the chain of command for one of the 26th Regiment's tanks. A tank was dispatched to the airfield, which greatly sped up my efforts," said Ōmagari. The work continued for the next few months as aircraft regularly arrived and were destroyed on the ground in American air raids. Some of the aircraft hulks that Ōmagari cleared off the field were converted into air raid shelters.

The secondary role of the maintenance men was to fill in American bomb craters on the airfield. It was important to maintain a serviceable runway for the Betty bombers that usually arrived from Japan around 4:00 p.m. for their late-night missions to the Marianas. Ōmagari's men would refuel the thirsty Bettys that were headed to bomb the captured airfields at Saipan, Guam and Tinian. The ladies would trundle off around 7:00 p.m., drop their bombs on their respective targets around midnight, thread the gauntlet of night fighters and make it back to Iwo Jima around 4:00 a.m. Rushing to beat the inevitable retaliation raid that would come the following day, Ōmagari's sleepy-eyed men topped off the bombers' fuel tanks for the return trip to Japan.

After the Betty bombers left, Ensign Ōmagari's men scuttled back underground to wait for the inevitable air raid. As the American bombers came and went, Ōmagari and the others popped out of the ground to repair the damaged field with shovels, pick axes, handcarts, a few trucks and mechanized rollers. Ōmagari says his men were exhausted by the grossly inefficient and labor-intensive work, "Division wanted the airfields repaired after every raid. We did our best, but it was backbreaking work that took a heavy toll on my men. We should have gone along with the Army's plan to abandon the airfields, and focus our efforts on digging more tunnels and bunkers." After the war, Ōmagari was not shy in sharing his feelings, "The Imperial General Headquarters Staff sat behind desks pouring over production figures, reports and maps. They made unrealistic demands on both men and machines. They should have visited the frontlines to understand what was really going on."

The 3rd Aircraft Maintenance Unit's commander Lieutenant (jg) Hideo Koshi gave his ensigns another task; to supervise the offloading of SB(T) landing craft, and smaller Daihatsu boats, that braved enemy submarines to bring in troops and supplies from Chichi Jima. Once the vessels arrived, usually during the night, the materials were off-loaded onto trucks and distributed to various army and navy supply depots across the island. On occasion, an army supply clerk would appear at Ōmagari's bunker complaining of being shortchanged on food. Ōmagari kept meticulous records that proved the army was allowing boxes to "fall off the truck." Ōmagari refused to budge, knowing that others would demand to be reimbursed for their so-called losses, too.[59]

Naval airman Haruo Yoshino spoke of the pilfering that took place on Iwo Jima. They even had a nickname for men who stole from other units; the thieves were called *ginbae* (blowflies). Yoshino claimed that supplies had to be hidden or placed under guard or they would be spirited away by sneaky *ginbae*.

After the disastrous air battles of July 1944, Iwo Jima's surviving Zero fighters and flight crews were evacuated to Mobara Air Field in Chiba Prefecture. Some of the pilots were later sent to the Philippines as escorts on Kamikaze missions, while others were sent back to Iwo Jima.[60] Some of more famous Zero pilots who survived Iwo Jima were; Isamu Miyazaki, Kazuo Tsunoda, Minoru Honda, Ryōji Ohara, and Saburō Sakai.

Ensign Kazuo Tsunoda was one of the few that were sent back to Iwo Jima with the reorganized 252nd Naval Air Group in August 1944.[61] However, heavy losses forced Ensign Tsunoda and the other Zero pilots to leave Iwo Jima on August 19, 1944. Tsunoda's last memory of Iwo Jima was of sitting in the shade listening to birds singing in the bushes. He recalled watching a young pilot take a caramel candy from his emergency rations kit, and place it in the sun until it was gooey. The mischievous pilot then spun the viscous caramel around a twig, and halfheartedly attempted to snare a warbler that was perched in the bushes singing a happy tune. This angered Tsunoda who scolded the younger man for trying to harass such a sweet, trusting creature. Tsunoda's outburst sent the little bird to flight.

More Letters from Iwo Jima

We can see through Lieutenant Genichi Hattori's letters that the Army was not receiving supplies regularly. Due to the US Navy's submarine warfare, the mail bound for Iwo Jima was often sent to the bottom of the sea. In letters to his younger brother dated July 30, August 13, 18, 30, September 17, 18, 21, and 29, Hattori complained he was not receiving any mail. In one letter he wrote, "It seems like you aren't getting my letters because I am getting nothing from you." He repeatedly asked his younger brother to send him care packages with canned crab, canned fish and meats, canned fruit, dried foodstuffs, tobacco and photos of his daughter Chikako. He complained that the Army depended on cargo ships for mail but they were unreliable. Meanwhile, he bitterly noted that the island's naval personnel regularly received postcards, letters and care packages via air mail.

Lieutenant Hattori was openly unhappy with the uneven mail delivery system and that stationery was scarce on the island that some men couldn't write home at all. As proof of this, some of Hattori's own letters from Iwo Jima were written in the margins of pages carefully cut from magazines. Lieutenant Hattori wrote, "Please send stationery, local newspapers and magazines. Novels are good too, even if they are old and tattered." Hattori also wrote, "We heard the enemy has landed on Yap and Peleliu. It won't be long before they come this way."

What makes Hattori's letters so unique is that the overwhelming majority of letters sent from Iwo Jima lacked details of the actual situation. Military personnel were not permitted to write "Iwo Jima" or mention anything that would cause their families concern. The senior officers, who strictly censored their subordinates' letters, however were themselves free to write openly. Hattori's letters from Iwo Jima are a valuable historic record of life on Iwo Jima before the Marines landed.

In Hattori's letter dated October 5th, he wrote that he received his first letter from home. The letter, which arrived via the Army's slow-moving seaborn mail delivery system, contained a photo of his daughter. "Thank you!" he wrote, "I placed Chikako's photo inside the notebook that I keep in my breast pocket. I look at her cute face many times each day." In this same missive, Hattori stated that his men were suffering from malnutrition, exhaustion, dysentery, jaundice and night blindness. He asked for a magnifying glass because his own vision was failing.

In addition to tins of tobacco, Lieutenant Hattori wanted rice crackers, canned food, rock candy and newspapers. Hattori acknowledged that it was against regulations, but asked his younger brother to mark the care package "military priority," and use his connections at the Kisarazu Naval Air Base to get them loaded onto aircraft bound for Iwo Jima.

Hattori ended one particular letter informing his brother that "…air mail first goes to the Navy Headquarters then gets moved three or four more times before it arrives in our sector's military mail section. I have to retrieve my mail after it goes through several other hands, so please mark the package 'Executive Officer, Matsushita Battalion' to ensure it is treated with the proper care."

A House Divided

Being an officer, albeit a junior one, Ensign Satoru Ōmagari was privy to many of the problems that plagued Iwo's command structure. The officers in the *Nanpō Shotō* Air Group bunker took their meals together as if on a ship at sea. Although normally the junior officers were not permitted to dine with the senior officers, but because there were only two-dozen officers, Ōmagari and his naval reserve classmates ate with Captain Inoue. "Our daily rations of cooked rice scarcely filled a mess kit lid, but we also had soup, canned fish, canned beef, dehydrated carrots and other dried vegetables." Ōmagari described the strict naval class system that existed even in the bunkers, "During meals we junior officers listened while the senior officers talked."[62] It was at one of these meals that Ōmagari learned of the bickering between Captain Samaji Inoue and the head of the *Keibitai*, Commander Tsunezō Wachi. There had risen a dispute over the firing of the island's anti-aircraft guns at US Army bombers that were clearly out of range. Captain Inoue petitioned Commander Wachi to stop this practice, arguing that the ammunition should be reserved for blasting US Marines once they came ashore. Commander Wachi claimed it would be dereliction of duty not to fire his AA guns as long as enemy aircraft were overhead. Inoue reported to RAdm Ichimaru that Wachi was wasting valuable ammunition that could not be easily replenished.

Ōmagari said that Inoue and Wachi made little attempt to conceal the bad blood between them.[63]

In early October, Captain Inoue instructed Ensign Ōmagari to accompany him to a special meeting. The conference was held in a wooden structure in the north. Normally, the *Nanpō Shotō* Naval Air Group's accounting officer would travel with Captain Inoue to such meetings, but on this day Ōmagari was instructed to carry the captain's briefcase and take the meeting minutes. Due to Ōmagari's junior status, he did not warrant a seat at the table, but stood against a wall. He was intimidated by the number of staff officers dripping with shoulder cords that had flown in from the mainland. General Joichirō Sanada and Vice-Admiral Tasuku Nagazawa and their staff had flown in from Imperial General Headquarters, and Commander Kiyoshi Urabe flew in to represent the Third Air Fleet. RAdm Rinosuke Ichimaru and Capt Samaji Inoue were at the meeting to represent the local Navy presence. The Army's local representatives were MajGen Makoto Ōsuga, MajGen Sadasue Senda, Major Yoshitaka Horie, Major Fujie Shirakata and Colonel Koichi Hori.[64] At the head of the table was the man responsible for the entire island, Lieutenant General Tadamichi Kuribayashi. This was the first of only two times that Ōmagari saw Kuribayashi in person. The meeting was held to discuss how to effectively deal with the expected US invasion. Kuribayashi said that he would listen to the opinions of the Army and Navy representatives before making his decision.

According to Ōmagari, Commander Urabe campaigned for the traditional "waterline defense strategy" (*Suisai Gekimetsu Sakusen*), the same defense that failed at Tarawa and Saipan. MajGen Ōsuga, Captain Inoue, and staff officer Colonel Hori agreed with Commander Urabe who said, "The Navy will transport the necessary supplies for the Army to build 300 blockhouses concentrated at the southern beaches. There is no other place for the enemy to come ashore. We will destroy them as they land."

LtCol Kaneji Nakane, Kuribayashi's right hand man, argued against the beach defense strategy. Nakane wanted an in-depth siege defense saying, "Only a child would think bunkers could stand up to the big guns that the US Navy will bring to bear. We must dig in deep and make them pay dearly."

LtCol Nakane asked Commander Urabe for his own personal opinion on the matter, but Urabe continued to state he was there to represent the Navy High Command and was not in a position to share his own opinions. Urabe's refusal to state his own opinion sent Nakane into a tailspin that escalated into a shouting match. Nakane roared, "The Americans have control of the air and sea, yet the Navy High Command expects us to meet them on the beaches? Have they lost their minds?!"

Nakane presented the case of the defenders of Peleliu, an island half the size of Iwo Jima that was invaded two weeks prior but was still holding out. Until the battles of Peleliu and Biak, the Japanese had tried to defend the beaches and lost. But on Peleliu, Japanese combined forces moved into caves and bunkers in the center of the island to engage in a stubborn, no-retreat battle. At the time of this meeting, the final outcome of the battle for Peleliu had not been determined, but the evidence was encouraging to LtCol Nakane who continued to push for the siege defense. He requested the Navy transport supplies so the Army could build inland defenses at the high ground areas.

During the meeting that lasted for hours, Ōmagari took detailed notes and recalled high levels of tension between the two factions. It wasn't a simple "Navy vs. Army" argument. The navy and some of the army officers supported the beach defense, but the Peleliu-inspired defense strategy was an army only proposition.

According to Ōmagari, Kuribayashi said, "I have listened to, and understand both sides. I agree with LtCol Nakane's plan for an in-depth defense." Even after Kuribayashi openly sided with the siege defense plan, Commander Urabe would not budge so the meeting adjourned without a consensus being reached. The key difference was the defense of the airfields. The Navy saw the Chidori and Motoyama Airfields as an all-or-nothing prize to be protected, while the Army was prepared to hand over the airfields like a chess piece in a protracted siege. Neither side would bend, but a compromise was necessary in order to move forward with either plan. Tempers flared as everyone recognized that precious time was being wasted arguing about how to proceed.

Ensign Ōmagari learned that after several months of in-fighting between Commander Wachi and Captain Inoue, General Kuribayashi stepped in to settle the feud. Kuribayashi contacted the Naval General Staff in Tōkyō to request a transfer for Wachi. On October 15, 1944, roughly eight months after arriving as the island's naval commander, the former spy was promoted to captain and flown to Kisarazu Air Base. As Wachi's transport plane lifted off the dusty runway, he felt sad about leaving his men behind. He wrote, "That was the most unwilling transfer I experienced in my naval career."* He was granted an unprecedented 30-day shore leave, which he spent with his son at a hot springs in Atami. Wachi's position as *Keibitai* commander was folded into Captain Inoue's *Nanpō Shotō* Naval Air Group.

Kuribayashi requested replacements for officers who disagreed with his in-depth defense strategy. In December 1944, Kuribayashi fired 2nd Mixed Brigade commander MajGen Makoto Ōsuga, and replaced him with MajGen Sadasue Senda. Colonel Tadashi Takaishi replaced Chief-of-Staff Colonel Shizuichi Horie who was sent to Chichi Jima. Kuribayashi also fired two of his battalion commanders who failed to back him on the in-depth defense plan.[65] [66] Unlike the newly-promoted Captain Tsunezō Wachi who was sent back to Japan, the dethroned MajGen Makoto Ōsuga and Colonel Shizuichi Hori stayed on Iwo Jima where they later died.

Ōmagari said that a compromise regarding the in-depth defense was reached in a subsequent meeting. The Navy agreed to transport for the Army: an unspecified amount of machine guns; ammunition; 12,000 tons of cement; 60 tons of nails; 15 tons of steel wire; and 750 tons of reinforcing rods for bunker construction. There was a condition, the Army had to agree to supply the manpower to build the Navy's beach defenses. In the end, it seems neither side got what it wanted or needed. Half of the materials that arrived on the island were used for the Navy's shoreline bunkers, and the other half was used

---

* In December 1944, Tsunezō Wachi was assigned to SouthWest Fleet HQ. Wachi was then re-assigned in February 1945, to command the Torpedo School in Nagasaki Prefecture. His final posting came in March 1945, as commander of the 5th Special Attack Fleet of Suicide boats (*Shinyōtai*) in Kagoshima, Kyūshū.

to create the Army's inland fortifications.⁶⁷ Instead of fully investing in a single defense plan, Ōmagari feels that the compromise weakened both designs.

Care Packages and the Rocket Men

Lieutenant Genichi Hattori's younger brother developed a friendship with a naval officer named Lieutenant (jg) Kazuo Yamada, so was able to circumvent standard Army channels to get his mail on a supply aircraft destined for Iwo Jima. On October 24th, Lieutenant Genichi Hattori received his first airmail care package; it arrived on a Tabby transport plane in a large wooden box marked "Military Priority." His younger brother Genji had previously sent five care packages via the Army's mail system, but none of them ever arrived. This box that came on the naval transport plane was the first to make it to Iwo Jima. Lieutenant Genichi Hattori wrote a thank-you letter that began with large, bold letters, "Dear Brother, thank you!" He then further conveyed his appreciation by writing, "thank you" eleven more times in a row. He continued, "There was a happy commotion when I opened the box. I shared the contents with the other officers and the NCOs in sickbay. The others asked how I was able to get such a wonderful care package when no one else was even getting postcards. I bragged about you, my clever younger brother."

In a scene reminiscent of passing out candy on Halloween, Hattori described handing out treats to grateful officers who crowded around him. In that thank-you letter (that the family still has) Hattori listed the contents of the care package: "Daily use items- Tins of tobacco, cigars, toilet paper, soap, small towels, shirts and other things; Edibles- candy, snacks, *Katsuo* (blocks of dried tuna); Letters- one each from you and Mother; *Omamori* (good luck charms)- one each from (the temples) Naritasan, Fugen, Moritasan, Ikomasan and others; Miscellaneous- two notebooks, a map, handmade cloth dolls and other items."*

At the end of the list Hattori wrote, "thank you" six more times in a row. Hattori wrote that a ship arrived that very night bringing his first Army mail call in three months. He received a total of nine letters; three from his wife

---

* *Omamori* are made from paper or wood, and kept inside a brocade bag with a religious inscription. *Omamori* are still available at both Shinto shrines and Buddhist temples.

Sawako, three from his mother Kurie, two from friends, and one from his younger brother. The postmarks on the letters varied from two weeks to two months prior. Hattori then wrote, "Today was a wonderful day. It was like my birthday, New Years Eve and the *Obon* summer festival all rolled into one!" He ended the missive by asking for two 1945 calendars and more tins of tobacco. The closing line read, "Thank you dear brother, when I return home I will pay you back ten times, no, I will pay you back 100 times over for the money you will spend on my care packages."

On November 14, 1944, in a letter to his younger brother, Lieutenant Genichi Hattori described B-24 and B-29 air raids on the island. "When our planes attack Saipan, the Americans are courteous in their instant, and overwhelming, return of the favor," he wrote with a hint of dark humor. In this letter, he asked for "seeds to grow vegetables that won't attract bugs; such as onions, green onions, scallions, and ginger." Hattori also wrote, "We endured a tremendous naval barrage on the night of November 11th that lasted until 2:00 a.m. A dozen enemy gunships shelled the island and fired star shells that illuminated the area like daylight. It was impressive, frightening and beautiful."

On November 18, 1944, amid a welcome rainstorm, a flight of four Tabby transport aircraft from the 1023rd Naval Air Group landed on Iwo Jima. According to the diary of one of the plane commanders, the C-47 lookalikes were carrying *sake* bottles filled with water, and fresh vegetables; *daikon* radishes, spinach, sweet potatoes, and yams.[68] A plane captain on one of the planes in this supply run was Ensign Yoshiyuki Nakasone who later died on February 28, 1945, on a transport run from Kisarazu to Iwakuni. Nakasone's plane flew into a blizzard and crashed into a mountain in Mie Prefecture killing all twelve men aboard.*

Due to regular visits by US Army P-38s and B-24s, it was no longer safe for the Betty bombers to use Iwo Jima as a forward operating base. As a result, Iwo Jima was left with a large stockpile of 60 kg and 250 kg bombs.[69] A plan emerged to re-purpose the bombs by turning them into rockets. In the beginning of November, Ensign Satoru Ōmagari greeted a planeload of

---

* He was the younger brother of future Prime Minister Yasuhiro Nakasone. During the war, Yasuhiro Nakasone served aboard the battleships *Aoba* and *Nagato* with the rank of Lieutenant junior grade.

engineer eggheads that were culled from private industries, such as Mitsubishi and Nakajima Aircraft Works, and commissioned as officers. In charge of the group was Ensign Chozaemon Morishita, an engineering officer from the 2nd Naval Arsenal. The collective brain trust arrived to conduct field tests on a new weapon.

The team would attach rocket motor tubes to the leftover bombs and launch them from wooden chutes. Iwo's naval troops would provide the brawn for transporting the bombs and fabricating the Rube-Goldberg-looking launching frames that resembled rain-gutters on stilts. The program needed a local junior officer to function as a liaison for the engineers. Ōmagari's classmate Ensign Kaneko was selected to help the newly arrived boy geniuses. Ōmagari said, "I teased Ensign Kaneko for having drawn such a harebrained assignment with no chance of success."

On November 30th, Hattori sent a letter to his brother thanking him for a group of three care packages that arrived together. In the letter, Hattori asked about their ailing father and requested that his brother send "incense money" to the families of two of his men who were killed. He thanked his brother again, writing the words "thank you" five times in a row. Hattori wrote that the boxes he received contained magazines, newspapers, high quality tinned tobacco, cigars, military-issue cigarettes, peanuts, rice crackers and dried peas. There were sweet treats as well: cherry flavored candy, rock candy, *mochi*[*], *yokan*[†], and *tanbaguri* chestnuts. "My fellow officers are deeply grateful to you," wrote Hattori.

Corporal Nishi and the Oscars

On November 29, 1944, a flight of four Army Ki-67 Peggy bombers landed on Chidori Airfield carrying Corporal Shinjirō Nishi and a group of army aircraft mechanics, their equipment and gear. Shinjirō Nishi was born in 1923, in a little country village in Kagoshima, Kyūshū.[‡] Nishi's father was Dr. Morinoshin Nishi, a physician and chairman of the Kagoshima Medical Association. As the son of a physician, Shinjirō Nishi's four sisters and three

---

[*] Steamed rice pounded into compact balls or "cakes."
[†] *Yokan* is a thick, jellied dessert made of red bean paste, agar and sugar.
[‡] No relation to LtCol Takeichi Nishi, commander of the 26th Tank Regiment.

brothers lived a life of affluence, that is, until their father passed away from kidney failure in 1936.

Nishi's doting mother couldn't afford to send him to a private college, but thanks to his excellent grades, he was accepted into a government-run college in Tōkyō and deferred from the draft. While a college student, Shinjirō Nishi lived with his uncle Haruhiko Nishi, a civilian official that had previously been personally appointed to the Japanese consulate in Tsingtao (Aoshima) by Mamoru Shigemitsu. Haruhiko Nishi was later called back to Japan by Foreign Minister Shigenori Tōgō and appointed Vice-Minister of Foreign Affairs. It was at this time that Shinjirō Nishi lived with him and learned a great deal about life and the outside world. Vice-Minister Haruhiko Nishi maintained that he had no foreknowledge of the attack on Pearl Harbor, and resigned his post along with Foreign Minister Shigenori Tōgō on September 2, 1942.

In October 1943, University student Shinjirō Nishi joined the tens of thousands of other college, university, and trade school students across the Empire that were harvested for military service under the "Great Student Draft."* Shinjirō Nishi, despite being enrolled in college, would be drafted as a private in the army. Unlike ROTC volunteers Ensign Minoru Tada and Ensign Satoru Ōmagari, Shinjirō Nishi did not volunteer for the military. He chose not to join the ROTC where he could have become an officer. Nishi said, "Most of us university students resented the college draft. We felt that it wasn't *our* war. We didn't start it, so why did we have to fight?" The college draft is represented by film footage taken of a somber parade of rain-soaked students in their school uniforms carrying rifles as they march around Meiji Jingu Shrine's track and field arena. Since 1924, the Olympic quality track had been used for sporting events, but was now had turned into the scene for a parade of future residents of the Yasukuni Shrine.

Nishi's mother gave the reluctant soldier a typical sendoff party at which time she presented him with a hand-stitched *sennin-bari* (1,000 stitch good luck belt). It was customary for boys and men entering the military to receive a wide cotton or silk belt with hundreds of red stitches sewn into it. They would wrap them around their stomachs under their uniforms. The belts could take

---

* This *Gakutō Shutsujin*, or college draft, included those born and raised in Japan's colonies.

weeks to assemble as women visited friends and relatives to collect stitches. Each girl or woman said a prayer as she dropped a single stitch in the pattern. Females born in the year of the tiger were considered good luck, so they could contribute ten stitches. Tiger motifs are common on 1,000 stitch belts, due to the expression, "A tiger will roam a thousand miles and always return to its den." Shinjirō Nishi's belt has both a 5-sen and a 10-sen coin as symbols of his mother's wish that he experience neither suffering nor death. A mystery, even to him, is the addition of a stone-hard nut that his mother sewed into the fabric. He thinks she intended for him to be resilient like the tough nut, but never thought to ask her to explain it before he left for basic training.

Shinjirō Nishi reported for duty in the Army on December 1, 1943. His basic training was at the Army's Seibu 101st Maintenance Training Unit. He said, "The Japanese Army was a sadistic machine, well-oiled with the sweat and tears of the recruits." In April 1944, Nishi went for advanced training with the 1st Air Force Aircraft Maintenance and Armor School in Mie Prefecture. Nishi befriended a Tōkyō University student named Hirō Hachiya who was also caught up in the college draft. Their college credits and test scores earned both of them spots in the Army's Officer Candidate Course. Nishi and Hachiya were on the fast track to becoming 2nd Lieutenants as aircraft maintenance specialists.

In August 1944, Nishi and Hachiya completed their training and were both promoted to corporal. They proudly sported cloth wings on their chest to denote they were in the Army Air Force. Pilots wore an additional second set of wings above the standard service wings worn by non-flying personnel. They were assigned to the 10th Air Division's 23rd *Hikō Sentai* (Air Combat Group) at Inaba Airfield.* By November 1944, the 23rd Air Combat Group was equipped with the Nakajima Ki-43 (II) "Oscar" fighter and the Nakajima Ki-44 (II) "Tojo" fighter. Shinjirō Nishi and Hirō Hachiya worked on the Oscars fighters that regularly engaged B-29s over Tōkyō and the Kantō Plain.

On November 30th, the 23rd Air Combat Group ordered twelve Oscar fighters and related ground crews to Iwo Jima. The Oscars would provide an umbrella of protection for transport vessels bringing men and supplies to the island fortress. Corporals Shinjirō Nishi, Hirō Hachiya and thirty other

---

* Now known as Haneda International Airport.

maintenance men flew out a day early aboard a flight of four, twin-engine Peggy bombers. The planes were packed to the gills with men, duffle bags, tools, food, tents, and *sake* bottles filled with fresh water. Nishi was glad that he and his buddy Hirō Hachiya had been assigned to the same plane for the long flight. The formation rose to 12,000 feet, passed the Izu Islands before flying three hours south, and crossing over the islands of Chichi Jima and Haha Jima. The Peggys flew the last leg at the gas-guzzling low altitude of 1,500 feet to avoid roaming American carrier-based fighters.

Nishi pressed his face against a window to get a better look as the Peggys circled the island. Unlike Naval radioman Tsuruji Akikusa, who first saw Iwo Jima from the rolling deck of a ship, Nishi got his first glimpse from the air. Nishi saw hulks of twisted ships beached on the western shore, half sunken, their bows poking above the surface like turtles in a pond. A rickety wooden pier gave a silent warning, pointing in the direction of the unseen advancing US Navy.

As each of the bombers descended, Corporal Shinjirō Nishi saw wrecked aircraft lining the runways and initially assumed they were American, but none of them were. "Our planes looked like they been swept away by a giant broom. I felt then that we had lost the war," Nishi said. As the Peggys touched down on Chidori Airfield, Corporal Nishi felt a wave of despair. Nishi climbed from the plane and followed the others to the *Nanpō* Air Operations tent as Ensign Ōmagari's ground crews swarmed to unload the bombers. For the return journey, the Peggy bombers were loaded with wounded men and sacks of mail. Even before Nishi and the others had finished logging in with the air operations officer, the Peggys were grumbling loudly down the dusty runway. No pilot in his right mind would tarry a minute longer than necessary.

The army maintenance men boarded trucks for a bumpy ride to Motoyama Airfield where the Oscar fighters would be landing the following day. Nishi stood in the back of an uncovered truck as it rolled along, and was surprised to see very little of what he expected to encounter. *Where were all of the defenders?* The trucks approached the airfield and a scan of the apron revealed only four operational aircraft - the rest were damaged, or undergoing maintenance or repairs. The trucks came to a dusty stop amid a crowd of smiling sailors who were awaiting their arrival. Nishi said, "The navy boys shouted 'Welcome', 'Glad you're here' and 'It's great to have the Army Air Force with us'. They wanted to know how things were back home."

The sailors were starving for fresh news. General Kuribayashi and Rear Admiral Ichimaru decided that morale concerns dictated that bad news – a growing supply of which was available by the time Nishi landed on Iwo Jima – was carefully screened for consumption by the enlisted ranks. The maintenance men brought with them valuable uncensored news from the homeland.

The navy troops helped Nishi's group unload the trucks and set up tents. "Despite so much destruction, there was no despair in their eyes. Their friendly smiles seemed out of place on that depressing island. They made me feel optimistic again," said Nishi.

A petty officer guided Corporals Nishi and Hachiya to their barracks, which was a wooden house that once belonged to a local family. The house had polished wooden floors and *tatami* straw mats. After stowing their personal gear, they climbed back in the trucks to attend a briefing at the airfield. The meeting was conducted in a musty canvas tent with the sides rolled up for ventilation and a ceiling that was well ventilated with shrapnel holes. Nishi learned that the command of the Army's fighters would fall under Navy Captain Samaji Inoue who attended the meeting in his white uniform. He stood out in contrast against the other officers in green uniforms. The army mechanics would be getting their water and meals from the Navy. This was good news for Nishi because he said it was well known that Navy chow was better than Army grub.

An naval enlisted man entered the tent and calmly interrupted the meeting by announcing, "Enemy planes are approaching." Unflustered, the naval personnel packed up their papers, folded the table and easel, and dropped the tent flat. The group walked towards a cave entrance in a small hill. Inside was a concrete and rebar reinforced U-shape tunnel with three-foot thick concrete blast walls protecting both entrances that faced the airfield. The tunnel had electric lighting and could hold about 100 men. In the center of the bunker was an angled shaft leading up to the crest of the hill. It provided ventilation and acted as an exit to the top of the mound that was crowned by a pole with a striped windsock, a 25 mm twin-mount anti-aircraft gun, and a modest wooden lookout tower. The Motoyama Command Center had a direct landline to the island's radar station, so it received constant news of all radar contacts. When the radar station picked up enemy aircraft sixty-miles out to sea, it would phone with the distance and direction. This information was fed up to the lookout that would announce it via megaphone to the ground crews working below on the airfield. He would update and repeat this announcement as the enemy aircraft advanced. This allowed the men to work as long as possible before heading for safety.

The briefing continued inside the bunker under the glow of electric lights. Minutes later Nishi heard a long eerie complaint from a hand-cranked siren. It was the five-minute warning from the observation tower; the Americans had approached to within thirty miles. Nishi said as the bombers drew closer, the lookout used high-power optics to observe the B-24s' bomb bay doors. Once the bomb bay doors rolled open, the lookout would issue a warning to the men inside the bunker using a sound power phone (like the kind used on ships). Once the bombs began their arching trajectory, the lookout would descend the steps of the angled shaft down into the safety of the bunker.

When the lookout slid into the bunker, Nishi mimicked the actions of the men around him. As a defense against the shock waves, the men crouched down, covered their ears and opened their mouths. Nishi got his first taste of war as dozens of 500-lb bombs crashed around the airfield. The concussive blasts spread out like ripples on a lake, only much faster. "The bombs didn't go 'boom, boom' like in the movies, it was more like very fast thunder. It was terrifying," Nishi said. He felt the changing air pressure inside his chest; the ground trembled like an old wooden roller coaster. He recalled the cacophony of sounds; whistles, shrieks, whirring growls, and thunderclaps. "My ears were ringing so badly that I thought my ear drums had burst," said Nishi. The roars were mixed with a typhoon-like shower of debris falling back to earth. "I worried about losing my composure in front of my friend Hachiya, but neither he nor anyone else paid attention to me," said Nishi. The bunker's entrance was filled with the overwhelming acrid smell of gunpowder and fine, yellow dust.

After the all-clear signal, trucks jammed with troops rushed out of underground bunkers to fill in the bomb craters. They drove small tractor rollers to pack down the earth. "There were large pieces of heavy, jagged shrapnel everywhere, some were stabbed into the earth like tombstones," said Nishi.

As for the island's response to the attack, Nishi said, "We didn't send up any aircraft, and the enemy lazily flew back to Saipan." He added, "I still don't like the sound of fire truck sirens."

Following the raid, a mess steward brought food to the bunker. "The Navy ate better than us to begin with, but the naval aviators had it even better. We were issued delicious rations of canned pork, mackerel, sardines, and even beef," said Nishi.

The next day, November 30, brought the arrival of the twelve Oscar fighters. The aircraft wore camouflage coats of green speckles over unpainted aluminum skins. Their wings and fuselage bore the distinctive *Hinomaru* red circles on wide white bands. This new recognition system was a response to trigger-happy homeland gunners, much like the black and white invasion stripes on Allied aircraft in the Normandy invasion. The Oscar pilots touched down at Motoyama Airfield and were greeted by enthusiastic army troops who boiled out of the ground like ants. Nishi pushed his way through the eager crowd and heard something familiar; it was his native Kagoshima dialect. Nishi discovered that these Army troopers were from the Kagoshima 145th Infantry Regiment. "How wonderful it was to talk with men from home," Nishi said. One of those Kagoshima boys might have been Teruo Sasamine, an enlisted machine gunner who had been aboard the *Noto Maru* with Lieutenant Genichi Hattori.[*]

Like at Chidori Airfield, the troops gathered around the newcomers and asked questions about the home front. The 145th Infantry Regiment had been on Iwo Jima since July and they hungered for fresh news. The Kagoshima infantry boys pitched in to push the planes off the airfield into U-shaped revetments. In addition to transport vessel escort duty, the 23rd *Sentai*'s fighters were expected to pick up where the Navy's Zero fighters left off.

At dawn, Nishi and the other maintenance men pushed the fighters out of their revetments in preparation for the expected mission. The maintenance men performed their walk-a-round inspections followed by an oral checklist. Nishi sat in one of the cockpits waiting for the attention of the starter truck. Once his radial engine sputtered and barked to life, Nishi carefully throttled it up while monitoring the gauges for abnormalities. After confirming all was in order, the Oscars were shut down, topped off with aviation gasoline and ready

---

[*] Teruo Sasamine was captured shortly after the March 17th banzai attack, and sent to a POW camp on Hawaii.

to go at a moment's notice.

At noon, a call came from the radar station that an enemy formation had been picked up sixty miles away. The ground crews started their fighters' engines as the pilots dashed to the flight line.* The sound of a dozen engines growling to life was inspirational to the defenders who resembled prairie dogs as they poked their heads out of their bunkers to watch the spectacle. It had been a long time since they had seen so many fighters start up at once.

Carrying the hopes of many on their wings, the Oscars rose to meet the incoming B-24 bombers. The Oscars had no luck in bringing down the large four-engine bombers. The only things that fell from the sky were American bombs. Some of the explosives were of the time-delay variety that would ignite up to two hours later. "We hated those bombs the most," said Nishi.

The 145th Infantry machine gunner, Teruo Sasamine, said the Japanese fighters were no match for the American bombers or fighters. "As a machine gunner, I could easily identify the different sounds of American machine guns and our own aircraft machine guns. Our planes had a much slower rate of fire," said Sasamine.[70]

A day or two later, the 23rd *Sentai*'s pilots and ground crews were ordered to assemble at 8:00 a.m. for a greeting from the island's supreme naval commander, Rear-Admiral Rinosuke Ichimaru. As the airmen stood in formation outside the Motoyama Command Center bunker, a luxury car appeared. A door opened to reveal the figure of Admiral Ichimaru in his dark blue uniform, billed cap, white gloves and sword. The Admiral stepped out of the command car and climbed a short flight of steps to a wooden podium. He shot a long, purposeful gaze out over the small group of men, then he bellowed out in a foghorn voice saying, "Officers and men of the Army's 23rd *Sentai*, the war situation is grave." Admiral Ichimaru paused to make eye contact to convey his sincerity. In a staccato military manner he said, "I ask you to act as with one beating heart, a heart pumping in fierce stubborn determination to fulfill your duty." He punctuated each syllable with emotion. "I beg of you, every man must do his best." Unlike other speeches Shinjirō Nishi had been forced to endure in the past, the Admiral's sincere words made a lasting

---

* The Zero's engine was started with a two-man operated crank, but the Oscar's engine required a heavy torque mechanical starter, usually mounted on a truck.

The Attack on Saipan

On the evening of December 6th, a flight of seven Betty bombers (K704th *Hikōtai*) and ten Army Peggy bombers (110th *Sentai*) landed on Iwo to refuel. Each was armed with a single 1,600 lb bomb for a night raid against the B-29s parked on Saipan. Shinjirō Nishi joined the other maintenance men in gassing up the planes. There would be a few hours to kill, so the airmen gathered in a tent to eat and rest. The airmen were in high spirits as they passed the time. "They sang and laughed loudly, so I think some of them were drinking," said Nishi.

The Bettys and Peggys began taking off around 10:45 p.m., and arrived over Saipan four hours later. They identified the B-29s parked on the airfield easily because the area was bathed in floodlights. After dropping their bombs, roughly half of the aircraft failed to return; two of the Bettys and six of the Peggys were lost to American AA gunfire. The raid destroyed four B-29s, damaged an additional twenty-three B-29s and left approximately 200 Americans dead.

The ground crews hurried to get the aircraft back in the air because they knew there would be a retaliatory American strike. After the surviving bombers departed for the homeland, Nishi and the others waited in their bunkers as the sun rose on December 7th, but nothing happened. Bad weather over Saipan had prevented the Americans from striking back that day. On December 8th, Nishi and Hachiya rode bicycles over to their Oscar fighters to warm and check the engines in preparation for the expected mission. Nishi said that while Iwo Jima's radar station could provide ample warning of approaching enemy bombers; there was no defense against the marauding low-flying P-38s. The twin-engine fighters would zoom in under the radar to strafe the airfields. In the event fighters snuck in, the lookout, or whoever happened to spot them, would bang an empty oxygen cylinder or fire off several bursts from a machine gun. Nishi said, "Hearing either sound was terrifying. There was no time to get to safety because the *Katsuobushi* zoomed in, shot us up and disappeared like phantoms."*

---

* To the Japanese, the P-38 Lightning's profile resembled a block of dried

Nishi completed the checklist and climbed down from the Oscar fighter. Nishi looked over to see the familiar site of his pal Hirō Hachiya performing the pre-flight warm-up on another fighter. Over the roaring of the idling Oscar aircraft engines, Nishi's attention was grabbed by a clanging sound piercing the air. He looked up to see the lookout banging on an oxygen cylinder. Nishi shut off the engine, jumped from the cockpit and dashed for cover as the P-38s plowed the airfield and vanished. After waiting several minutes, Nishi and the others rushed out of their holes to discover Corporal Hirō Hachiya on the ground lying in a muddy pool of blood.

Hachiya didn't hear the warning in time and was cut down as he bolted for cover. Nishi knelt over his friend's body as a medic stuffed gauze into the deep wounds.

Nishi accompanied Hachiya's crumpled body as it was lifted onto a truck and driven to the 2nd Mixed Brigade's field hospital. Nishi was distressed to discover that the so-called field hospital was a cave overflowing with the sick and dying. There were a few makeshift canvas lean-tos, but most of the wounded men were in the open. Stretchers were scarce, so the patients were rolled onto blankets outside the tunnel complex. Nishi did his best to comfort Hirō Hachiya, whose face had turned an ashen hue, and promised to return to visit him in the morning.

One of the medics assigned to work at the field hospital was Shūji Ishii, the pre-war cameraman who worked for Mainichi Shimbun newspaper. Ishii said that the medics did their best to work with ever dwindling supplies, but admitted the hospital was simply overwhelmed.

The following morning, Nishi rushed back to the field hospital to visit his friend. Corporal Hachiya's cold, lifeless body was right where Nishi had left it; someone had pulled the blanket over his face to keep the flies off. There was no wood available for a cremation, so Nishi said a prayer, borrowed a pickaxe, and scratched out a shallow grave in the rocky soil. He gently wrapped his friend in the bloodstained blanket and eased the body into ground with the promise, "I'll come back for you."

Corporal Hirō Hachiya was not the only wounded man who suffered from a near total lack of medical supplies. The arrival of the 23rd Fighter Squadron

---

skipjack tuna called *Katsuobushi*.

coincided with an outbreak of amoebic dysentery that swept the island. Due to the constant bombings and shelling, the men had to urinate and defecate in their caves. The cause of the rapid spreading of the illness was the blowfly.* Men, who were weakened by months of hard labor and reduced rations, were further decimated by diarrhea and dehydration. "The blockade meant that we ran out of medicine," said Ishii. Due to the American air raids and submarine action, the appearance of friendly ships carrying supplies was becoming a fond memory. However, in mid-December a glimmer of hope arrived on the wings of seven Japanese bombers.

Bad News

One of the patients languishing in the field hospital was Private Toshio Koshimura of the 2nd Independent Machine Gun Battalion, 1st Mixed Brigade. Thirty-four-year-old Koshimura was drafted in January 1944, and after six months of training was sent to Iwo Jima in mid-July 1944. He arrived on a decrepit cargo ship crammed with supplies and other greenhorn replacements. In the following half-year, Koshimura spent more time digging tunnels than doing anything else.[71] That is, until November 1944, when he was diagnosed with typhoid fever and quarantined. He spent the next few weeks waging a losing battle against the illness. Sometime in mid-December, a medical orderly told Koshimura he would be among those evacuated back to the mainland.

There had been several attempts at getting the severely sick and wounded off the island by boat, but Koshimura's hopes had been dashed so many times he didn't dare believe it anymore. But this time it seemed different since the orderly passed out a stack of cotton hospital robes bearing a red cross on the sleeve. The orderly told the men to change into the robes because they were part of a larger group of twenty-three men who were being evacuated by plane.

Did he say plane? Could it be true? Koshimura pulled off his filthy uniform and slipped into the thin cotton robe. *Why are we suddenly given hospital robes?* Koshimura had been a patient for months but was never issued a clean uniform, let alone something like this.

Perhaps it was a psychological boost for those on the airfield who would

---

    *   *Calliphoridae*, known as blowflies, carrion flies, bluebottles, greenbottles, or cluster flies.

witness a group of men who were outwardly identified as deserving evacuation. Or was there to be a reception in Japan as the sick and wounded came off the plane? Perhaps the powers-that-be didn't want the evacuees showing up in Japan resembling the walking dead, and thought the hospital gowns would give the impression, albeit totally false, of ongoing proper medical care.

As the sun was setting on November 30th, an orderly shouted for the evacuees to board a truck to the airfield. Once there, the patients were assembled for an early morning flight back to Japan.

The next morning, wearing a white cotton hospital robe, typhoid patient Private Toshio Koshimura scanned the skies for his deliverance from this tomb called Iwo Jima.

Koshimura first heard the planes, and then spotted them, "It felt odd to see planes and not hear air raid sirens," he wrote. He was startled to see several black puffs of smoke appear between the planes. It seems one of the AA gun crews failed to get the word about the inbound friendly aircraft. The seven planes circled Chidori Airfield, but one of them was trailing a wake of thick, ominous smoke.

As the seven bombers landed, an officer approached the evacuees holding a clipboard. He read their names aloud, forming the sick and wounded into seven boarding groups. Koshimura waited for his boarding group number to be called and grew anxious as he watched others board the bombers, and then, one after another, five bombers took off. Something was wrong. The maintenance crews were busy examining the last two bombers.

Koshimura felt a pit in his stomach when the clipboard officer conferred with another officer. The clipboard officer sucked air through his teeth and then shared the bad news; due to repair work, the last two planes couldn't take off until the following morning. This news hit Koshimura like a ton of bricks. American bombers had attacked the airfields every day and night for the past month. If these two planes didn't get off the ground today they would surely be blasted to pieces. He watched in silent despair as the maintenance men evaporated from the stricken planes taking their tools with them. It was getting too dark to see, and using lights was out of the question. Koshimura's hopes of getting off the island were once again dashed. It was late to be trucked back to the field hospital, so he and the others spent the night in one of the airfield bunkers. Koshimura gave up hope. *What's the use of praying? The Americans would come the next day to smash the airfield and the planes anyway.*

According to Koshimura, at 5:00 a.m., the clipboard officer appeared and told the evacuees it would take five hours to conduct the repairs. A horde of naval maintenance men swarmed the planes. Like ants disassembling a dead grasshopper, they cannibalized pieces and parts from one plane to fix the other. Only one plane would be able to fly out, that is, if the Americans didn't show up first and destroy them both. The trigger-happy AA crew had ensured that an entire planeload of wounded men would not be going home. Koshimura deduced that even more of the wounded men would be left behind to make room for the crew of the damaged plane that could no longer fly.

As the work progressed, the officer read off only four names. When Koshimura heard his name he was filled with joy, yet felt pity for the others that were quickly trucked back to the field hospital cave.

At 9:30 a.m., the officer ordered Koshimura and the other three men to board the plane. Koshimura tried to hide his excitement as engines whined and sparked to life with a roar and a cloud of exhaust. No sooner was the hatch closed, than the plane began to rumble down the dusty runway. Back on the ground, Ensign Ōmagari's men pushed the stricken bomber to the edge of the airfield where it joined the growing pile of aircraft in the bone yard.

Despite being one of the lucky ones to leave the island, Koshimura was filled with guilt. After the war he discovered he was the sole survivor of the 288 men of the 2nd Independent Machine Gun Battalion.

Roughly two weeks after this mercy flight, Ensign Ōmagari was angered to read a message from Yokosuka to Admiral Ichimaru's command requesting that no more patients be evacuated to the homeland. The reason given was that the patients from Iwo Jima often died within four to five days of admittance to the Yokosuka Naval Hospital. The message claimed that it was bad for the morale of other patients in the facility, and a waste of resources. Ōmagari said that these same men who were described as a drain on resources had originally come to Iwo Jima healthy and fit. But within a few months of hard labor they were burnt-out hulks. With little medical care, or hope of evacuation, those admitted into Iwo Jima's field hospitals were offered nothing more than a cruel form of hospice.

At the end of December, a navy reconnaissance pilot arrived and told Ensign Ōmagari about a massive earthquake that devastated two Nakajima aircraft assembly plants in Handa city, Aichi Prefecture. The Nakajima Aircraft Company's Yamakata plant and Yoshino plant were both destroyed, and that aircraft parts, including pistons, rods, screws, nuts, bolts, and cables were now under tons of rubble. The plants produced Nakajima's B6N *Tenzan* Jill torpedo bomber, and the C6N *Saiun* Myrt reconnaissance plane. The pilot believed it would take six months to repair the damage and sort the parts. This brought a standstill to Nakajima's aircraft production of the Jill and Myrt, two key aircraft in the Navy's air arsenal. "I already knew the war was lost. Those in command must have known it, too. I don't know why we didn't sue for peace. It would have saved hundreds of thousands of lives," said Ōmagari. News of the incident was withheld from the public until after the war.[72]

By this time, all twelve of the Army's Oscar fighters from the 23rd *Sentai* had been destroyed. Army aircraft maintenance specialist Corporal Shinjirō Nishi was excited when he learned that four Peggy bombers would be arriving to evacuate the men of the 23rd *Sentai*. But, instead of four bombers, only two arrived at the end of December to take home a select number of pilots and senior maintenance men. Nishi was heartbroken when he failed to see his name on the boarding roster. He and sixteen other maintenance men were forced to wait for the next evacuation flight, that is, if there was one. Nishi felt he had been left to die.

After the pair of bombers departed, Corporal Nishi and the others were transferred from Captain Inoue's *Nanpō* Naval Air Group back to the Army. "That meant no more tasty navy chow for us. Instead, the army gave us stale hard tack to eat," said Nishi. "We were not incorporated into a battle plan, but shuffled away and told to wait for orders. On one hand, it was a blessing to be *persona non grata* because we were exempt from digging. On the other hand, with nothing to occupy ourselves with we became anxious," said Nishi. The night after the pair of Peggy bombers left for Japan, Nishi had a premonition of never seeing his mother again.

At about this same time, deep inside Admiral Ichimaru's 27th Air Flotilla Headquarters Communications bunker, one of the radiomen remarked to Akikusa, "Tomorrow is Christmas Day. The Americans are Christians so they won't bomb us, right?" Akikusa didn't have a clue, but hoped the man was correct. Akikusa was tired of the raids that kept everyone bottled up underground. Akikusa said that by this point he were ordered to make only the shortest of radio transmissions, because the enemy would home in on the transmission source and drop bombs right on top of their position. "There were times we were ordered to tap out only a predetermined code to signal that the island had not yet fallen," said Akikusa.

Ensign Ōmagari attended a year-end staff meeting at Kuribayashi's headquarters at which the various Army and Naval staff officers presented their status reports to Division. The staff officers unanimously requested a break for the exhausted troops. The men were collapsing from the hard labor and meager rations. The men were digging their own personal platoon-size bunkers as well as working on their HQ bunkers and fortifications.[73] The heat and hard labor took a toll on the malnourished and perpetually dehydrated men. Some officers suggested that the Navy send bombers loaded with vitamin drinks, medicine, and high calorie foods to distribute to the men to celebrate the New Year. Ōmagari stood against the wall, listening in total agreement, but was stunned by Kuribayashi's complete refusal, "There will be no deviation from the plan." Ōmagari wondered, *what is the point of digging bunkers if we all die before the enemy even lands?*

Radioman Akikusa worked as usual on December 31st, but when his shift ended, he and the other radiomen celebrated the best they could by talking of home. They reminisced about the special New Years dishes that their families would be enjoying. Akikusa sweltered in the underground tunnels, dreaming of big fat snowflakes landing softly on his roof of his parents' home. His extended family would gather to eat the traditional New Year dish of *mochi* rice cakes carefully roasted over charcoal flames in the floor-set fireplace. The small flames licked softly at the rice cakes, resting on a metal rack causing them to blister and release a wonderful smell. His grandmother and mother were busy for days preparing the special New Year's dishes; *ozoni* soup, mashed sweet potatoes, sweetened chestnuts, sweetened black soybeans and other delicacies. And who could forget the *toshikoshi* noodles served on New Year's Eve? The noodles were a symbol of longevity. Akikusa remembered his grandmother's words, "It is bad luck not to eat noodles on this night."

Deep underground in the hot, foul smelling tunnels, Akikusa imagined the sounds of New Years Eve back home; starting at midnight the deep resonant tone of the temple's heavy bronze bell would begin tolling. In a ceremony called *Joya no Kane*, Buddhist priests across Japan would strike a large bronze bell 108 times. Japanese Buddhism teaches that humans have 108 earthly desires, which are the source of all suffering. Across the cities, farms and villages of Japan, the deep sound of the bells is as much a tradition as the Christmas bells in London.

On this night, another Iwo Jima defender was thinking of home. On New Year's Eve, Lieutenant Genichi Hattori wrote a letter to his wife Sawako. He penned four traditional one-line *Haiku* poems for her:

Our 'Joya no Kane' is the air raid bell announcing another enemy attack.
We welcome the New Year in the shadow of enemy aircraft.
As 1944 passes, we welcome the New Year inside our bunkers.
A beam of light from the New Year's dawn strikes the entrance [of the bunker] as water drips from an Octopus tree.

In his letter, Hattori described the blessing of fresh water in the form of a heavy rainsquall that struck on New Year's Eve. There were no temple bells tolling for the redemption of the defenders; the island's modest temple had been destroyed in air raid.

Kuribayashi's Oath of Combat

On January 1, 1945, while monitoring the radio frequency used by the B-29 bombers, Akikusa was taken aback by the sound of a woman's laughter echoing through his headset. He could distinguish the sound of male voices and the high-pitched, melodic female laugh. *Why did they have girls on their aircraft?* he has wondered for decades. Akikusa claimed that on one occasion, US aircraft dropped empty 55-gallon drums,* and a high heel shoe over the airfield.†

Kuribayashi rang in the New Year with a mimeographed copy of his three-part manifesto: "Five Oaths (to) Properly Train (one's) Spirit" (Hon Seishin Rensei Gosei); "The Oaths of Combat" (Kantō no Chikai); and twelve practical pieces of advice for "Courageous Soldiers to Remember in Combat" (*Tanhei no Sentō Kokoroe*).[74]

---

* The barrel might have been a Napalm bomb that failed to detonate.

† Perhaps there is a former WWII US airman who can solve the mystery of the woman's voice and discarded shoe. If so, please contact the author who will be happy to inform Mr. Akikusa.

Bill D. Ross, a USMC combat correspondent who landed on Iwo Jima, and later authored *Iwo Jima: Legacy of Valor,* wrote, "Marines found copies (of the oaths) in the first destroyed bunkers on the beaches, and they would find others in caves, tunnels, pillboxes and other bunkers - and on the bodies of the enemy dead - everywhere on the island."

Each line of "The Oaths of Combat" is numbered as being the *first* since all are equally important, just like the five principles of a soldier's code of conduct. (Author's translation. The original Japanese text is in the endnotes as a reference.)

<u>The Oaths of Combat[75]</u>
1. We will wield all of our strength to protect this island.
1. We will carry explosives and pulverize the enemy tanks into dust.
1. We will rush into the enemy's midst as *kirikomi-tai* to annihilate them.[*]
1. We will hit our targets, killing an enemy with each shot.
1. We must not die until we have each taken ten enemy lives.
1. We will hold out using guerrilla warfare to harass the enemy.

If this cheery New Year's card from the island commander wasn't bad enough, the following day Akikusa and Kageyama were ordered from Admiral Ichimaru's heavily fortified headquarters bunker in the north back down to the Tamana-Yama Communications bunker. While Tamana-Yama was well defended, it was much closer to the invasion beach. By now the island had been bombarded and attacked relentlessly, so it was only a matter of time before the Americans landed. Akikusa said he much preferred the safety of Admiral Ichimaru's Headquarters. The good news was Akikusa and Kageyama made the move together.

On January 2, 1945, while Akikusa was making the move from Adm Ichimaru's headquarter bunker to Tamana-yama, another man was moving as well. Thirty-four-year-old Private First Class Mitsuru Higuchi, 2nd Mortar Battalion, fell gravely ill and was taken to the 2nd Mixed Brigade Field Hospital. The doctor, Captain Noguchi, diagnosed a thiamine deficiency

---

[*] *Kirikomi-tai* means a "quick rushing attack" like a knife cutting into an object.

known as beriberi, but, as medic Shūji Ishii noted, there was a shortage of all types of medication so none was provided to Higuchi. PFC Higuchi was carried the following day to the Independent 312th Infantry Battalion's "rest facility bunker" near Mount Suribachi. Higuchi succumbed to his preventable illness on January 5, 1945, leaving behind a wife and two sons, aged six and ten-years-old. PFC Higuchi's physical remains were never recovered, but he left behind his shaving kit, which was picked up by Corporal Owen Agenbroad of F Company, 2nd Battalion, 27th Marines, 5th Marine Division (F/2/27). Agenbroad picked up Higuchi's straight razor, a sharpening stone, an army-issue aluminum drinking cup and a large beautiful cowry seashell. He presented the items to PFC Higuchi's grateful son Yoshikazu Higuchi, on March 19, 2014, during the annual ceremony on Iwo Jima.*

A few days after PFC Mitsuru Higuchi died from beri beri, Ensign Satoru Ōmagari was on the southern beach with his clipboard monitoring the unloading of a newly arrived Type-2 transport ship. In addition to food and ammunition, SB(T)154 was packed to the gills with hundreds of neatly twine-wrapped bundles of sticks to be used as kindling to cook rice. The ship's crew had lowered the bow ramp, and Ōmagari was busy ticking items off the manifest when from behind him a stern voice said, "His Excellency is calling for you." Ōmagari turned to see an army officer wearing a green staff aiguillette. Ōmagari saluted and followed the man who led him to a group of other staff officers. Ōmagari snapped to attention like a mousetrap as the oldest man spoke, "You there. What is all that?" The entourage of officers, the man's age, and the walking stick all pointed to one thing – this was none other than Lieutenant General Tadamichi Kuribayashi. The General pointed his walking stick at the wood-filled gaping maw of the vessel and repeated his query, "I say, what is the meaning of all that?"

Ōmagari was stunned into silence, and wondered as to the true intent of the rhetorical question. He wanted to reply, *In the Navy we call it 'firewood' sir. What does the Army call it?* Instead he wisely said, "It's firewood, sir!" Kuribayashi shot him a look of disdain. The General demanded to know why firewood was showing up on his island when he needed more water, concrete, weapons and ammunition. Ōmagari's brain raced into overdrive trying to come

---

* The author was honored to translate for the occasion.

up with an appropriate answer. No matter how factual, the reply of "Because Imperial General Headquarters sent it, sir" was not going to work. Instead, Ōmagari held his tongue and remained ramrod straight. Kuribayashi snorted in disgust and spun on his heels with his staff officers in tow.* Ōmagari's description of Kuribayashi's micro-management style dovetails with several other survivors' accounts.

On January 7, 1945, Army Corporal Shinjirō Nishi and sixteen other aircraft mechanics from the 23rd *Sentai* received great news, something that was in short supply on Iwo Jima; Peggy bombers were flying in the next day to take them home. That night, Nishi was too excited to sleep. *Would the bombers get shot down on the way in?* After a restless night, the small group of maintenance men assembled in front of their partially demolished wooden billet to wait for a truck to take them to the airfield. Nishi was not prepared to see Kuribayashi come marching down the road. As Kuribayashi and his staff walked past the mechanics, which were by now standing at attention, Kuribayashi turned and approached the senior man in the group and asked why they were standing around. The leader replied that they had been ordered back to Japan, and were waiting on ground transportation. Kuribayashi briefly addressed the men, thanking them for their hard work and sacrifices, and then continued on his way. This was the first and only time Shinjirō Nishi saw Kuribayashi, and was impressed that the supreme commander had taken an interest in the lowly aircraft maintenance men.

Shortly after this chance encounter, the trucks arrived to take Nishi and the others to the pair of Peggys that had arrived with supplies. Nishi and the other maintenance men boarded the aircraft along with several officers that Nishi had never seen before. As the bombers lifted off the runway, Nishi was thankful to be leaving, but at the same time, felt guilt-ridden about leaving the body of his friend Hirō Hachiya behind in an unmarked shallow grave.

Nishi spent the next few months continuing to work as an aircraft mechanic for the 23rd *Sentai* fighters that battled B-29s over Tōkyō. His premonition of never seeing his mother again was tragically accurate. On June 17, 1945,

---

* "SB(T) 154" was sunk near Iwo Jima on January 5, 1945. Her 90-man Army *senpaku* crew, and the wounded men who were being evacuated, died after delivering this load of firewood and other supplies.

Nishi's hometown of Kagoshima was razed by B-29s from the 315th Bomb Wing on Guam. His mother, Hata Nishi, was one of 2,316 people killed in the air raid. Shinjirō Nishi said, "The 1,000 stitch belt she made for me is the only thing I have to remember her by."

Not long after Nishi and the other maintenance men were evacuated, Ōmagari's classmate Ensign Kaneko told him that the "eggheads" from the Yokosuka Naval Air Technical team would be testing their rockets, and that he should come watch the fireworks. The rocket-men were assigned to an area located about 300 yards from the beach, above the East Boat Basin. According to Ōmagari, about 200 men gathered to observe the maiden flight of the so-called "new secret weapon." The team used a block and tackle to lift a 250 kg bomb onto a "V" shaped wooden launching platform which was angled up at 45 degrees, pointed out to sea. Ōmagari said, "The device looked ridiculous." After the observers took cover, the engineers remotely ignited the rocket using wires attached to what looked to be a standard car battery. The switch was thrown and there were a few sparks, then nothing. Just when it seemed the rocket was a dud, it whooshed to life loudly belching a thick plume of smoke. The rocket screamed off the wooden trough and flew out over the sea leaving a squiggly trail of smoke. For a moment, it seemed to be held aloft by the "oohs and aahs" from the surprised onlookers. The rocket-bomb soared for several hundred yards before it wobbled, then tumbled end-over-end splashing into the sea without exploding. Ōmagari said he was one of many who sounded their disappointment.

Ōmagari witnessed three other tests that were conducted with similar results. The weapons seemed to have a mind of their own, with unpredictable flight patterns and landing wherever they pleased. Ōmagari's personal opinion was, "The secret weapon was a joke. What kind of weapon travels through the air so slowly one can watch it with the naked eye?" He continued to rib Ensign Kaneko about the wonky-looking contraption. Other officers smirked too, but the engineers seemed strangely optimistic. Their goal in conducting the tests was to determine if a bomb could be delivered with an attached rocket. The rocket-bombs only needed to fly 1,000 yards to reach the invasion beach, and they didn't need to fly straight because there would be plenty of targets.

Not to be outdone by the Navy, the Army's Research Center No. 7 was busy developing similar rocket-bombs of their own. The Army's Type-4 20 cm rockets were designed to be fired from a tube, but could also be fired from an angled launching platform. The Army's larger 40cm rockets were fired from wooden platforms only. Both weapons were used on Iwo Jima and Okinawa.[76]

Shortly after the rockets were tested, something wonderful happened on February 1, 1945. Akikusa was sleeping under the stars when he was awakened by a soft tapping his face. "Rain!" he shouted as he ran into the bunker to share the good news. Hundreds of men spilled out of the various exits into the darkness carrying buckets, pans, trays, and tent shelters to capture the life-giving liquid. The rain sizzled hard through the leaves of the octopus trees as the men quickly and carefully put out anything that catch water.* The water was carefully handed back inside the bunker via bucket brigade. Thankfully, the rain lasted long enough to fill all of the canteens However, it was a mixed blessing since the heavy rain created a muddy sludge that tended to plug the caves' ventilation shafts, so great care was taken to ensure the surface points were cleared out.

The Last Flight Out

The defenders received some good news. On February 10th; Lieutenant Shigeru Hanazawa would lead an element of five Betty bombers bringing in special rations of fresh vegetables, red bean rice, ammunition, water, and mail.[77] The planes were from the K704th *Hikōtai* Attack Squadron (752nd Naval Air Group) stationed at Kisarazu Airfield. On the return flight, each Betty would carry out fifteen wounded men and mail.

The plane captain of Betty No. 2 in the element was navigator Ensign Masayoshi Nemoto, a graduate of the 13th Naval Reserve Class. As the plane captain, Ensign Nemoto was responsible for the ship and crew. Prior to coming to Iwo Jima, Nemoto had been on Luzon Island when, on January 9, 1945, General Douglas MacArthur fulfilled his famous promise to the people of the Philippines, "I shall return." Nemoto was one of the many Japanese naval aviators whose planes were demolished by American air raids. In order to evade capture, the aviators marched north to Tuguegarao Airfield where most were evacuated to Taiwan. Also on the long march were Zero pilots Kazuo

---

* Japanese helmets had 4 small holes in the top for ventilation, which rendered them useless for catching rainwater.

Tsunoda, Isamu Iwakura, Toshimitsu Imaizumi, and Pearl Harbor veteran Haruo Yoshino.[78]

PO1/c Iwao Yamada was one of two wireless operators assigned to Ensign Nemoto's plane. Iwao Yamada decided to enlist after the Pearl Harbor raid, but had to wait until he was old enough. He said he was shocked because there were Japanese on the islands making a living as farmers, businessmen, fishermen, etc. "The Hawaiian Islands were a place to build one's dreams. I didn't know why we attacked Pearl Harbor, but I felt it was my duty to join up," Yamada said. On April 1, 1943, one month shy of his seventeenth birthday, hoping to become a pilot, Yamada took and passed the Navy's *Yokaren* Youth Aviation Course exam.* However, after basic training he learned he hadn't made the final cut for the pilots course, so he became a flying radioman. After completing the abbreviated wartime *Yokaren* course in March 1944, Iwao Yamada went on to his final phase of practical training in Betty bombers with the K704th Attack Squadron.

There was a different unit that normally conducted transportation runs to and from Iwo Jima; the 1023rd Naval Air Group that flew the Nakajima L2D Tabby, but due to crippling losses, the cargo planes were restricted to domestic transport duties. In February 1945, the K704th squadron received a special mission to deliver critical supplies to Iwo Jima. Yamada said, "We had the newer Model-22 version of the Betty." It was equipped with aerial radar, engines with increase horsepower, increased defensive firepower, self-sealing fuel tanks, and armor for the fuel tanks and crew. "We we had a better chance at getting through the blockade than the transport planes," Yamada said.

The February 10th mission was carefully timed so the Bettys would be in and out of Iwo Jima before the daily arrival of American planes from the Mariana Islands. However, there was an unfortunate *snafu* in the loading process. In their haste, eager sailors incorrectly loaded one of the bombers, so they had to empty and re-load it. This cost valuable time that carved away at the already slim margin of safety. "That loading error would cost the lives of a lot of men," Yamada said.

Yamada recalled being nervous enough about going to Iwo Jima without fighter escorts, but the foul up made him downright fidgety. His nerves were

---

* *Ko-Shū* Cycle 12.

further frayed because his plane was loaded with one ton of ammunition. The Betty bomber was notorious for going up in flames, and with this much ammunition on board it would take only a single trigger pull from an enemy fighter to send them all to kingdom come.

The five bombers made the trip to Iwo Jima without incident. However, during Yamada's final approach to Chidori Airfield, some of the ammunition shifted which disrupted the plane's center of gravity. Lacking enough air speed to come around for a second attempt, the pilot was forced to make a hard landing that damaged the tail wheel. The plane ground to a loud and abrupt stop. On initial inspection, Yamada was concerned they would be stranded because the broken tail wheel had gouged a long furrow in the runway.

Ensign Ōmagari's eager ground crews set to work divesting the Bettys of their bounty. Ōmagari's men were motivated to work fast because it wouldn't be long before the punctual Americans showed up to wreck the airfield. Ōmagari recalled inspecting the contents of the first bomber that landed and noticed a nostalgic, sweet fragrance. He traced the grassy aroma to the deck of the bomber; stored under the crates of vegetables, bottles of water and wooden crates of ammunition, were bundles of six-foot long freshly cut bamboo stalks that could have passed for *mono hoshizawa* clothes drying poles. Ōmagari scratched his head wondering what he was supposed to do with the bamboo poles. *Do we plant them around the bunkers to grow camouflage? Are we supposed to hang our uniforms on them?*

It seemed odd, so he interrupted the nearest airman's conversation, "Say there, what's with the laundry poles?" to which the airman replied, "They say you're supposed to make spears with them."[79]

Ōmagari repeated the words in disbelief as his face grew flush with anger, "Is this some kind of a joke? Bamboo spears? You can't be serious." The rest of the aircrew averted his gaze. With a wave of his arm and a sharp cluck of his tongue, Ōmagari ordered his men to discard the poles by the side of the airfield.

Decades later, Ōmagari spoke about the incident, "Even a child would understand that the cargo space should have been used to transport something more important. The men were dying of thirst, with barely enough ammunition for a brief firefight and they sent us 'panda food'. Someone had to harvest, tie, and transport those bamboo poles to Kisarazu Airfield. Someone had to unload, count, inventory, and handle the poles before they were put on the bombers. At no point did anyone stop to think if we needed bamboo poles? Did *no one* think that more rifles and ammunition would have been a better idea? (Only one-third of his aircraft maintenance men had rifles.) If weight was a problem, how about loading more dehydrated foods, powdered soup stock, or hardtack biscuits? The airmen risked their lives for bamboo spears. Our men were starving and they sent us panda food?"

Almost 70 years later, Ōmagari is still upset about the bamboo incident. He said it was if the Japanese Imperial General Staff was still fighting the *last* war, where bayonet attacks were the norm. Ōmagari said, "I accepted the fact we were expendable, but why not give us proper tools with which to fight? Did they expect our soldiers to hide in caves with poles sticking out like sea urchins? I get a knot in my stomach whenever I pass the bamboo grove near my home. It reminds me of the day we unloaded the spears."

As radioman Yamada's plane was being unloaded, the flight engineer asked the ground crew to change the spark plugs in the starboard engine; it was running rough. What the engine needed was a thorough once-over but there was no time for that. Other maintenance men set to work repairing the tail wheel, which would take some time. Lieutenant Hanazawa decided to have all of his planes take off together rather then leave one plane behind. It would prove to be a decision that nearly fifty airmen would not live to regret.

Knowing they had an hour or more to kill, Yamada's crew sat down with their box lunches in the shade of some large bushes and a copse of trees at the edge of the airfield. The airmen were happy to dig in to their special three-tiered *bentō* lunches. The food was prepared for them back at Kisarazu Air Base to commemorate "National Foundation Day." Their crew chief wasn't confident the Bettys would make it back for the actual celebration the following day, so he ordered the special lunches for them to enjoy a day early.

No sooner had Yamada cracked the lid on his lunch box than it was covered with aggressive blowflies. The Betty crewmen all swatted away the disgusting pests but soon noticed it wasn't just the flies that took an interest in their meals. A small knot of gaunt soldiers emerged from behind an aircraft revetment, with questions of home and glancing looks at forgotten delicacies. One of the aviators polished off his lunch, and without thinking, tossed the square tray aside. A skinny soldier leapt on it, scraping out the last bits of rice that was stuck in the corners. Yamada said, "I suddenly felt ashamed. We handed them what was left of our lunches." He also gave away a pack of cigarettes; a bottle of lemon-flavored soda, a box of caramels and a small bag of rock candy from his emergency flight ration kit.

On the airfield, the planes were being loaded with a group of wounded men. Yamada watched a parade of sick and wounded men limp and hobble towards the planes for the trip home. Ensign Nemoto was disturbed by what he witnessed during the loading process of Lieutenant Shigeru Hanazawa's lead plane. On the heels of the last wounded man to climb aboard, an army officer arrived claiming to have urgent reports requiring hand delivery. One of the wounded men was pulled off the plane to make room for the officer. Ensign Nemoto and Yamada both wrote that they were angry about this event.

Fifteen sickly men lined up at Ensign Nemoto's plane patiently waiting to board. However, after consulting with the maintenance chief regarding the status of the starboard engine, Ensign Nemoto had to make a painful decision, he couldn't risk taking them all. He counted off the first five wounded and then lowered his arm. The others looked at him with pleading eyes, but all Nemoto could do was apologize and explain they could only take five men because of an unreliable engine. He told the remaining wounded not to worry because another flight would arrive soon. After the five wounded men were carefully helped into Nemoto's plane, a military postal clerk dropped off a sack of outgoing mail. The mailman was one of the civilian postal workers drafted into the military for their clerical work experience.

Once all of the planes were loaded, Lieutenant Hanazawa gave the order to take off. Five pairs of 1,800 horsepower aircraft engines banged and growled back to life. Lieutenant Hanzawa taxied into the lead position, and prepared to take off. Behind him should have been Ensign Nemoto's plane, but the tail repairs had caused a delay that put Ensign Nemoto and his radioman Iwao Yamada in the tail end slot.

Lieutenant Hanazawa's Betty took off followed by the second plane, but as the third plane lifted off the runway, it dipped its wing and fell out of sight as P-38 fighters flashed overhead. The American raiders had snuck in under the radar catching the Bettys flatfooted.

The crews of the remaining two Bettys that were still on the ground cut their engines ran for shelter leaving the wounded men behind on the planes.

The P-38s made one pass then vanished like phantoms. Lieutenant Hanazawa's plane managed to make it back to Japan, but the second and third Bettys that took off behind him went down into the sea taking their wounded men with them. By some miracle, the P-38s caused only minor damage to the two Bettys that were still on the ground. Yamada attributes it to divine intervention. It all happened in less time than it took to read this paragraph.

The six P-38 pilots were from the US Army VII Air Force's 19th and 333rd Fighter Squadrons. They were conducting a fighter sweep as part of a photo-reconnaissance escort mission when they happened upon the Bettys: From the 19th Squadron were Lt Harry M. Stampme and 2nd Lt John R. Donahue; From the 333rd squadron were 1st Lt Wayne A. Duerschmidt, 2nd Lt Harry W. James, 1st Lt Everett Balkum, and Captain Judge Wolfe.[80] The six pilots claimed a total of seven kills that day with each claiming a bomber or a fighter, with the last man claiming two victories.

Yamada and Nemoto both stated that only two Bettys were shot down that day, so there is some confusion regarding the number of kills claimed by the P-38s. There might have been other aircraft in the air that Yamada was unaware of. Or perhaps the Americans claimed the other Bettys on the field as "kills." Confusion seems to be the very nature of war.

On the flight back to Japan, Yamada stared at the white canvas mail sack stuffed with cards and letters. "After the war, I felt guilty. I should have made a list of some of the names on those cards. I could have contacted their families after the war and told them where their loved ones had died. But at the time I didn't know we'd be the very last plane off Iwo Jima," said Yamada.*

According to K704th Squadron gunner Hikōji Nozaki, the following day there was talk of staging another mercy mission to Iwo Jima. "I was worried that it would be my crew's turn to go on the next trip, but we were determined to be too 'green' for the supply mission," said Nozaki. In the end, Nozaki said that due to the threat of a sizable enemy fleet so close to Iwo Jima, further mercy supply missions were judged to be too risky.

---

* Soldiers and Sailors were prohibited from writing their location in correspondence.

Prelude to Invasion

On a transport ship headed for Iwo Jima, Private First Class Eric "Sonny" Ojerholm Jr. (D/2/27) penned a letter to his parents back in Newtown, Massachusetts.[81] Out of respect, the missive is presented *exactly* as it was written by this man who quit college to enlist in the Marines:

February 9, 1945 "En Route"
Dear Folks,

Hope my letters have been coming through halfway regularly so you wouldn't worry. Mother, daddy, Barbara, Joan, Michael, David and last but not least Ruthie, I hope you're all well and happy!

Myself, at present, I'm aboard ship bound for combat & as fine as I could be under the circumstances!

Needless to say, I miss you all very much & hope the day that I will see you all again isn't far distant.

I have have tried to write a letter like this before & I don't know quite how to begin.

Soon, in the very near future we will attack Japanese occupied & strongly fortified territory - that is obvious.

That some of us won't be coming back is also quite obvious! It is going to be hot and heavy! I hope & pray – God willing. I'll be spared.

I'm in the state of grace, & that fact alone gives me great consolation. I'm not going to try to tell you all that I'll not be scared. I'll be scared-stiff! I just hope I can give a good account of myself. In spite of my resignation to God's will, being in a state of grace, and a sort of fatalism, I don't want to die. I suppose that's just natural.

But if the worst should occur, I really hope you'll not take it too hard - just pray for me. The only difficult thing for me will be missing you all because I love you all very much. Tonight, as I write this, you are all many thousands of miles away, but there are bonds & ties that time and space cannot diminish.

By the time you get this letter you probably would have read of the strike of our outfit, so this will be old news but, this is the last chance I'll have to write for a long time.

I can't think of much else to say except that the weather is fine and the chow exceptionally good.

Guess that's about all for now. Write soon.
Love to all,
Sonny

At 8:00 a.m., on February 13, 1945, As PFC Ojerholm and tens of thousands of Americans were steaming towards Iwo Jima, Admiral Ichimaru ordered a pair of Tenzan torpedo bombers out on a reconnaissance mission to the Mariana Islands. He was searching for the American Task Force that he suspected was coming to kick in his front door. *Were the Americans actually going to Okinawa as predicted by Imperial General Headquarters, or coming to Iwo Jima?* One of the planes was commanded by Lieutenant (jg) Bun Hayase, a young naval reserve officer, who at 11:30 a.m., tapped a coded message reporting on a massive enemy fleet that he discovered north of Saipan. It would turn out to be Admiral William "Spike" Blandy's Amphibious Support Force 52.2, which was scheduled for the invasion of Iwo Jima. Lieutenant Hayase returned to Iwo Jima and made a detailed report on his observations.

The following day, Vice-Admiral Ichimaru ordered a high-speed Myrt recon plane, from the 102nd *Hikōtai* (752nd Naval Air Group at Kisarazu Air Base), to come to Iwo Jima to assist with tracking the enemy task force. At 11:15 a.m., the plane captain of the Myrt, Lieutenant (jg) Seijrō Narita, reported that he was trailing 170 ships moving northwest, eighty miles north of Saipan. He then vanished.

Despite this information that Lieutenant Seijrō Narita and his pilot paid for with their lives, Imperial General Headquarters was still convinced that the Americans were heading to Okinawa. IGHQ was further convinced of the Okinawa aspect after they received a message that a US task force was spotted near Amami Ōshima Island, located over 100 miles north of Okinawa. The report, which was sent to Iwo Jima as proof of the Okinawa first theory, later proved to be inaccurate.

Following the disappearance of Lieutenant Narita's Myrt, General Kuribayashi placed the entire island on full alert. Admiral Ichimaru once again called on Lieutenant (jg) Bun Hayase's pair of Jill torpedo bombers to find and track the US task force. The pair of planes reported seeing a large enemy formation of ships 150 miles south east of Iwo Jima, and then both aircraft disappeared without a trace.

Admiral Ichimaru ordered another Myrt from Kisarazu Air Base to assist in tracking the enemy fleet. Ensign Hiroki Otsubo spotted the Americans south east of Iwo Jima then joined the others on the growing list of those who went missing in action. Despite what Imperial General Headquarters claimed, there was no longer any doubt that the Americans were coming to Iwo Jima first.

At noon on February 14th, Lieutenant Commander Sosonosuke Tachikawa ordered Ensign Satoru Ōmagari to plant makeshift landmines on Chidori Airfield that night. Ōmagari thought it was suicide so suggested, "If we do that, our aircraft won't able to use the airfield." Ōmagari reminded Tachikawa that all of their efforts had been to keep the airfield in operation. Tachikawa was unmoved, and repeated his order.

At 5:00 p.m., Ōmagari loaded twenty men, with shovels and picks, into a pair of trucks and then headed to the bomb storage bunker to requisition thirty 60-kg aerial bombs, and an equal number of anti-vehicle yardstick mines.* He had his men dig holes in which they placed bombs topped with yardstick mines, and then covered them with soil. The yardstick mines alone were filled with enough picric acid explosives to disable a tank track, and it was hoped that the 60 kg aerial bombs beneath them would take care of the tanks' supporting troops. As his men worked, Ōmagari kept one eye on his men, and the other on the skies, anxiously scanning and listening for enemy night fighters. It was nearly 10:00 p.m., when Ōmagari called it quits. They were only able to plant twenty-four landmines. Ōmagari entered the *Nanpō* HQ bunker and presented the landmine map to LtCdr Tachikawa who scolded him for not planting all thirty of the mines. Ōmagari returned to his own bunker and sulked, the efforts and bravery of his men went unrecognized.

Rear-Admiral William H.P. Blandy's Task Force 52 arrived off the coast of Iwo Jima on Friday, February 16, 1945. Naval radioman Tsuruji Akikusa said that a thick fog blanketed the island that day. Akikusa peered through the mist to see ominous silhouettes of several ships anchored in the distance. The clouds gently lifted to reveal dozens of gray ghostly ships. Akikusa said, "The American ships were sitting ducks. Why didn't our planes come out to attack them?"

---

*   The Americans dubbed these 10.5 lb explosives "yardstick mines" due to their length.

With so many surface warships, submarines and aircraft in the Ogasawara Islands, the Americans enjoyed complete control over the sea and sky. Resupply for the Japanese was out of the question; the entire area was locked in a ring of steel that stretched below the water line and up through the clouds. Akikusa said at that time he wondered, *how many ships could the enemy possibly have? They have several hundred ships pinning us here at Iwo Jima, yet they can simultaneous strike Tōkyō? Their Navy must be three times as large as ours.*

A formation of B-24 bombers droned overhead to deliver their payloads. The blue-eyed flyboys were hoping to knock out any beach defenses that might have survived previous air raids. From the perspective of the ships at sea, the island disappeared in explosive splashes of red that flickered along its purplish hump and spine, forming billows of dark smoke and dust. The smoke from the aerial bombs gave straining eyes aboard the ships only periodic glimpses of the island's volcanic cone.

Akikusa estimated that 100 or more US Navy F6F Hellcats and Mariana-based P-38 fighters arrived overhead. On seeing the swarm of fighters, he was reminded of the clouds of hungry dragonflies that prowled the rice paddies back home. The fighters repeatedly strafed the island, but did little more than provide a buzzing distraction as they carpeted the island with spent .50 caliber brass shell casings and steel links.

As a result of the US Navy's radio jamming operations, Japanese message runners had to dash through the tunnel systems hand delivering messages and status reports. The runners often had to travel above ground because all of the positions were not yet connected with tunnels. In addition to delivering messages, the runners were expected to return with their observations about the condition of the other bunkers, defenses and numbers of wounded.

The noose of dark gray camouflage-patterned American warships grew tighter; Akikusa observed several battleships to the south. He had never seen a battleship, not even a friendly one, and was entranced by the enormous size. Offshore were the battleships USS *New York*, *Tennessee*, *Nevada*, *Texas*, *Arkansas* and *Idaho*. The cruisers USS *Pensacola*, *Tuscaloosa*, *Chester*, *Salt Lake City* and *Vicksburg* joined the battleships and destroyers. There were even more ships out beyond the second and third rings of navy gray. Akikusa felt that the blanket of US warships might even have reached as far as Kita Iwo Jima and Minami Iwo Jima. *The battleships are moving now, jockeying into position, getting ready to fire,* he noted. The Marines had requested a ten-day naval bombardment, but due to unfavorable weather and concerns over ammunition, the leathernecks would only get three days worth of pre-invasion support.

Akikusa watched a lone battleship belch a silent orange flash. The other ships followed suit, firing their guns at the island. Akikusa witnessed fat shells arching in slow motion that ripped the earth open when they struck. Shells churned up the ground around Tamana-yama and Funami-dai. It looked as if a giant rotor-tiller had been thrust down into the soil launching truckloads of rocks and sand sky high. The smoky debris showered back to earth with a thudding roar, sounding like a herd of stampeding horses. Many times, there was little Akikusa could see because of the massive plumes of dust and dirt that were repeatedly sucked off the ground.

Then, low hanging, heavy rain clouds covered the island. The rain prevented the US naval gunnery officers from accurately determining where the shells were hitting so the bombardment was temporarily halted.

"We opened our bunkers to collect rainwater, but were careful not to move far from the entrances," Akikusa said. The rain soon passed, and the Japanese dashed back into their holes drenched to the skin, carefully cradling their containers of precious rainwater. The ships began firing again, almost as if the American gunners were jockeys, each trying to get to their racehorse out of the gate first.

At noon, the ships' gunners took a breather while American aircraft arrived to strafe and drop bombs. Akikusa said the machine gun fire hitting the ground outside the bunker sounded like "heavy spring rain pounding on the roof." To this day, he finds the sound of heavy rain discomforting. This pattern of bombardment from the sea and air continued until roughly 4:00 p.m. An entire day of rolling thunder, rocking explosions, and vibrating earth set Akikusa's nerves on edge; he welcomed the sunset but feared it might be his last.

As the evening fell, the warships moved back out to sea to open some distance between themselves and the island. There would be no rest for the shell-shocked Japanese troops. The darkness meant digging, excavating and backbreaking lifting in confined spaces for thousands of defenders as they dug out their collapsed bunker and tunnel entrances and air vents. There were fears the Americans would land that very night. There had been so many false alarms in the past, but perhaps this was the real thing; the defenders had experienced nothing so concentrated before.

The US Navy was determined to give Kuribayashi and his troops no rest. The support ships fired star shells over the island that hung suspended from parachutes lighting up the terrain like a nighter at Yankee Stadium. The illumination rounds dangled like spiders, gently swinging to and fro, casting long, eerie shadows. The blinding flares put out 800,000 candlepower until their three-minute lives were extinguished.[82] "When the flares died, they smoked and sparked like the *senkō hanabi* sparklers we played with as children," Akikusa said.

The star shells also cast an ghostly pale light out to sea, faintly revealing silhouettes of darkened ships. "It looked like a mountain range had risen up out of the sea," Akikusa said.

On this same day, Admiral Shigeyoshi Miwa (6th Fleet), ordered four submarines to prepare for action against the Americans operating off the coast of Iwo Jima; RO-43, I-44, I-368, and I-370. The three "I" submarines formed an underwater kamikaze unit called "*Chihaya-Tai.*" They would use *kaiten* one-man suicide submarines that were carried into battle on the deck of a mother submarine. The pilot, or captain, of each *kaiten* would ram his human torpedo into an Allied ship. The *Chihaya-Tai* submarines began immediately practicing simulated *kaiten* attacks on towed targets in the Seto Naikai Inland Sea. The fourth submarine, RO-43 a non-Kaiten-carrying submarine, had already left for Okinawa, but it turned around and headed straight for Iwo Jima to conduct standard torpedo attacks.

The four submarines carried a combined total of nineteen *kaiten* human-torpedoes and sixteen Type-93 *Sansō Gyorai* (Long Lance torpedoes), which had the combined potential to sink thirty-five ships.[83]

Maps and Illustrations p.2

Iwo Jima Elevation Map

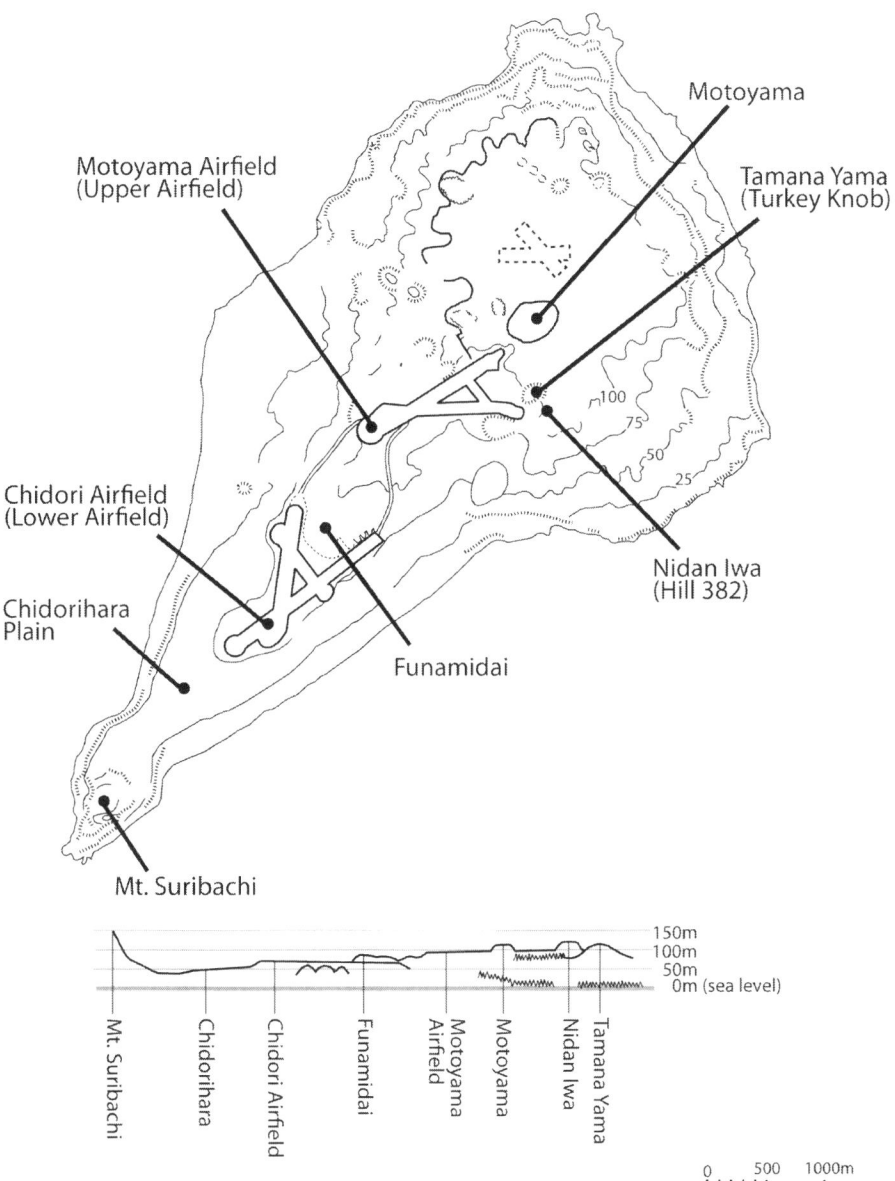

Source: adapted from information by Tsuruji Akikusa

Japanese Defensive Zones

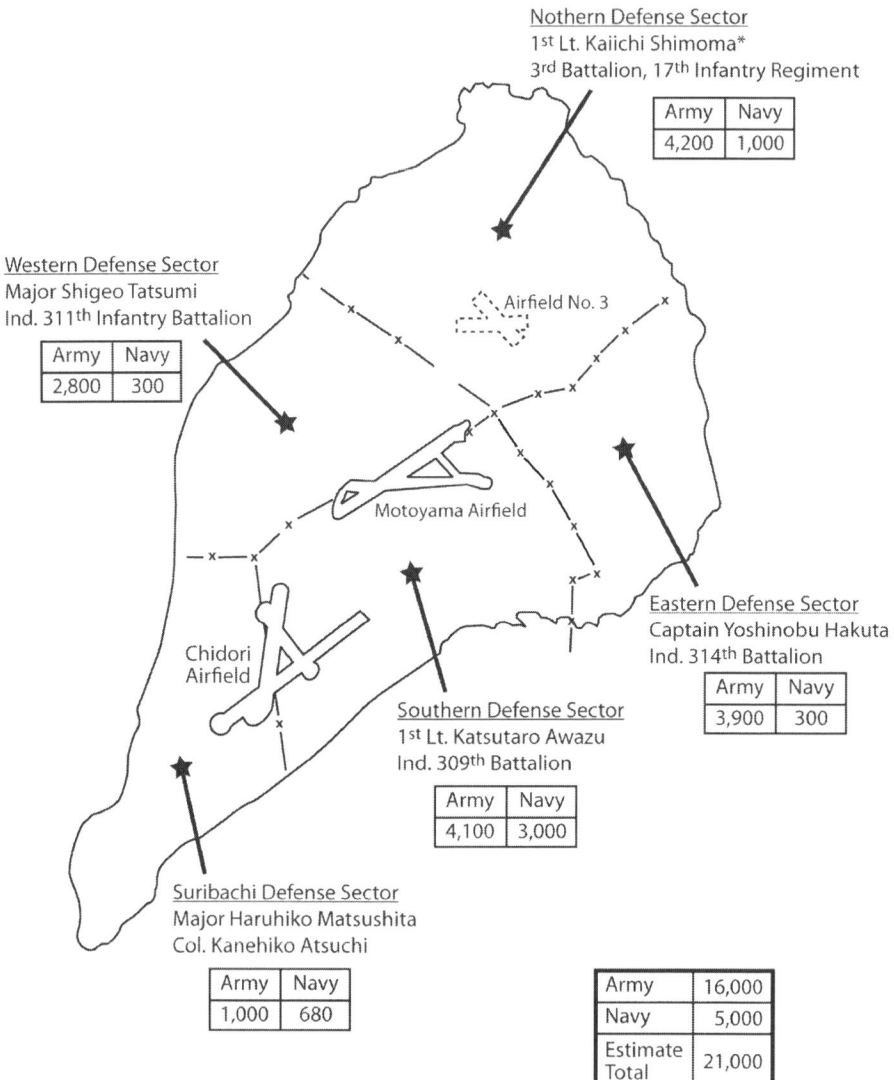

Source: Iwo Jima Association of Japan.

*Major Kan Fujiwara was sent back to Japan to attend Army College. 1st Lt. Shimoma took over in January 1945.

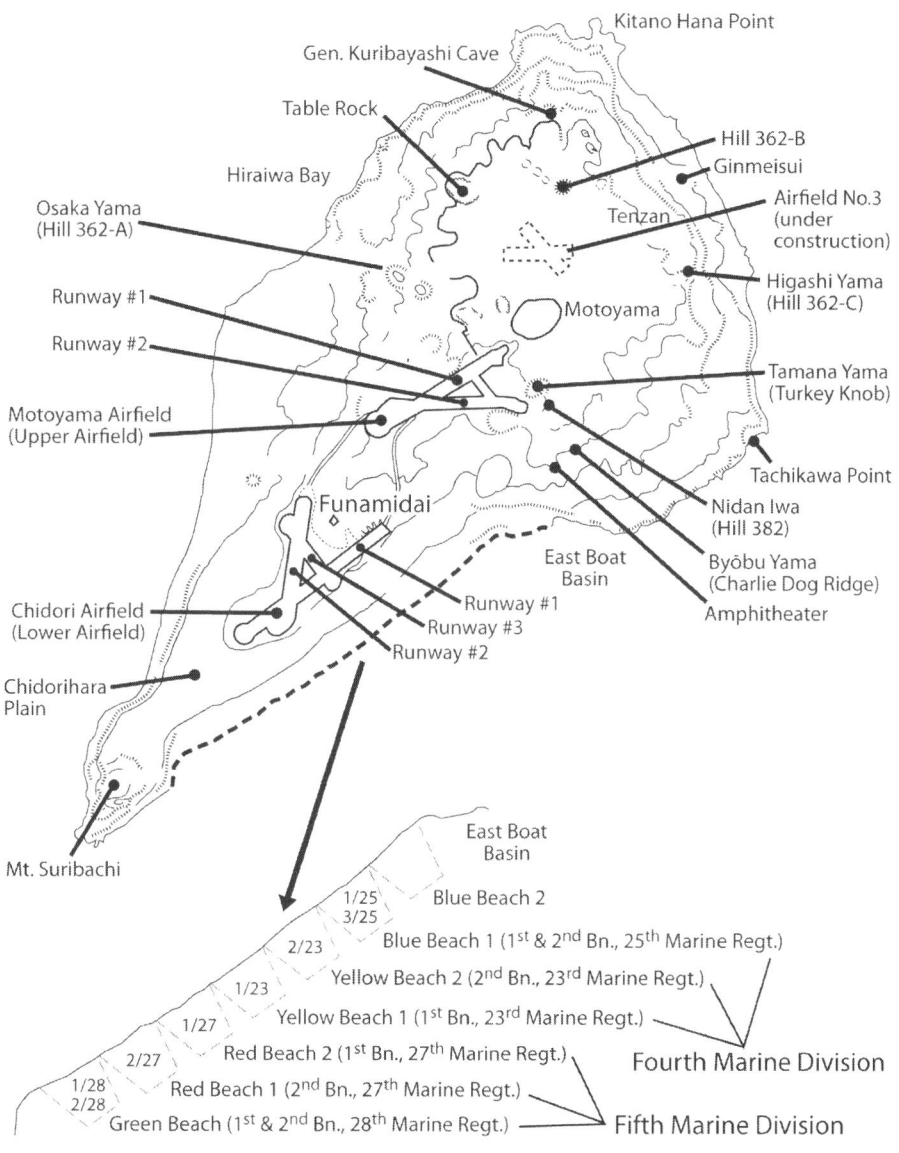

Maps and Illustrations p.5

Places & Dates of Importance

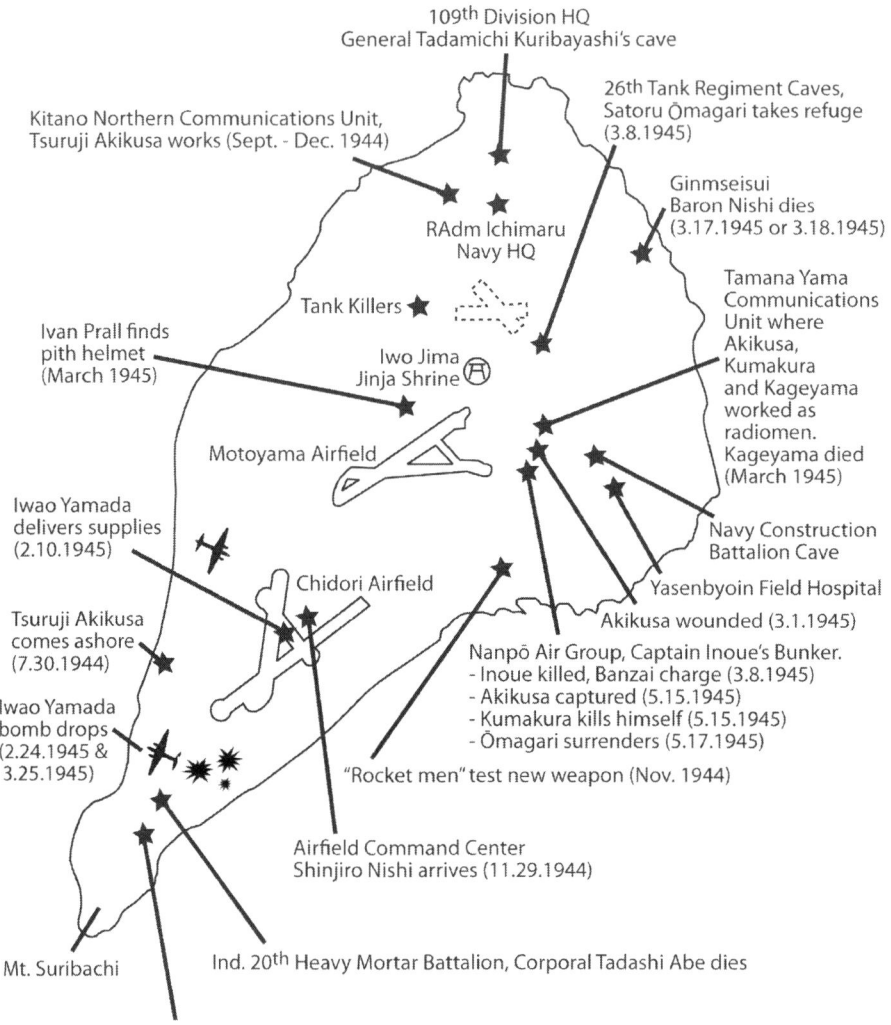

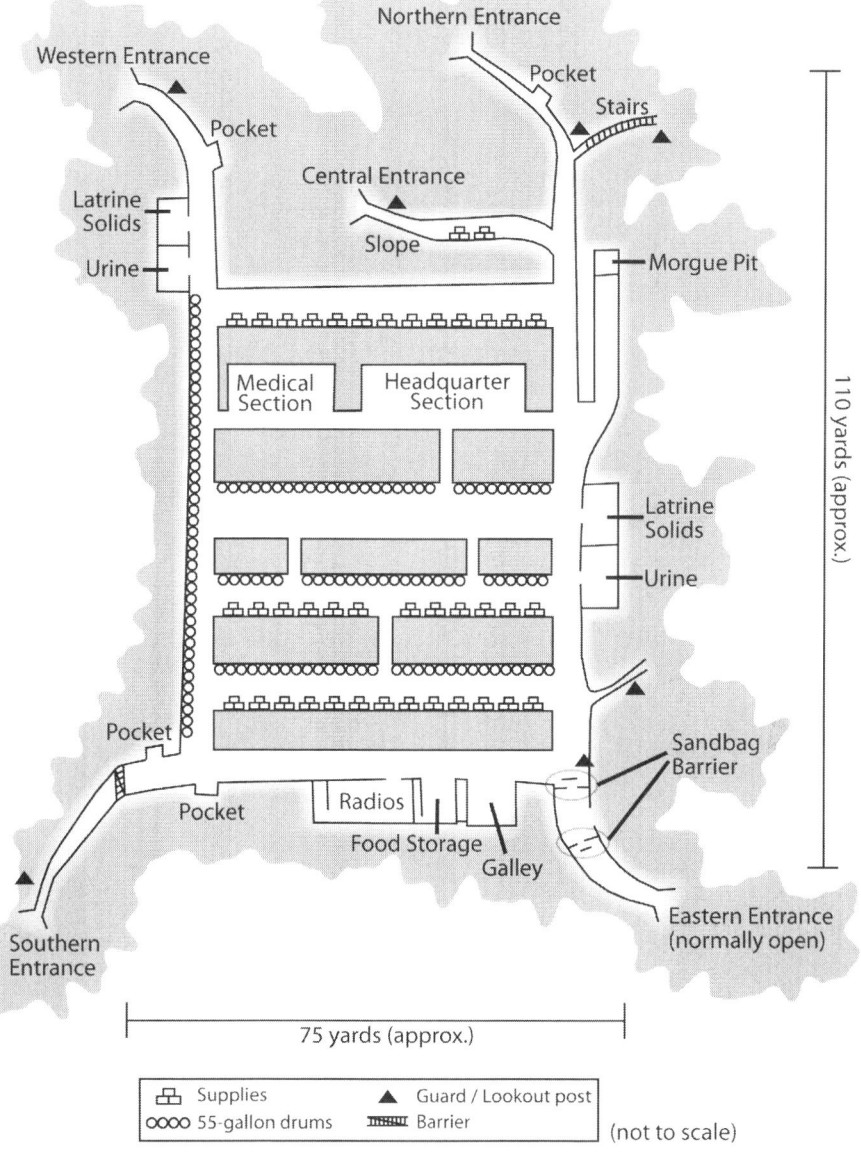

Maps and Illustrations p.7

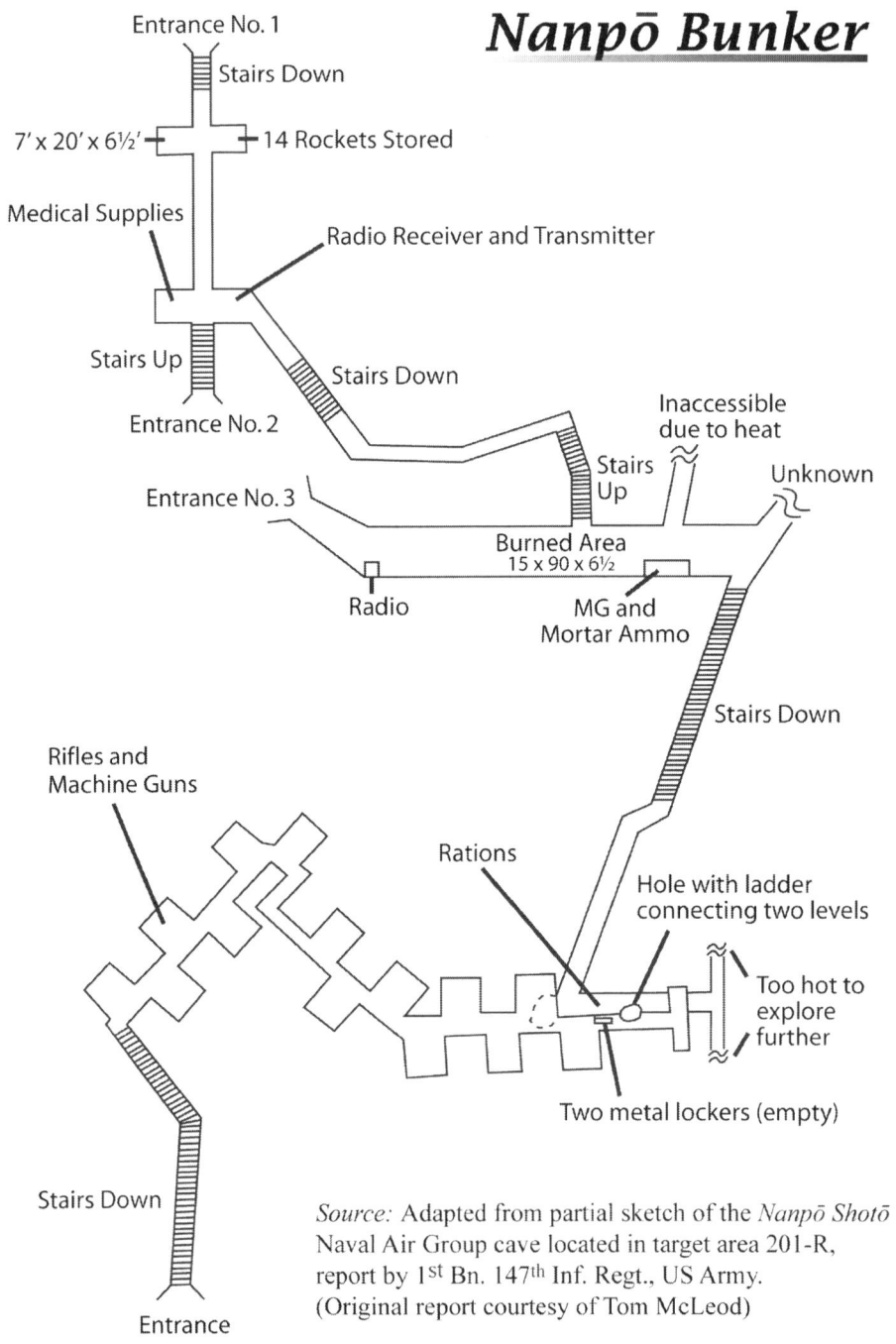

Breakdown of Japanese personnel captured between March 24–April 30, 1945

625 Combatants + 80 Military Non-Combatants + 84 Civilians = 789

Civiians: 11% (84)

Navy: 15% (120)
(includes 6 that claimed to be non-combatants)

Army: 74% (585)
(includes 74 that claimed to be non-combatants)

Japanese Personnel Captured by

US Seabees: 5% (39)

USMC: 13% (104)

US Army: 82% (646)

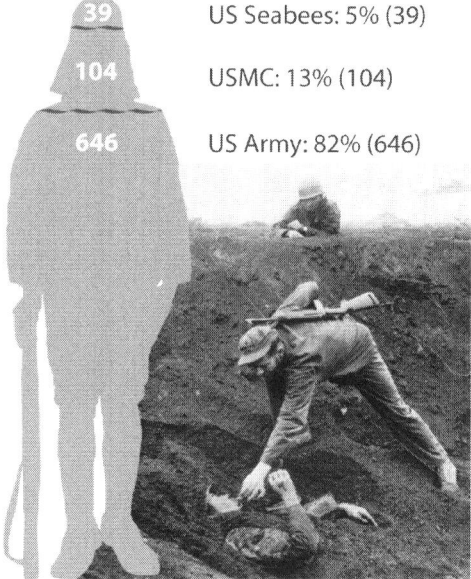

Source: 18-page report with details of names, ranks and capture dates of 789 Japanese personnel that were taken between March 24 and April 30, 1945.

Note: While not a comprehensive list, it provides a general timeline in which the Japanese defenders began to surrender, and by whom they were captured.

Department of the Navy, National Archives Identifier: 2939451
(http://research.archives.gov/description/2939451)

Photo p.1

Tsuruji Akikusa, circa 1942. (Tsuruji Akikusa)

Akikusa at Yabegawa Elementary School. It was here that the village held a joint funeral for all of their men who were killed in the Pacific War. (Author)

Yabegawa Elementary School class photo. (Tsuruji Akikusa)

Photo p.2

Kōhei Akikusa while in the Army in China. (Tsuruji Akikusa)

Akikusa's cousin, Corporal Nobuo Aoki, was in the *Kempeitai* Military Police and died in China. (Tsuruji Akikusa)

Akikusa's sister Iku joined the Red Cross as a nurse. She was drafted into the Army and worked in a field hospital in Manchuria. (Tsuruji Akikusa)

Tsuruji Akikusa's father served two tours in the Army in China. His scrapbooks are filled with letters from his family, pressed flowers, photos of fellow soldiers, cigarette pack labels, movie tickets stubs, and a log listing the dates and location of every town his unit visited. (Author)

Aide-de-Camp to Emperor Hirohito, LtGen Bunzaburo Kawagishi, was a friend of the family. (Tsuruji Akikusa)

Akikusa's uncle, Ensign Yoshinori Aoki, was a naval bomber crewman with the Takao Naval Air Group stationed in Taiwan. His unit attacked the Philippines during the opening days of the war. He wrote a book about his experiences. (Tsuruji Akikusa)

Akikusa's uncle, MajGen Shun Akikusa founded the Army's Nakano Gakkō Espionage School. He is seen here (Front row, 3rd from the right) with a group of Russian Nazis in Harbin, Manchuria in 1934. He is buried where he died in 1949, at the Vladimir Gulag near Moscow. (Tsuruji Akikusa)

Photo p.4

Akikusa's grandmother (front center left, in hat) begged him to be careful saying, "Flowers don't grow in graveyards." (Tsuruji Akikusa)

Yabegawa River where Akikusa swam and played as a boy. He rode a horse across this same bridge in 1942 on his way to enlist in the Navy. (Author)

Tenshin Shrine, Yabegawa Village, circa 1942. (Tsuruji Akikusa)

Akikusa stands in front of the rebuilt Tenshin Shrine. (Author)

Photo p.5

Tsuruji Akikusa in his sailor's uniform in 1942. The cap tally reads, "Yokosuka 2nd Kaiheidan." (Tsuruji Akikusa)

Sailors try on their new uniforms during the first day in the Navy. This staged photo belies the beatings that would come in the following months. (Andrew Strom)

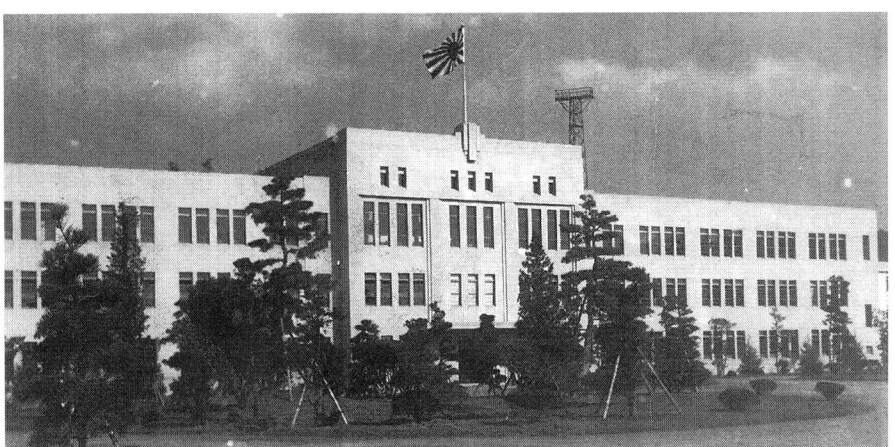

Japanese Navy Communications School at Kurihama. (Tsuruji Akikusa)

"Side view of a Japanese radio receiver, type B, in a cave on Miyako Island. Signal Corps Photo." This is similar to one used on Iwo Jima. (National Archives)

Tsuruji Akikusa undergoing radio training, 1943. (Tsuruji Akikusa)

Leading Seaman Tsuruji Akikusa sporting the double blossom efficiency rating on this left sleeve indicating he has completed his training, 1944. (Tsuruji Akikusa)

Field trip to Kunōzan Temple in Shizuoka, 1943. (Tsuruji Akikusa)

Photo p.7

Yokosuka Mutsuai *Buntai* in Fujisawa, 1944. (Tsuruji Akikusa)

Senior Seaman Tsuruji Akikusa with his cousin Sachio Akikusa while stationed at the Yokosuka Mutsuai *Buntai*, 1944. (Tsuruji Akikusa)

This statue of Masashige Kusunoki was erected in 1900 next to the Imperial Palace. Kusunoki committed *seppuku* after suffering a defeat in the one-sided battle of Minatogawa in 1336. His family herald crest of a mum floating on water and his phrase, "But that I had seven lives to offer the Emperor" were adopted by Imperial forces during WWII. (Author)

Photo p.8

Minatogawa Shrine in Kōbe city where Akikusa stopped to pay his respects to the spirit of samurai warrior Masashige Kusunoki, patron saint of the Japanese Navy. The shrine was later heavily damaged in US bombing raids but rebuilt after the war. (Author)

The gravesite of Masashige Kusunoki. Akikusa visited this very spot in 1944. (Author)

The author and Tsuruji Akikusa during their first meeting in 2006. (Author)

Photo p.9

This civilian transport vessel was converted by Japan and re-named *Enjū Maru*. (Wikipedia)

Akikusa uses a map to explain his movements around Iwo Jima. (Author)

Akikusa holds a portrait of his friend Yasuo Kumakura. (Author)

Akikusa and the author in the veteran's home, December 2013. (Jim Crawford)

Photo p.10

After the war, Akikusa erected this memorial for his village's war dead. (Author)

Akikusa is pointing to the name of his childhood friend Tadashi Mita. The pair rode their bicycles to the Nakajima Aircraft Factory. Mita enlisted in the Navy as an air crewman and was killed in 1945. (Author)

Tsuruji Akikusa and Tadashi Mita. Akikusa was a student at the Nakajima Aircraft Factory's Youth Engineering School, 1943. Mita was a year older and was an employee of the same factory. (Tsuruji Akikusa)

A USMC war dog investigates a suspected Japanese holdout. Akikusa was discovered and captured by a K-9 team from the US Army's 147th Infantry Regiment. (Harris Done)

Tsuruji Akikusa, Takashi Matsuda, Ayako Akikusa, and US Army Major (later LtCol) James Crawford in the Akikusa home. The three men traveled together to Iwo Jima in 2008 courtesy of the US Army. Akikusa was captured (he says "rescued") by a dog handler with the US Army's 1st Battalion, 147th Infantry Regiment. (Tsuruji Akikusa)

Photo p.11

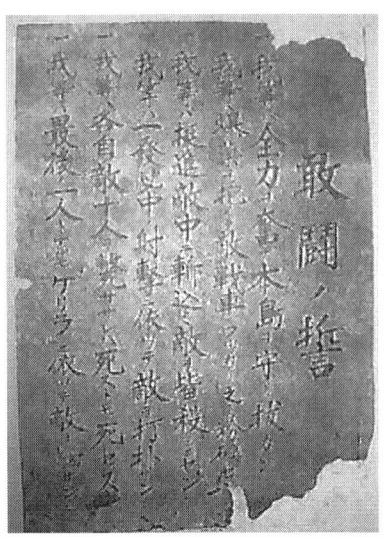

A grainy photo of one of the mimeographed copies of General Kuribayashi's "combat oath" that was issued to the troops on Iwo Jima on January 1, 1945. Among other things, it orders the defenders to kill ten of the enemy before dying.

The bunker entrance to Rear Admiral Rinosuke Ichimaru's 27th Air Flotilla Headquarters cave in 1945. (Chris Marks)

The same bunker as it appears today. (Chris Marks)

Photo p.12

Tsuruji Akikusa chants a Buddhist mantra for the souls of the dead at one of the entrances to the *Nanpō Shotō* Naval Air Group Bunker. (Takashi Matsuda)

The location where Akikusa spent the last few months of the war. (Takashi Matsuda)

With Suribachi in the background, Tsuruji Akikusa explains what he witnessed the day the US Marines landed. Note his missing fingertips. (Takashi Matsuda)

Photo p.13

Tsunezō Wachi as a Lieutenant. (Rose Wachi-Ogawa)

Even as a naval officer, Tsunezō Wachi enjoyed riding horses. (Rose Wachi-Ogawa)

Original caption, "Sunday afternoon on Amsterdam Street, Mexico City." Photo taken when Wachi was working for the Japanese consulate as a naval attaché. (Rose Wachi-Ogawa)

Commander Tsunezō Wachi, upon taking command of Iwo Jima in March, 1944. (Rose Wachi-Ogawa)

This 5.5 inch naval rifle was once completely enclosed in a 3-foot thick casemate. US bombings and naval shelling turned it to rubble that was cleared away after the war. (Author)

A Japanese 5.5 inch naval rifle, part of Commander Wachi's *Keibitai* unit. It is seated at the base of Suribachi and could fire at any target in the south. (Author)

Marines examine a Japanese naval 120 mm anti-aircraft gun. (Scott Freund)

A Japanese naval 120 mm anti-aircraft gun, part of Commander Wachi's *Keibitai* unit. (Anonymously contributed from Japan)

One of the beach defense bunkers shows the logic behind Kuribayashi's decision to move his troops underground.
(Todd Morris and Ivan Prall)

An aircraft fuselage was turned into an air raid shelter for the crew of this Japanese Type-10, 120 mm naval anti-aircraft gun. (Todd Morris)

Photo p.15

A Marine surveys a Japanese naval 25 mm twin mount anti-aircraft gun; possibly one of Ensign Tada's battery of ten guns. (Scott Freund)

A mobile Type-96 dual mounted 25 mm anti-aircraft gun on a metal sled with rings. These guns could be pulled into position with vehicles (or manpower) and relocated if attacked by enemy aircraft. (Ivan Prall)

Tsunezō Wachi became a Buddhist priest after he was released from Sugamo Prison in 1946. He dedicated his life to gathering the remains of the Japanese that died on Iwo Jima. He founded the Japanese Iwo Jima Association and was key in organizing the first joint US-Japan Reunion of Honor in 1985. Wachi displayed respect and admiration towards his former enemies. (Rose Wachi-Ogawa)

Photo p.16

As B-24 bombers drop bombs on Chidori Airfield, Japanese Zero fighters are flying above them dropping Type-3 anti-aircraft cluster bombs aimed at bringing down the American bombers. What appears to be anti-aircraft fire is actually these "Octopus Bombs," so called by the Japanese pilots for their appearance when they exploded. The specialized cluster bombs have exploded beneath the B-24s so the magnesium "tentacles" reach down into empty air space below the bombers.
(Chris Marks)

American bombers concentrate on Chidori Airfield to the left, and Motoyama Airfield to the right. Note the taxiways connecting the airfields. (Chris Marks)

Photo p.17

Chidori Airfield (Motoyama No. 1) under attack by planes from USS *Lexington*, August 4, 1944. (Chris Marks)

Photo taken by elements from USS *Wasp* in an air operations report from June 30 – July 4, 1944. The berms that the Marines struggled to get over are visible in the center of the photo. (Chris Marks)

Photo taken by elements from USS *Wasp* in an air operations report from June 30 – July 4, 1944. The landing beaches are at the top of the photo. Mount Suribachi is off to the right out of frame. (Chris Marks)

Photo p.18

Photo of Motoyama Airfield taken June 15, 1944 by aircraft from USS *Langley*. This shows wooden buildings, water cisterns, and damaged aircraft. Also note the patchwork of farms. A this time, the island was still home to roughly 1,000 civilians. (Chris Marks)

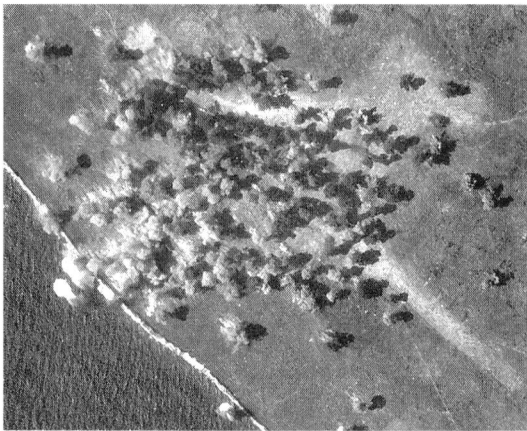

Guam-based US Army B-24 bombers plaster Chidori Airfield. (Chris Marks)

Photo of Motoyama Airfield taken June 15, 1944 by aircraft from USS *Langley*. This photo shows the various wooden buildings. The aircraft revetments are empty because the Zeros are in the air. (Chris Marks)

Photo p.19

Photo taken of the quarry at which a large number of civilians were employed before the invasion. Photo taken June 16, 1944. (Chris Marks)

Original caption, "Aerial strike on Iwo Jima in the Bonin Islands, by Navy carrier based planes. Jap aircraft lie shattered and burning on the airstrip. This was done in summer, 1944, to protect Marianna Islands Operations, and was not directly connected with the invasion (of Iwo Jima)."
Note the buildings and farms near Chidori Airfield. In the summer of 1944, the Japanese were still living aboveground. (National Archives)

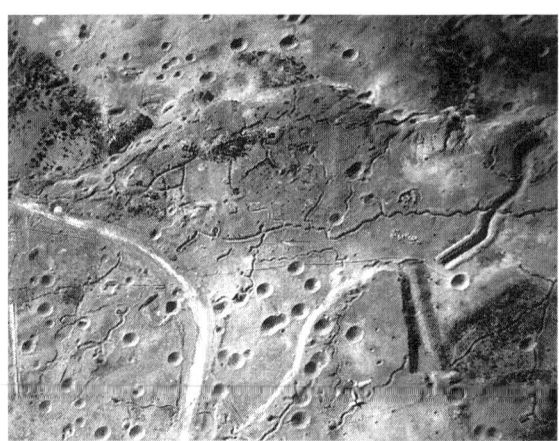

Original caption, "A stubborn enemy position on Iwo Jima has been blasted by SB2c-4's from USS *Hancock* (CV19), a unit of invading US task force. The effects of concentrated bombing and shelling are visible." (National Archives)

Photo p.20

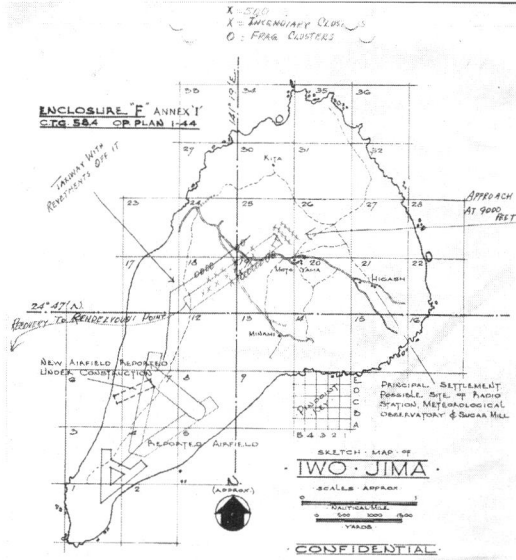

The Xs and Os mark the locations of the three types of bombs dropped by the Avengers from VT-32, USS *Langley*, on June 15, 1944; 500-pound general purpose, Incendiary Clusters, and Fragmentation Clusters. The original map is marked with blue and red grease pencil. (Chris Marks)

Pre-invasion bombing by B-24s target the beaches and Chidori Airfield. (Mark Stevens)

A TBF Avenger piloted by Lt David Marks flies over Iwo Jima on June 15, 1944. (Chris Marks)

The entrance to one of the Independent 309th Infantry Battalion's machine gun company underground positions. (Chris Marks)

Original caption, "Fires and explosions on Iwo Jima, airfield, Bonin Islands caused by heavy bombardment from U.S. heavy cruisers of Cruiser Division 10. Photo taken by reconnaissance aircraft from USS *Boston* (CA-69), July 4, 1944." (National Archives)

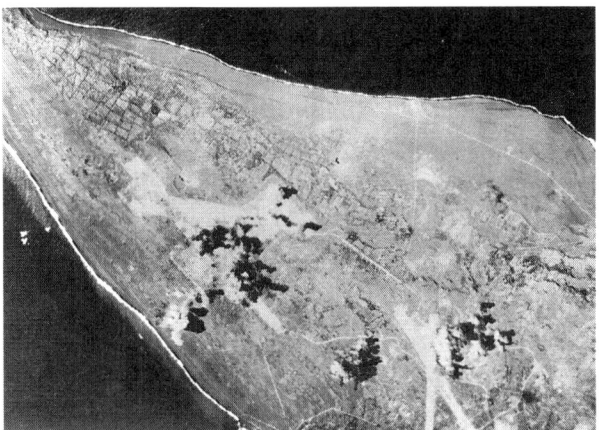

Chidori and Motoyama airfields under attack by American bombers. Mount Suribachi is off camera to the left. (Mark Stevens)

Close up of Japanese fleeing under strafing attack. (National Archives)

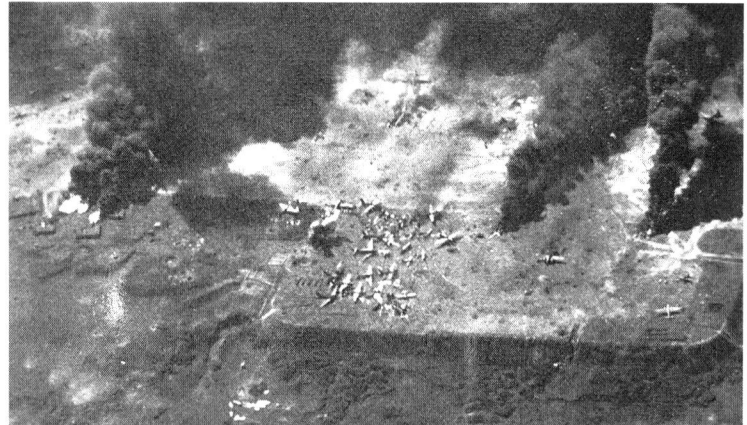

Close up of damage done to Iwo Jima airfield on July 4, 1944. (National Archives)

Original caption, "Damaged and partially destroyed, this Jap Zero won't make trouble for the U.S. anymore. U.S. Army P-38 skims top of trees at Iwo Jima Island prior to the invasion. Defense Department Photo, US Navy." (National Archives)

The three runways of Chidori Airfield (Motoyama No. 1) can be seen in this pre-invasion photo. (Mark Stevens)

Photo p.23

Sachio Kageyama, Teruko Abe with Gen James T. Conway, former USMC Commandant following the ceremony on Iwo Jima in March, 2010. (Author)

Marker for the Independent 20th Mortar Battalion, Iwo Jima. (Contributed anonymously from Japan)

Corporal Tadashi Abe behind his future bride Teruko Kageyama and fellow nurse in Korea, circa 1939. (Teruko Abe)

Photo p.24

Engineering Seaman 3/c Kiyoshi Kageyama (Teruko's brother) and her future husband Corporal Tadashi Abe. Kiyoshi Kageyama was killed on 12/23/41 during the pre-dawn landing on Wake Island. (Teruko Abe)

A Japanese 320 mm spigot mortar that was in the process of being assembled. Note the lifting handles and the instructions on the lid that state, "Place at top of body, top of warhead." (Scott Freund)

Original caption, "320 mm spigot mortar emplacement showing motor [sic] attached to baseplate with other threaded parts, body and head, in foreground." possibly one seen by Army combat photographer Ivan Prall. (Mark Stevens)

The author, Teruko Abe and Sachio Kageyama examining the *yosegaki* signed flag that was presented to her by patients she treated while working as an army nurse in China. (Author)

Photo p.25

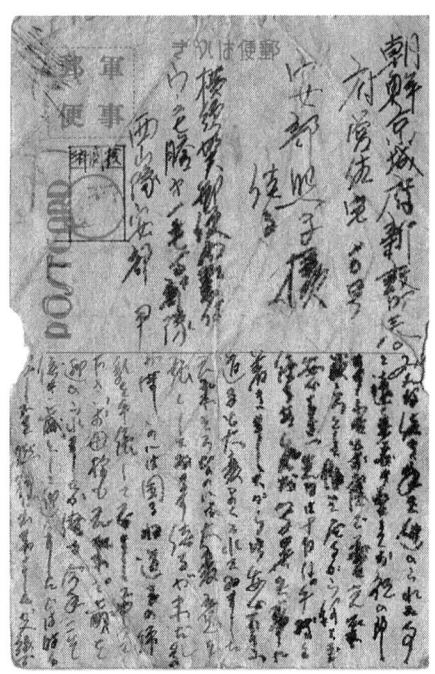

The only postcard Teruko Abe received from her husband after he went to Iwo Jima. (Teruko Abe)

The postcard is addressed to Teruko and daughter Yoshiko at an address in Seoul, Korea. "I trust you were able to greet the New Year. I celebrated the New Year under an unfamiliar sky in a place far away. Rest assured that I am working hard and doing my best. Thank you for your letter with photos (of Yoshiko and Michiko) dated (December) 10th. Michiko looks very cute in the photo. I see that Yoshiko still wants breast milk, too. You should wean her soon. Please file the paperwork to obtain formula for (the youngest) Michiko (so that neither girl will be breastfeeding). I will write again soon. Were you able to obtain enough coal to heat the house? Bye for now. (Teruko Abe)

Peace bells and envelopes that were handcrafted by Mrs. Teruko Abe for US Marines and their families who visit Iwo Jima each year. (Author)

Photo p.26

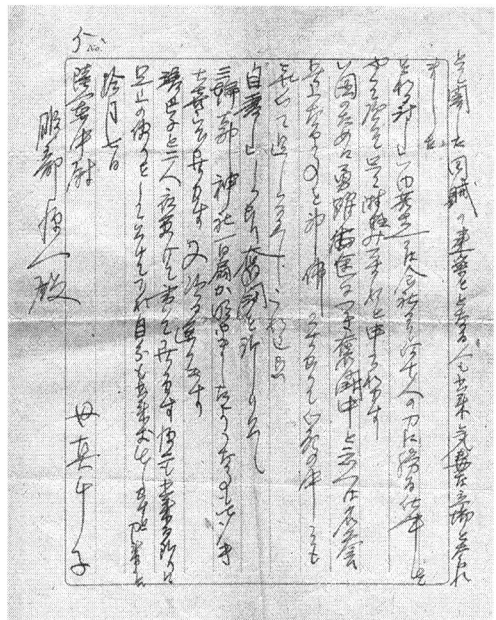
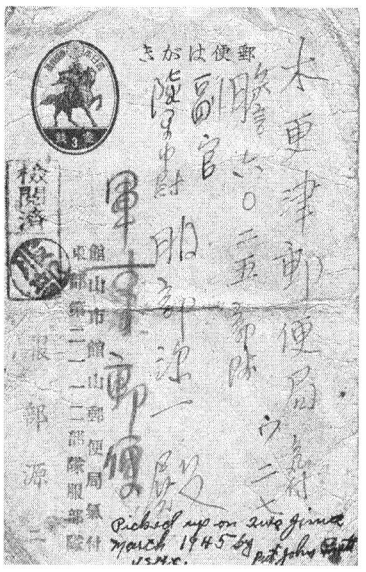

The last page of the letter from Kurie Hattori to her eldest son 1st Lt Genichi Hattori who was killed on Iwo Jima on the night of February 21, 1945. During the battle the letter was taken as a souvenir by John Puett, 5th Division, US Marines. (Author)

The postcard sent via naval airmail from Genji Hattori to his elder brother 1st Lt Genichi Hattori on Iwo Jima. (Author)

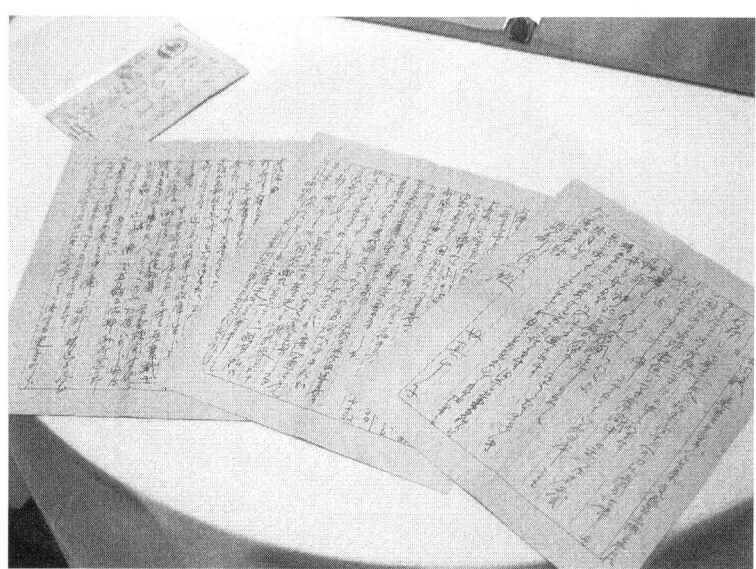

True life "Letters from Iwo Jima" that were returned to the Hattori family by Rex Butler. (Author)

Photo p.27

Mihoko and Motoki Hattori. The couple came to Oceanside, California in 2011 to accept the letter and postcard that were taken during the war. The items are now treasured family heirlooms. (Author)

1st Lt Genichi's younger brother, the late Captain Genji Hattori. Next to his photo is his army officer's cap. Genji wrote a book about his older brother and published all of the letters the family received from Iwo Jima during the war. Sadly, Genji passed away never knowing about the final Iwo Jima letter and postcard. (Author)

Motoki Hattori presents the letter from Iwo Jima to 1st Lt Genichi Hattori's daughter Chikako. (Motoki Hattori)

Photo p.28

Photo of the Hattori family at *Tomi Jinja* shrine in Sakura city, Nara, on New Year's Day, 1944. (L – R) Genuchi Hattori, Captain Genji Hattori, Kurie Hattori, and 1st Lt Genichi Hattori. The family visited the shrine to pray for good fortune and protection. (Motoki Hattori)

Tomi Jinja shrine was built in the 11th Century. (Author)

At *Tomi Jinja* shrine in 2012 in Sakurai city with Kinuko, Gentaro and Motoki Hattori. (Author)

The Hattori family was grateful to receive the letter and postcard after almost 70 years. The dead officer's daughter, Chikako, is seated front row second from the right. (Motoki Hattori)

Photo p.29

Kurie Hattori had a nightmare on the very night that her son 1st Lt Genichi Hattori died on Iwo Jima. She wrote in her journal of a vision of her son rushing towards her covered in blood waving his sword. (Hattori Family)

1st Lt Genichi Hattori was posthumously promoted to Captain. (Hattori Family)

Offerings to the spirit of 1st Lt Genichi Hattori, killed on Iwo Jima. The letter that was returned from the USA is seen on the left hand side of the table in an open box. (Motoki Hattori)

Photo p.30

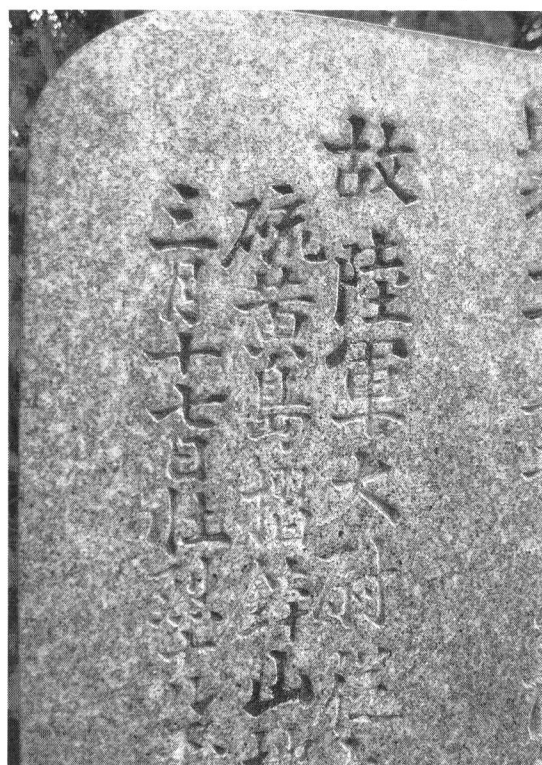

Genichi Hattori's remains were never recovered, but his family held a funeral and placed his name on the family tombstone. The place of death listed on the headstone is "Suribachi, Iwo Jima." (Author)

The roots of a "Tako no Ki" or Octopus Tree. (Author)

A pair of Type-1 47 mm anti-tank guns similar to those used by Lt Hattori's 10th Anti-Tank Battalion.
(Pacific War Museum, Guam)

Photo p.31

Satoru Ōmagari and the author in 2006.

Satoru Ōmagari and Japanese historian / author Yukie Sasa in 2012.

Satoru Ōmagari and his class of soon-to-become Naval Reserve Ensigns visited the Tsurugaoka Hachiman gu Shrine in Kamakura to commemorate their graduation. The shrine is home to *Hachiman*, the patron saint of warriors. (Satoru Ōmagari)

二 種 軍 装

Satoru Ōmagari and the 17th *Buntai*, 13th Cycle Naval Aircraft Maintenance Reserve. The caption reads, "Type 2 Uniform." (Satoru Ōmagari)

A Japanese 250 kg "rocket bomb" discovered on Iwo Jima as seen in a 1945 US intelligence bulletin "Japanese Artillery Weapons."

A Marine examines a Japanese 60 kg naval rocket-bomb, the type described by Ensign Satoru Ōmagari. (Scott Freumd)

The natural spring called *Ginmeisui,* is the approximate location of Baron Nishi's death. (Submitted anonymously from Japan)

Due to the amount of growth in this bunker, it suggests this is one of the beach defenses, the construction of which was halted by Kuribayashi's siege-defense plan. (Richard Stotz via Bruce Hirt)

Photo p.33

The cargo ship *Noto Maru* circa 1934. Lt Genichi Hattori, and Baron Takeichi Nishi were two of her passengers on the voyage to Iwo Jima.

Nestled behind a tree lies the turret of a Type-97 *Chi Ha* tank that was converted into a machine gun pillbox. The author encountered a similar one on Chichi Jima in 1992. (Mark Stevens)

The fresh coat of camouflage paint is a sign that this Type-97 *Shin-Hoto* tank came to Iwo Jima fresh off the assembly line. It does not yet bear the 26th Tank Regiment markings on the turret or hull. (National Archives)

Satoru Ōmagari witnessed a similar scene when he was with Baron Nishi's "Tank Killer Teams." (Scott Freund)

A Japanese Type-97 *Chi Ha* tank that was destroyed in the battle. (Ivan Prall)

US film Footage taken from inside a Sherman tank showing a Japanese soldier who was possibly a member of a "Tank Killer Team" like the one described by Satoru Ōmagari. (Scott Freund)

One of Baron Nishi's Type-97 *Shin Hōtō* tanks that was captured intact. (Scott Freund)

The top of a Japanese Type-97 *Shin Hōtō* tank on Iwo Jima. (Author)

Screenshot from a 1944 Japanese propaganda film about Iwo Jima shows a Type-97 *Shin-Hōtō* tank in the foreground.

A Japanese Type-95 *Ha Go* tank. Akikusa described a horrible encounter with a Japanese tank. (Scott Freund)

A Japanese soldier lies dead next to a Type-95 *Ha-Go* tank. It is in a dugout for improved defensive protection. It appears to be relatively undamaged and might be the one taken to Guam for evaluation. (National Archives)

Photo p.35

The Nishi family, Shinjirō is 2nd from the left. (Shinjirō Nishi)

Shinjirō Nishi, age 7, circa 1930. (Shinjirō Nishi)

Shinjirō Nishi displays the 1,000 stitch good-luck band his mother hand stitched for him. She was killed in a B-29 bombing raid in April 1945. (Author)

Ambassador Haruhiko Nishi. (Shinjirō Nishi)

Shinjirō Nishi in February 2014. (Author)

LtGen Larry Snowden (USMC-red) and Shinjirō Nishi are both Iwo Jima veterans that met on Guam in March, 2012. (Author)

PFC Jack "Beer" Blankenhorn rests under the shade of a Japanese Army Oscar fighter on Iwo Jima. Jack was the friend of PFC Don Lawson who was a flamethrower operator (3rd Battalion, 26th Marines, Fifth Division). Blankenhorn was killed two weeks into the battle. (Stephen Lawson)

Original caption, "Alert Navy and Marine pilots destroy Jap fighters & bombers on ground at Motoyama Airfield, Iwo Jima. Official Navy photo." (National Archives)

Photo p.37

PO 2/c Iwao Yamada (circled) and other members of the K704th Attack Squadron, March 1945. (Iwao Yamada)

Four members of Yamada's Betty bomber crew: (L-R) CPO Mitsuo Tachibana (pilot), Lt (jg) Masayoshi Nemoto (Navigator), PO 2/c Kazuo Tabata (co-pilot). and seated in front is PO 2/c Iwao Yamada (Wireless operator). Photo taken in April 1945 at Matsushima Naval Air Base. (Iwao Yamada)

Photo p.38

Photocopy of Iwao Yamada's mission report from the March 25th night time bombing raid on Iwo Jima. (Iwao Yamada)

Photo taken from the ground of Yamada's March 25th bombing raid against Iwo Jima.

Iwao Yamada with a replica of his Betty bomber that was built for a Japanese documentary about his February 10th mercy mission to Iwo Jima. (Iwao Yamada)

Iwao Yamada and his grandson Masato Yamada during interview in 2011. (Author)

A photo that was found in a Japanese camera by a member of the US Army 386th Air Service Group. A smiling officer (left) and an enlisted man stand in front of the barracks that the defenders lived in before the battle. (Mark Stevens)

Photo captured on Iwo Jima shows Japanese troops in Manchuria. (Ivan Prall)

Photo of Japanese soldiers in cold weather gear that was discovered in a bunker during the battle. (Ivan Prall)

Family photos captured on Iwo Jima. (Ivan Prall)

Family photos captured on Iwo Jima. (Ivan Prall)

US Army combat photographer Ivan Prall on Iwo Jima. (Ivan Prall)

US Army combat photographer Ivan Prall (right) exploring caves on Iwo Jima. (Ivan Prall)

A US Marine and Prall posing with a captured flag, Japanese helmet and Type-94 semi-automatic pistol. (Ivan Prall)

A Japanese Navy 400 mm rocket launcher in front of two Army Type-41 75mm field guns. To the right is the front of a Japanese Type-97 tank. (Ivan Prall)

US Army photographer Ivan Prall exploring caves on Iwo Jima. The large wooden poles that are evidence of the Japanese having scavenged building materials from warehouses and buildings across Iwo Jima. (Ivan Prall)

Photo p.41

Interior of Japanese tunnel. (Ivan Prall)

The interior of the pith helmet is written, "Shinji Ehara, Shibuya Unit Headquarters." (Author)

The Japanese Army enlisted man's tropical pith helmet that Ivan Prall found in a headquarters cave in 1945. It was later returned to the soldier's younger brother. (Author)

Thank you letter and current photo of Shōzō Ehara, along with WWII-era photo of Shinji and Shōzō Ehara. (Author)

Photo p.42

Original caption, "H & S of 147th Infantry prepare to land on D-Day (Feb. 19, 1945), Iwo Jima Island." (Tom McLeod)

The single stripe on this man's green cotton cap, shows he was a naval petty officer. He was with one of the four IJN units on the island; *Nanpō Shotō* Naval Air Group, Iwo Jima *Keibitai*, 204th Construction Battalion, or 27th Air Flotilla. Next to him is a 7.7mm late war "last ditch" Type-99 rifle without a sling. There is foliage tied into the net on his helmet. (National Archives)

Japanese who died in General Kuribayashi's March 26th airfield attack. (Todd Morris)

Aftermath of General Kuribayashi's final coordinated attack on March 26, 1945. (Bob Garey, 45th Fighter Squadron)

Original caption, "Killed by a Yank shell, Japanese dead lie in shell hole near airfield at Iwo Jima. Official Navy Photo." (National Archives)

Original caption, "U.S. Marines and Japanese dead give mute testimony of fierce battle by U.S. Marines to establish a beach head at Iwo Jima. Official Navy Photo." (National Archives)

Two Japanese naval troopers lie amidst the detritus of battle. A Type-97 hand grenade is near the man in the foreground. (Mark Stevens)

Dead Japanese soldiers from Kuribayashi's final attack in the fuel storage trench where they died on the night of March 26, 1945. (Mark Stevens)

Every day the Marines learned a new way to die. (Richard Stotz via Bruce Hirt)

A dead Japanese soldier lies with a grenade in his hand. (Richard Stotz via Bruce Hirt)

Photo p.44

Original Caption, "Marine Grave - died of three wounds taking pillbox – D-Day. Photo credit Sgt Stotz."
(Richard Stotz via Bruce Hirt)

First Lieutenant James Short (second from right standing) with flags captured by his fellow tankers on Iwo Jima before he was wounded. (Vicki Hawkins)

First Lieutenant James Short (front row, second from right in overseas cap) with fellow officers and men, Camp Tarawa, Territory of Hawaii, 1944. (Vicki Hawkins)

Photo p.45

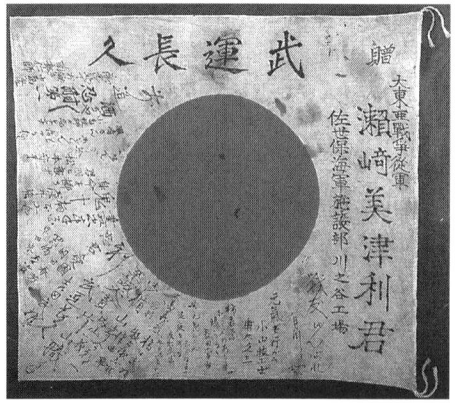

Japanese flag captured by First Lieutenant James Short on Iwo Jima. Its original owner was Mitsutoshi Sesaki, an engineer at the Kawanotani naval factory in Sasebo, near Nagasaki. (Vicki Hawkins)

James Short with the scar he received on Iwo Jima, circa 1980. (Vicki Hawkins)

A Marine Corps M4 Sherman tank knocked out by Japanese defenders. (National Archives)

US Navy personnel examine a Marine Corps M4 Sherman tank on Iwo Jima. (Author)

Owen Agenbroad returns a war souvenir to Yoshi-kazu Higuchi, son of PFC Mitsuru Higuchi who died of beri-beri in January, 1945. (Author)

Photo p.46

PFC Mitsuru Higuchi left behind two young sons when he died on Iwo Jima. (Yoshikazu Higuchi)

Corporal Owen Agenbroad after the war. He would return to Iwo Jima to meet the son of PFC Mitsuru Higuchi. (Owen Agenbroad)

PFC Eric Ojerholm wrote to his family about his concerns regarding the battle for Iwo Jima. (David Ojerholm)

John McKenzie was 17-years-old when he drove a landing craft onto the beach. (Doug McKenzie)

Ed Mervich and his son Gregg on the invasion beaches with Suribachi in the background. (Author)

US Army Corporal Ed Mervich after Iwo Jima. (Ed Mervich)

Photo p.47

P-51 pilot Captain Jerry Yellin, US Army, 7th Fighter Command, "Sun Setters." (Jerry Yellin)

Jerry Yellin's P-51 "Dorrie R" taking off from Iwo Jima on a VLR (Very Long Range) escort mission for B-29 bombers heading to Japan. He lost three of his wingmen on similar missions. (Jerry Yellin)

P-51 fighter pilots Lieutenant Dan Mathis and Captain Jerry Yellin swap stories on Iwo Jima. Lt Mathis was lost in a storm while escorting B-29s to Osaka on June 1, 1945. (78th Fighter Squadron, via Mark Stevens and Jerry Yellin)

Thousands of US Army air crews, like the one on this B-29, were saved by being able to land on Iwo Jima. (Richard Stotz via Bruce Hirt)

Navigator Saburō Kojima (601st Naval Air Group) holds a flare gun in front of a naval fuel truck. He would die in the "2nd Mitate" Kamikaze attack against Iwo Jima on February 21, 1945. (Harue Masuda)

Photo p.48

One of the ten Nisei members of the US Army 309th Intelligence Detachment (led by Lt Manny Goldberg) sent to Iwo Jima. The 309th landed in March, 1945, with the mission of translating enemy documents, but many Nisei went out on patrols. This Nisei is wearing his US Army field jack with a Marine Corps camouflage field helmet. The POW is carrying an IJA enlisted mess kit. (National Archives via Mark Stevens)

A Japanese POW whispers into the ear of a US Marine.
(National Archives via Mark Stevens)

Once captured or they decided to surrender, some prisoners were helpful in identifying locations of other POW holdouts. (National Archives via Mark Stevens)

A Japanese prisoner is perhaps stunned by the transformation of the island by US forces. (National Archives via Mark Stevens)

Tsuruji Akikusa, Satoru Ōmagari and other starving holdouts took great risks sneaking into US Army billeting areas at night to steal food and water.

Photo p.49

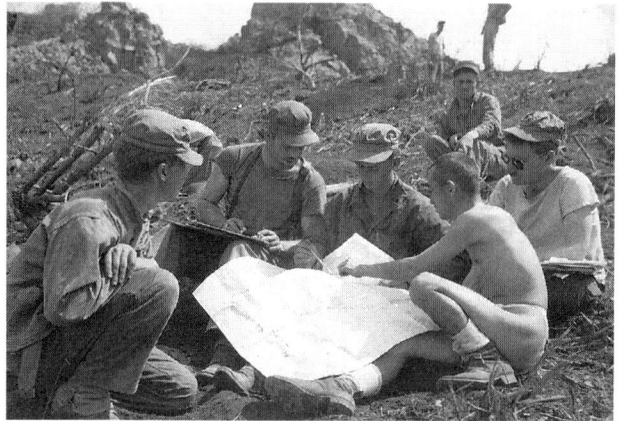

A Japanese prisoner shares information with soldiers of the US Army's 147th Infantry Regiment, which were sent in to "mop-up" the Japanese. (National Archives via Mark Stevens)

It seems not all Japanese POWs were sick and starving. This group appears to be in good health wearing mixed US and Japanese uniforms. (72nd Fighter Squadron John Skripek via Mark Stevens)

US soldiers try to smoke out Japanese holdouts in a cave. (Todd Morris)

Large caves under the airfield. (Todd Morris)

Photo p.50

Chidori Airfield was repaired and widened by the 386th Air Service Group that was sent to Iwo Jima to support the 15th Fighter Group and its new fighter planes: P-51 Mustang and P-61 Black Widow night fighter. One Japanese officer had a plan to steal one of these transport planes. (Mark Stevens)

Ensign Satoru Ōmagari discovered a case of beer that was misplaced possibly by US personnel who were celebrating after the battle. (Mark Stevens)

Japanese aircraft in the area used by the US Army's 386th Air Service Group, ASG. (Mark Stevens)

Looking east from Chidori Airfield to the invasion beaches. (Mark Stevens)

Members of the US Army's 386th Air Service Group seal a tunnel using a 1.5 yard Northwest Shovel. (Mark Stevens)

Photo p.51

An American cameraman utilizes one of the myriad of types of underground air raid shelters built by the Japanese. This one consists of quarried stone and concrete. (Mark Stevens)

A US Army combat photographer demonstrates how the Japanese cave position could have been used by snipers. (Mark Stevens)

VIIth Air Force pilots and cameramen enjoy a well-made Japanese bunker that was constructed from a Betty bomber fuselage and quarried stone blocks. (Mark Stevens)

Photo p.52

Soldiers from the 386th ASG search the entrance to a tunnel that is suspected of having been re-occupied by Japanese. (Mark Stevens)

Black Marines carry a wounded Japanese POW to the beach for evacuation. Akikusa recalled seeing African-American Marines on Iwo Jima. (National Archives)

POWs being guarded by Marines from 1/28. Note the Marine carrying the Japanese rifle over his right shoulder. (Richard Stotz via Bruce Hirt)

Photo p.53

An intelligence officer interrogates Japanese POWs as US Marines look on. The man standing with this back to the camera is a POW that surrendered and then volunteered to assist in coaxing others to surrender. (Mark Stevens)

A Japanese Army enlisted POW shares information with a Marine interrogator. The Japanese wrote his name, "Murasaka" (in *Kanji* and *Katakana*) on the US canteen that was given to him. (National Archives, Author translation)

A US Marine stockade for Japanese prisoners. (National Archives)

Photo p.54

Japanese POWs helplessly watch US Army P-51 fighters take off from Iwo Jima to escort B-29s to Japan. (National Archives)

Original caption, "Japanese surrender and are led to holding areas." (National Archives via Tom McLeod)

Close-up of previous photo. (National Archives via Tom McLeod)

Photo p.55

Japanese surrender to members of the US Army 147th Infantry Regiment. (National Archives via Tom McLeod)

Japanese surrender to members of the US Army 147th Infantry Regiment. (National Archives via Tom McLeod)

Japanese surrender to members of the US Army 147th Infantry Regiment. (National Archives via Tom McLeod)

Photo p.56

Original caption, "Iwo Jima's rugged terrain, northern Iwo Jima." (National Archives via Tom McLeod)

Some of the Japanese POWs were in poor health from deprivation and disease. (National Archives via Tom McLeod)

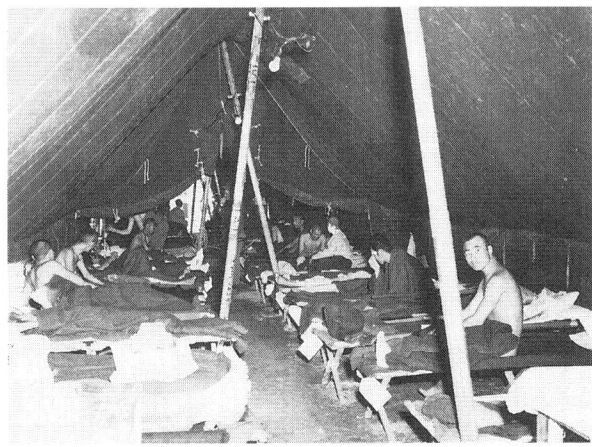

Japanese POWs await evacuation from Iwo Jima. (Mark Stevens)

Original caption, "The Captured Jap. The first to emerge from an Iwo Jima cave in which, with twenty other Japs, they had been hiding for several days, these Japs are astonished to find that they are treated kindly instead of being tortured as they had been led to believe would be their fate if captured. 3 April 1945" Captain Kolb, Co. A, 1st Bn, 147th Infantry Regiment is on the right. (National Archives via Tom McLeod)

Original caption, "Japanese Prisoners Types – These five Japanese, part of twenty taken alive by a mop-up squad several days after organized resistance had ended on Iwo Jima, found their captors were far from being the fanatics they had been led to believe all Americans were. The first thing they received were American cigarettes." The same two Japanese POWs seen in the famous photo can be seen in the center wearing a cap over his bandaged head, and the other with the shaved head is wearing a bandage over his left calf. The American in the center facing the camera is Lt James Hearn, Co. F, 1st Battalion, 147th Infantry Regiment, US Army. (National Archives via Tom McLeod)

Photo p.58

Original caption, "Iwo Jima – 1945, Two white shirted prisoners coax a Japanese to surrender." (Captain Kolb, A Company, 1st Bn, 147th Infantry Regiment) (National Archives via Tom McLeod)

Original caption, "Captain Kolb of Company A (1st Battalion, 147th Infantry, US Army) uses a flamethrower against Japanese, Iwo Jima." (National Archives via Tom McLeod)

Original caption, "Japanese troops await movement to compound." (National Archives via Tom McLeod)

Photo p.59

"US Army 147th Infantry medics treat wounded Japanese survivors."
(National Archives via Tom McLeod)

A POW on a stretcher is questioned by an intelligence team.
(Richard Stotz via Bruce Hirt)

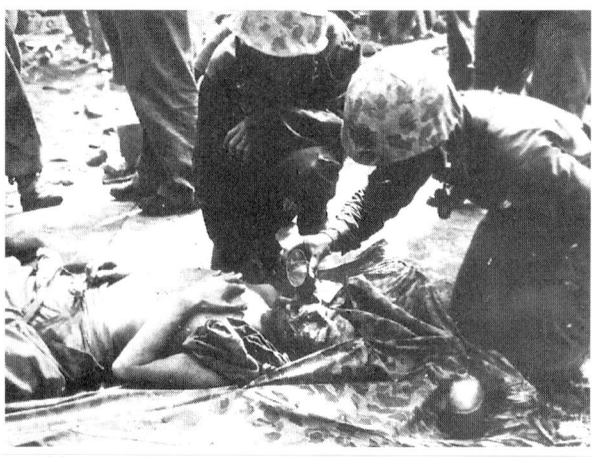

Marines show mercy to a thirsty Japanese POW.
(Richard Stotz via Bruce Hirt)

Flags from the Japanese field hospital are displayed by members of the 1st Bn, 147th Infantry Regiment. (Tom McLeod)

A Japanese Army POW convinces a Japanese naval enlisted man to surrender. (531st Fighter Squadron, Sgt Cossel via Mark Stevens)

The same Japanese Army POW with several newly surrendered POWs. Note the Type-99 Arisaka rifle with bent monopod on the Marine's shoulder. (National Archives via Mark Stevens)

Photo p.61

US Marines with a camouflage painted flamethrower and a bazooka. Hershell Williams recieved the Medal of Honor for his work with such a team. (Scott Freund)

Third Marine Division marked cannisters at a flame-thrower re-charging station. Possibly the one used by Hershel Williams. (Scott Freund)

US Army Flamethrowers are re-charged and ready. 1st Battalion, 147th Infantry Regiment. (Tom McLeod)

US Marines gawk at a rare sight, a living Japanese POW. Upon close examination there is evidence that the photo was retouched by a US censor who drew in a pair of "solid black trousers" so the photo could be released to the public.
(National Archives via Mark Stevens)

Photo p.62

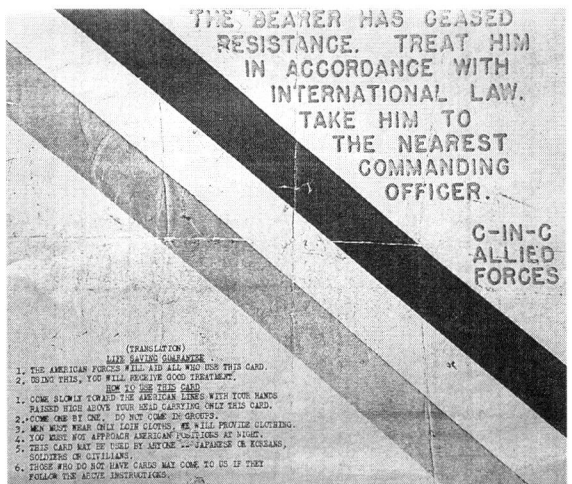

A US surrender leaflet with a special message to the Japanese on Iwo Jima. (Tom McLeod)

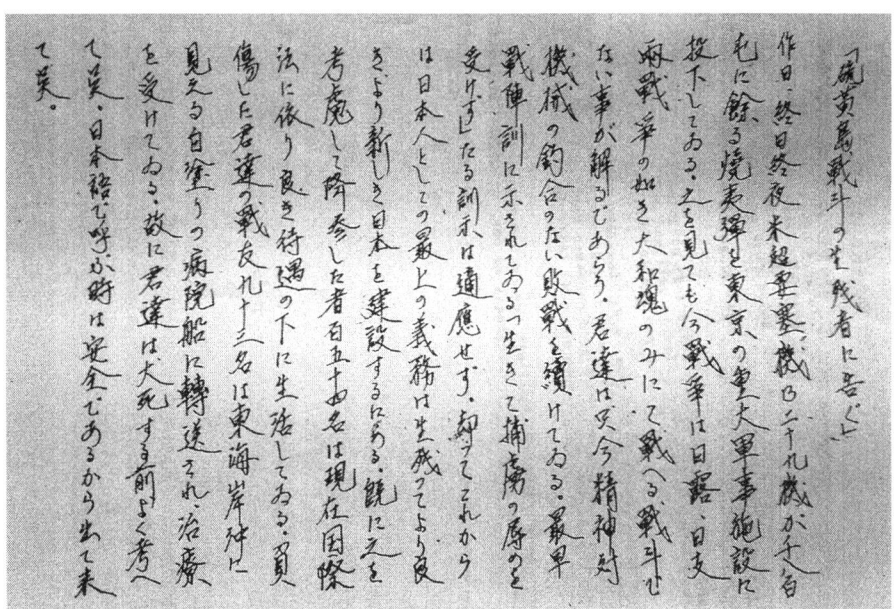

The reverse of the surrender leaflet says, " - To Personnel Remaining in the battle of Iwo Jima – Yesterday, all day and all night, American B-29 Flying Fortresses dropped over 1,800 tons of incendiary bombs on Tokyo's heavy industry installations. Judging by this one can see that this war, unlike the Russo-Japanese War and the Sino-Japanese War, is not one that can be kept going by *Yamato Damashi* (Japanese fighting spirit) alone. You men are continuing to fight a losing battle of spirit against machine. Instead of clinging to that first lesson of battle, 'One cannot live and bear the humility of being taken prisoner,' your supreme duty is to live and build a new and better Japan. 154 men have realized this and surrendered, and are living at present under humane treatment of international law. 93 of your wounded comrades have been moved and are being treated in that white hospital ship you see in the waters off the east coast. Therefore, think before you die like a dog. When you hear someone call to you in Japanese, it is safe. Come out, please."
WWII-era original translation. (Tom McLeod)

Photo p.63

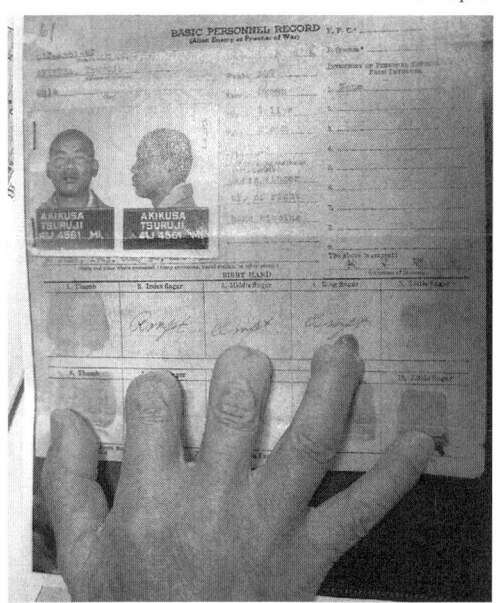

Akikusa lost three fingertips on March 1, 1945. (Author)

Akikusa's Basic Personal Record, 1945. (Tsuruji Akikusa)

POW camp located at Fort Eustis, VA. (Tsuruji Akikusa)

Pine Grove Furnace POW camp, PA., (Licensed for use by Cumberland County Historical Society)

Photo p.64

Original caption, "Japanese prisoners-of-war working in a POW camp kitchen." (US National Archives)

Pine Grove Furnace POW camp, PA. (Licensed for use by Cumberland County Historical Society)

A cave entrance on Iwo Jima today. (Author)

A Japanese Type-99 7.7 mm rifle with the Imperial 16-petal mum intact. (Author)

Japanese journalists examine a cave filled with broken shelving. (Author)

Photo p.65

A cave that is full of smashed furniture and shelving. (Author)

A cave full of smashed furniture and shelving. (Author)

55-gallon drums in a cave on Iwo Jima today are rusted and covered with dust. (Author)

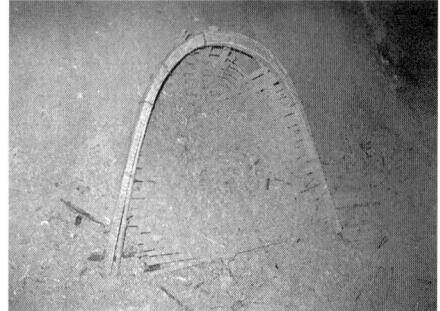

A wicker basket implement used in WWII to haul dirt to the surface. (Author)

Photo p.66

The human remains were recovered, but left behind are bottles, remnants of broken shelves, gas masks, navy dishes and a folding metal cot frame. (Author)

Tsuruji Akikusa respectfully places a pin at the USMC monument atop Mount Suribachi. (Author)

A US Army / Marine canteen and a Japanese Army enlisted canteen lay side-by-side on Iwo Jima. (Author)

PART 3
Invasion

The Americans Arrive

The dawn broke on Saturday, February 17th with not a cloud in the sky. As the darkness slowly dissolved, the outline of the American ships sharpened. Following an aerial attack from Mariana-based B-24s, eager US Navy gunners sent a salvo of good-mornings to the Japanese defenders at 8:00 a.m. Akikusa watched the battleships USS *Idaho*, USS *Nevada* and USS *Tennessee* fire point blank at their assigned targets. He tried to describe the sound of so many guns firing at once, and shook his outstretched hands with a wild look in his eyes. Akikusa said that shells ripped large chunks of soil from the hillsides, shooting geysers of volcanic rocks and soil high into the air. Some of the shells ricocheted, arching high and away. *Were the Americans trying to wake the volcano by punching a hole in it?* Akikusa wondered.

The ships pulled back to clear for the Underwater Demolition Team (UDT) operations. Four UDT teams were embarked in the Destroyer Transports *Bull*, *Bates*, *Barr* and *Blessman*. Seven destroyers provided cover for the landing craft carrying the frogmen to the beach. These UDT frogmen, whom Ernie Pyle, the famous war correspondent, tagged, "half fish and half nuts" rolled into the 59-degree water about 300 yards from shore wearing short pants.[84] "The first enemy troops I saw were the swimmers. They were bobbing up and down as they swam," said Akikusa. The UDT frogmen were pushing demolition bags and carried little tobacco sacks to gather sand for analysis.[85] As the men crawled out of the surf, Akikusa saw what he thought were dark-skinned Pacific Islanders. Some of the frogmen were covered in grease as a protection against the cold water, which might have made them appear dark-skinned.[86] Their primary jobs were to survey beach conditions and destroy beach obstacles. American planners needed firsthand assurance that tanks and jeeps could travel over the volcanic ash of Iwo's foreboding shoreline.

The defenders exhibited more of their stoic fire-discipline as American phosphorous rounds landed to provide a smokescreen for the audacious swimmers.

Akikusa estimated about 150 frogmen landed and occupied themselves with their work at the waterline. He expected to hear the bugle calls sounding the "commence fire" order. A feeling of panic gripped his chest, *why isn't anyone firing? Did the shelling kill all of our gunners?*

A heavy machine gun opened fire, scattering the frogmen. The swimmers dashed into the surf under ribbons of tracer fire and mortar round splashes. "Yes! Get 'em!" yelled Akikusa.

In an instant, 5-inch naval rifles opened fire from Suribachi hitting the support vessels. The large caliber guns were well camouflaged in heavy concrete casemate block house bunkers. The volcano, which was silent throughout past bombardments, exploded into light and sound as first one, then another vessel was hit by Japanese gunners. Other guns to the northeast unleashed and scored six hits on USS *Pensacola*, killing seventeen of her crew and wounding nearly a hundred more.

The heaviest fire came from a battery in the high ground just north of the beaches. The commander of US Task Force 54, RAdm Bertram J. Rogers, reported, "These batteries had remained concealed through over two months of softening preparation… because of their peculiar nature they could be neutralized only by point-blank fire."[87] The ships fired back with a vengeance and snuffed out the concrete casemates one-by-one.

Akikusa said the US Navy wasn't content to simply knock out the positions, they blasted them again, and again, to grind the broken rubble into dust. Had the Japanese held their fire until the actual landings two days later, it would have certainly resulted in a much higher butcher bill for the US Marines, soldiers and sailors involved in the first few waves. Akikusa guessed that the impatient Japanese gun crews had reached their emotional limit; they had endured months of shelling, bombing and strafing, and the sight of so many targets close to shore was too much to resist.

Lieutenant (jg) Rufus G. Herring, commander of one of the gunboats supporting the frogmen, was wounded yet kept his ship in action. Herring was awarded the first of twenty-seven Congressional Medals of Honor in the battle for Iwo Jima, fourteen of which were award posthumously.[88][89]

Shortly after 12:30 p.m., all but one of the swimmers from the eastern beach operation had been recovered. With every one of the supporting LCI(G)s damaged, none were available for the scheduled late afternoon reconnaissance of the western beaches on the opposite side of the island. Undeterred, the leader of the mission, Capt B. Hall Hanlon, asked for smoke planes, and for the ships to fire white phosphorus shells. The UDT frogmen made their second reconnaissance with little resistance and no casualties.

A possible explanation for the lack of resistance to the second UDT mission against the western beaches could be found in the smokescreen. When the planes released the white billows of smoke, Akikusa was convinced, (even until recently) that the Americans were releasing poison gas, or the insecticide DDT to incapacitate the defenders. Akikusa and the others donned their gasmasks and plugged their observation ports with blankets and sandbags, thus blinding themselves to the second UDT mission. One of the radiomen found dark humor in the perceived use of DDT, and quipped, "What do they think we are, head lice?" This misunderstanding on the use of DDT seems to have arisen from the holdouts that later watched American planes criss-cross the island spraying DDT after the battle to kill the swarms of flies that were feasting on the dead.[90]

After the second UDT mission, the defenders sent optimistic reports to Imperial General HQ that quickly found their way into NHK's daily English radio propaganda program called "Zero Hour" that aired at 6:00 p.m.* Following the playing of a few American songs, a female announcer who called herself "Orphan Anne" stated, "The brave defenders of Iwo Jima have repulsed the Marine Corps landing after the heaviest concentration of fire in the war." She went on to proclaim, "The Marines have turned tail and run [sic]."[91]

On February 18th, Kuribayashi ordered Colonel Kanehiko Atsuchi to leave the 109th Division HQ bunker to take command of the Suribachi Defense Sector. It is likely that Major Haruhiko Matsushita (10th Independent Anti-Tank Battalion) retained direct control of the Suribachi Defense Sector, while Colonel Atsuchi acted as an advisor. Colonel Atsuchi took his new post one day prior to the invasion, in the midst of a three-day bombardment. It is remarkable that he was able to traverse the island and move from the northernmost part of the island down to the foot of Mount Suribachi.

At the Tamana-yama Communications Unit bunker, radioman Tsuruji

---

    *   There were several female announcers who read the news in English, but the Americans called them all "Tokyo Rose." Iva Togri D'Aquino, aka "Orphan Anne," read scripts that were written by captured Australian news announcer Major Charles Cousens.

Akikusa's fragile optimism was shattered as the overcast dawn revealed countless ships jockeying into position to fire. The Americans were not going away. The weary defenders had worked through the night, repairing their fighting positions, cleaning debris from firing ports, and running messages. Rainclouds gathered over the island fortress as the ships moved to within a few hundred yards of the southern shore, so close that Akikusa thought they might scrape their hulls. At 8:00 a.m., the ships opened fire.

At the neighboring *Nanpō* bunker, Ensign Satoru Ōmagari received a messenger with an order to confirm rumors that the 5-inch naval gun at Kamiyama had been destroyed and enemy troops had landed. This casemated gun was located southeast of Tamana-Yama between East Boat Basin and Tachikawa Point in a rocky area. Ōmagari sent a petty officer and a squad of enlisted men to confirm the report. They returned to state the gun had been destroyed but no enemy troops had landed. Ōmagari needed to get this information to Captain Inoue's neighboring *Nanpō* HQ bunker so he rushed out into the zigzag communication trenches, keeping low as he moved. But the trenches were filled with debris, and in some places had collapsed. Ōmagari crawled the short distance to the bunker, with shrapnel snapping and buzzing overhead.

Once inside the Headquarter bunker, Ōmagari witnessed LtCdr Sosonosuke Tachikawa chew out a small group of men, saying, "How dare you desert your post in the face of the enemy!" Ōmagari quickly surmised the men were survivors from the Kamiyama 5-inch naval gun.* Tachikawa punched and kicked each man in turn, and then then drew his sword and threatened to execute them if they didn't return to their gun position saying, "The supreme commander of the island has forbidden retreat. All hands will defend their posts to the death."[92] The survivors of the smashed naval gun headed back out into the maelstrom.

At noon, now back in his own bunker, Ensign Ōmagari received a runner with a message from LtCdr Tachikawa. The messenger said, "Ensign Ōmagari is instructed to retrieve the landmines from the airfield. End of message." Ōmagari was aghast, and had the man repeat the outrageous message. *Had Tachikawa lost his mind?* Unwilling to question Tachikawa's orders and risk

---

    *   Ōmagari declined to use the man's name because the officer was still alive.

a summary execution, Ōmagari told the runner that he understand and would obey the order.

Ensign Ōmagari waited until dusk and gathered up his thirty-man team and headed to Chidori Airfield where he encountered a jaw-dropping view of the US task force assembled off shore. The airfield was almost untouched so he guessed that the Americans planned to use it soon. Upon seeing the condition of the airfield, Ōmagari felt that the enemy would be landing at first light.

Ōmagari's men moved to quickly, and carefully, recover all twenty-four landmines that they worked so hard to place. As darkness fell, they continued their labor under the light of illumination rounds fired from the ships. Ōmagari couldn't explain why they weren't fired on, but presumed the American naval gunners were ordered not to shell the airfield. Per the instructions he received from LtCdr Tachikawa, Ōmagari transported the bombs to one of the *Kugishō* rocket team bunkers (to be converted into rocket-bombs) and then drove back to the *Nanpō* HQ bunker. With his hands quivering from the adrenaline rush, Ōmagari made his verbal report to LtCdr Tachikawa, and then shared his own theory as to why the airfield was unscathed. Tachikawa shook his head in disbelief, saying that Ōmagari must be mistaken. Ensign Satoru Ōmagari returned to his own bunker in frustration.

The naval bombardment intensified on Monday morning, February 19th. The battleships USS *North Carolina* and *Washington* added their 16-inch shells to the orchestra of destruction. The cruisers USS *Indianapolis*, *Santa Fe* and *Biloxi* brought more 8-inch and 6-inch guns to the one-sided battle artillery duel. The island had been broken into target areas which bore numbers. Each numbered target area was further broken down into twenty-five smaller squares that were identified with letters. For example, the Nanpo Naval Air Group bunker was in target area 201-R. Each ship was given targets in their assigned areas. The US Navy was methodically trying to lay waste to Iwo Jima.

There were periodic lulls to allow carrier-based airplanes to bomb, strafe, and fire rockets as the curtain went up on the battle. A ship that had survived the Pearl Harbor attack, USS *West Virginia*, arrived later in the day to join the fracas.

The Marines are Landing

Akikusa watched boats carrying troops head towards the island, and described odd-looking tracked vehicles and tanks that came ashore ahead of the Marines.

Growing in the soil outside of Akikusa's vision port were a few lavender-colored flowers, looking much like morning glories. Akikusa had not taken notice of the delicate petals before, and felt it as a sign from heaven that he would survive the battle.

But as more and more vehicles and boats arrived, he grew worried. "The Marines were digging in down at the water's edge. There were so many of them," said Akikusa. "It reminded me of a crowd of baseball fans waiting for the stadium to open. I saw their numbers swell from several hundred to a few thousand. Each new wave piled on top of the last one," he said. He was worried that the lack of concentrated counter-fire meant that the Americans would overrun the island. *Why weren't our big guns firing?* he thought.

Akikusa was encouraged by the sharp sound of bugles echoing over the landscape. To the Marines in the first couple of waves, the staccato Japanese melody would have sounded like a cavalry charge from a John Wayne western movie. The cheery notes belied its dark lyrics, *dete kuru, dete kuru, minna minna korose* (Come out, come out, kill them all). The buglers' lips pressed hard, splitting against the metal mouthpieces, blowing with all of their might. They poked their bugles out of vent holes and observation ports to blow the the 4-second-long repetitive tune that cut through the ensuing explosions and gunfire.

Ensign Ōmagari heard the bugles, too, and exited the *Nanpō* tunnel complex to place his men in their spider holes.[*] For the sixty men under his direct control, Ōmagari had only twenty Type-38 Arisaka bolt-action rifles, two Type-89 50 mm "knee mortar" grenade launchers, and 120 Type-97 hand grenades. He told his men, "Iwo Jima will be our tomb."[93]

Radioman Tsuruji Akikusa said, "A runner brought a message from Kuribayashi's HQ asking if the enemy had landed. Another runner came with a message that congratulated us for repelling the invasion. This made me angry because it meant the Army wasn't engaged in the fight. It was the (naval) Southern Defense Sector doing all the work," Akikusa said. He saw Japanese

---

   * The spider hole, or "*tako tsubo*" (octopus pot), is a small fighting position that takes its name from the ceramic pots used by fishermen to trap octopi.

rocket-bombs explode on the heavily packed shoreline. The Marines were pushed back into the surf as mortars, machine guns and artillery rounds rained down on the crowded beaches. "The beaches were so full of men, boats and vehicles, that there was no way to miss them. Many were forced back into the water. Yet, I saw many small boats coming and going, bringing even more Marines," Akikusa said.

One of those boats was piloted by 17-year-old Boatswain's Mate Third Class (BM3/c) John McKenzie in LCVP No. PA-159-24, from USS *Darke* (AP-159). McKenzie was carrying thirty Marines, from the 4th Marine Division, and was about 200 yards away from Red Beach 2 when he was broadsided by another LCVP that was heading back out to sea. "The other boat's crew had their heads down so they couldn't see where they were going. I tried to steer clear but a fully loaded Higgins boat doesn't turn very well and the other guy smashed into our side. We started to take on water," McKenzie said.[94] He made it to the beach and offloaded the Marines, but discovered that he couldn't completely raise the bow ramp because the hull was damaged. McKenzie and his three crewmembers abandoned their boat and headed south towards Mount Suribachi in hopes of catching a ride back to USS *Darke*. "I don't know how we were able to move down the beach and not get hit by Japanese mortars," McKenzie said.

BM3/C John McKenzie continued down to Red Beach 1 where he found an LCM (Landing Craft, Mechanized) from USS *Darke* and hitched a ride. However, the mother ship had moved farther away from the island so McKenzie and his men spent the night aboard the LCM and transferred back to their ship the following morning. With their LCVP destroyed, McKenzie and the others would not be returning to Iwo Jima.

According to Ensign Satoru Ōmagari, on the night of February 19th, the Japanese received a shot in the arm from an American radio transmission. The Americans had not encoded the message that was intercepted and translated. The message stated that the Americans wanted more hospital ships. It also mentioned devastation from a "new weapon." Ōmagari was in Captain Inoue's bunker when the message came in and said that he scratched his head because he knew of no such "new weapon" that would send the invasion force into a panic.

Down on "Green Beach," Captain Dave Severance's E Company, 2nd

Battalion, 28th Marine Regiment (E/2/28) landed and quickly pushed across the narrow neck of the island to cut off Mount Suribachi. In neighboring F Company were BAR gunners Privates First Class George Dunn and William Sayer. The pair had gone through boot camp together and was inseparable. Alongside them was rifleman PFC Donald Ruhl. Neither Dunn nor Ruhl would live long enough to witness the flag raising captured by photographers Joe Rosenthal and Sgt Bill Genaust, and only PFC Sayer would survive the battle.

PFC George Dunn was shot in the head while assaulting a bunker at the foot of Mount Suribachi. PFC Dunn left behind a wife and a 2-year-old daughter Kathy.

PFC William Sayer was severely wounded in the face the following day and evacuated.

On the morning of February 21st, while still engaged at the base of the volcano, PFC Donald Ruhl jumped on a Japanese grenade that put him on the growing list of posthumous Congressional Medal of Honor recipients. PFCs Dunn and Ruhl were initially buried next to each other in the 5th Marine Division Cemetery on Iwo Jima.

One of the Japanese units stubbornly defending Suribachi was Lieutenant Genichi Hattori's Independent 10th Anti-Tank Battalion. They were using the Type-1 47 mm anti-tank guns armed with armor-piercing shells. The guns had a range just over four miles, but they would be engaging the Sherman tanks at distances that could be measured in first downs. The commander, Major Haruhiko Matsuhita, said that many of his guns ran out of ammunition or were put out of commission. However, his guns still managed to take a heavy toll on the first day when they blasted four Sherman tanks from the 5th Tank Battalion. One Marine recalled seeing an anti-tank round slice into a tank and kill the 5-man crew, "It punched through the cold armor plate as a finger is punched through putty," said Sgt Thomas Gallant.[95]

As is evident by photographs, and the lone Sherman tank that still rests on Iwo Jima, the Marines up-armored their tanks. They applied additional appliqué armor welded to the sides; poured-concrete siding and oak planks to defeat magnetic charges; and welded rebar steel cages, or large nails, to the tops of hatches to prevent Japanese infantry from placing satchel charges directly against the hatches. But due to the close range, Japanese anti-tank gunners were able to exploit weaknesses, such as the vision ports that had armored glass, which could be defeated by a well-placed armor piercing round.

The Marines tankers had a shocking surprise for the Japanese defenders; some of their tanks could spit fire. Prior to the invasion, the Sherman M4A3 flamethrower tank was adapted by an inter-service task force of Seabees, Army Chemical Warfare Service technicians, and Fleet Marine Force tankers at Camp Tarawa on the big island of Hawaii. According to Lieutenant Colonel William R. Collins, commanding the 5th Tank Battalion, (who received the Silver Star on Iwo) the tinkerers modified the Shermans with a Mark-1 flamethrower to operate from within the turret, replacing the 75 mm gun with a look-alike tube.[96] The Marines dubbed these special tanks "Ronson" and "Zippo" after the popular cigarette lighters of the day. The flame tanks were effective, but the *ad hoc* modification team had only sufficient time and components to modify eight tanks with a Mark-1 flame system; four each went to the 4th and 5th Tank Battalions for the Iwo campaign.

The Japanese anti-tank gunners fought hard but quickly ran out of ammunition. On February 19 and 20, Lieutenant Genichi Hattori and a squad of men were credited with dragging as many as fifty dead and wounded men into their bunkers.[97] However, at the end of the third day, with most of his men wounded or dead and ammunition exhausted, Lieutenant Hattori joined a banzai charge at 2:00 a.m., on the night of February 21st (morning of February 22). Parachute flares illuminated Hattori as he drew his sword and led five men out of his bunker towards the Marines. Hattori and all but one man were killed outright. The sixth man crawled back into the bunker where he died from his wounds a few hours later.

Major Matsushita and thirty survivors moved north and hid out for almost four months. On the night of June 2nd, Major Matsushita and his survivors moved along the western shore where they took refuge in a wrecked Japanese LST. They were discovered, and after a firefight that left as many as twenty Japanese dead, Major Matsushita and five of his men were captured by US Army troops. Of the original 303 men in the Independent 10th Anti-Tank Battalion, only these six survived the battle.

Lieutenant Hattori was given a posthumous promotion to captain. His headstone at the family cemetery in Nara is engraved with the death date of March 17, 1945, the blanket death date given to all of Iwo Jima's defenders. In December 1974, Major Matsushita visited the Hattori family home in Nara to introduce himself to the family of his Executive Officer. Matsushita felt guilty for surviving and wanted to share what he knew about Lieutenant Genichi Hattori's final hours. Thanks to Major Haruhiko Matsushita's testimony, the Hattori family learned the true date of Hattori's passing. Knowing the date of death is important for Japanese Buddhist funeral rites. Sadly, Lieutenant Hattori's father passed away in 1950, and never learned of his son's fate, but his mother Kurie, wife Sawako, and daughter Chikako were grateful to learn of Lieuteant Genichi Hattori's final hours. He didn't die on March 17th, as the government had told them, but in the early morning hours of Thursday, February 22nd at 2:00 a.m. Hattori's mother shared an entry in her diary dated the morning of February 22, 1945. She wrote of a nightmare she had of her son screaming, covered in blood, swinging a sword while charging towards her. The Hattori family was, and still is, at a loss to explain the incredible timing of her vision.

Further up the beach, towards the quarry, is where another company of Marines, led by Captain Lawrence Snowden (later Lieutenant General), came ashore. Snowden was a senior at the University of Virginia when the war started, and like many of his generation, went to the Marine Corps recruiting office to volunteer on December 8, 1941. The University of Virginia noted his exceptional academic record and extracurricular activities, which included the glee club and managing the basketball team, so permitted him to graduate early in April 1942. He received his college degree the day he entered Officers Candidate School, shortly after his 21st birthday.[98] Snowden was commissioned as a Second Lieutenant in July 1942.

By the time he arrived on Iwo Jima, Snowden held the rank of captain and was a veteran of the Roi-Namur battle in the Marshall Islands, and both the Saipan and Tinian battles. On Iwo Jima, 23-year-old Captain Snowden was the commander of F Company, 2nd Battalion, 23rd Marine Regiment, Fourth Marine Division. Captain Snowden and his company landed in the third wave at a place designated "Yellow Beach 2."[99] Snowden said that the latest intelligence photos had shown a gentle sloping beach, "So we expected to ride in our LVTs straight onto the airfield." But they were met by a 15-foot high sand berm that caused his LVT to spin and grind to a halt. "Get out!" Snowden shouted as men spilled over the edges of the vehicle. Snowden and his adjutant Sergeant Leonard Ash found cover in a bomb crater. "We couldn't dig in because the volcano ash was so soft that the sides caved in," he said. There were several LVT(A)4 armored amtracs, with snub-nosed 75 mm cannons, that were mired in the sand ahead of his position. The armored vehicles arrived ahead of the first wave to clear the way for the troop-laden LVT-2s and LVT-4s but had become bogged down by the terraces and the soft volcanic ash.

Captain Lawrence Snowden's position was among those farthest from Mount Suribachi, but one of the closest to the *Kugishō* rocket-bomb firing positions located above the quarry to the right. Snowden described in detail the nerve-rattling screech of the rocket-bombs and heavy spigot mortars that wobbled as they traveled overhead. Due to their appearance, some Marines nicknamed the 600-pound spigot mortar rounds, "flying ash cans."

"In order to track the heavy mortars I'd hold out my finger out in front of my eye, and if it moved left or right I'd know it wasn't coming down near me. But if my finger blocked it for more than a slit second, then I knew I was in trouble," explained Snowden. Sergeant Leonard Ash suffered a serious leg wound from one of these large mortar rounds. Seeing the horrific injury, Captain Snowden shouted for a corpsman and heard, "On the way!" When help arrived, Snowden reluctantly advanced leaving Sergeant Ash behind. "That is how we were trained, we had to keep moving forward," said Snowden. The pair were reunited years later and were thankful that the other had survived.

The corpsman that tended to Sergeant Ash might have been Hospital Apprentice Second Class (HA2/c) Danny Thomas, an 18-year-old Texas native who was a naval corpsman assigned to Captain Snowden's Fox Company. "I was in a shell crater, doing my job...plugging chest wounds, injecting morphine if needed. Then I was dodging artillery, mortars — you name it— to get to the next crater where more wounded lay," said Thomas.[100] The former corpsman also said, "The noise was unbearable, the chaos was unbelievable. There was intense smoke as our planes bombed the Japanese. I was so scared. I wanted to run and hide, but where? There was no cover, and the only way to go was forward. My buddies were being shot. I tried to help them ... to stop their bleeding, but all the time I was close to panic. I'd never seen dead people before, and they were piled up around me."[101]

Eight days after he landed, Captain Lawrence Snowden was wounded by shrapnel from a 320 mm spigot mortar and was evacuated to Guam. He talked his way back onto Iwo Jima but after a second wound, Snowden was evacuated for good.

US Army combat photographer Ivan Prall once encountered the wooden base for a spigot mortar on Iwo Jima. He described it as having a stepped appearance like a Mexican pyramid. It was buried partly underground and seated at a 45 degree firing angle. It was sanded smooth and coated with a glossy lacquer finish, and the joints of the heavy wood beams fit perfectly together. "The base of the heavy mortar was an impressive piece of woodworking. I wish I could've taken it home with me," Prall said.

The wooden base found by Ivan Prall possibly belonged to Corporal Tadashi Abe's 20th Independent Mortar Battalion. They are the ones that fired the spigot mortars that wounded Captain Snowden.

Corporal Abe's body was never recovered. He left behind his wife Teruko and two daughters, Yoshiko and Michiko.[102]

The Kamikaze

Third Fleet commander Vice-Admiral Kinpei Teraoka made the decision to send Kamikazes to hit US ships near Iwo Jima. Captain Toshiichi Sugiyama's 601st Naval Air Group was selected for this mission that would be known as *Dai 2 Mitate Tokubetsu Kogeki-tai* (Emperor's Shield, Special Attack Force, No. 2). Captain Sugiyama, selected thirty-two aircraft for the mission: twelve escort Zero fighters from the 301st Squadron; twelve Judy dive-bombers from the 1st Attack Squadron carrying 500-kg bombs; eight Jill torpedo-bombers from the 254th Squadron armed with a combination of 800-kg bombs and 800-kg aerial torpedoes. The planes would attack in five separate waves.

The Judys and Jills and had two and three-man crews so technically only the pilots were needed for the mission, but the "back seaters" refused to be left behind. According to one of the surviving Zero pilots, the crews of the dive-bombers and torpedo bombers said that since they had trained and lived together they wanted to die together. Following the mission briefing, the Kamikazes walked to *Katori Jinja* Shrine to pray for success, which meant their deaths.

Barely sixty minutes passed from the time the Marines landed on Iwo Jima before Admiral Teraoka personally announced his official orders to the pilots and aircrews who had volunteered for the one-way mission. In the late afternoon of February 21, 1945, roughly twenty of the Kamikaze planes of the 2nd *Mitate-tai* broke through the American Combat Air Patrols and AA gunfire to strike several US ships supporting the invasion. The Kamikazes sank the carrier *Bismarck Sea* (CVE-95), and damaged the carrier *Saratoga* (CV-3), the escort carrier *Lunga Point* (CVE-94), LST-477, LST-809 and the anti-torpedo net tender *Keokuk*. Chief Petty Officer Saburō Kojima was one of the navigators in the fourth wave of Jills that struck *Keokuk*.*

The Flag

Akikusa said he didn't see the famous flag on top of Mount Suribachi, but others observed it and the word spread quickly. "The Marines may have raised their flag, but we still held most of the island," Akikusa said.

February 23rd was a memorable day for another man, Corporal Hershel Williams of C Company, 1st Battalion, 21st Marine Regiment, Third Marine Division. He would use his flamethrower against the bunkers around Mount Suribachi containing troops from Lieutenant Hattori's Independent 10th Anti-Tank Battalion, and Corporal Tadashi Abe's Independent 20th Mortar Battalion. When Marine Corps tanks stalled in their advance through the maze of bunkers, Williams advanced with his flamethrower. For four hours Corporal Williams and a squad of Marines crawled along destroying Japanese positions with C-2 pole charges and a flamethrower.† Williams moved to and from the beach four times to retrieve fresh flamethrowers. It is unknown how many Japanese soldiers and sailors Corporal Williams engaged that day, but his actions helped the tanks break through and result in him being recommended for the Nation's highest award for valor.

William's Congressional Medal of Honor citation reads, in part, "... *Covered only by four riflemen, he fought desperately for four hours under terrific enemy small-arms fire and repeatedly returned to his own lines to prepare demolition charges and obtain serviced flame throwers, struggling back, frequently to the rear of hostile emplacements, to wipe out one position after another. On one occasion he daringly mounted a pillbox to insert the*

---

* Details on this attack will be addressed in the author's upcoming book about the Kamikaze.

† Composition C-2, a plastic explosive that came in one-pound blocks. Williams stated that the Marines would place C-2 on the end of a stick or length of lumber, and insert the explosive into a bunker.

nozzle of his flame thrower through the air vent, kill the occupants and silence the gun; on another he grimly charged enemy riflemen who attempted to stop him with bayonets and destroyed them with a burst of flame from his weapon. His unyielding determination and extraordinary heroism in the face of ruthless enemy resistance were directly instrumental in neutralizing one of the most fanatically defended Japanese strong points encountered by his regiment and aided in enabling his company to reach its' [sic] objective."

Hershel Williams, who goes by the nicknames "Woody" and "Hershey," told the author when they met in Charleston, West Virginia, in 1997, "I wouldn't call myself a hero. I was doing what I was trained to do." Williams, who is also a veteran of the Guam campaign, was wounded on March 6th and evacuated. At the time of this writing, 90-year-old Hershel Williams is the last surviving Medal of Honor Recipient from the battle of Iwo Jima.[103]

The Return of the Bettys

On the night of February 23rd, the same day that Hershel Williams earned his Medal of Honor, seven Betty bombers from the K704th Squadron left Kisarazu Airfield and set out to hit the US Marines on the beach. According to Ensign Masayoshi Nemoto, three of the Bettys turned back due to bad weather, two planes aborted due to engine trouble, and two Bettys disappeared without a trace.

A second attempt with only four Bettys was planned for the following night, February 24th. Ensign Nemoto's bomber, carrying radioman PO1/c Iwao Yamada, was one of the four Bettys assigned to the raid. This time, Yamada would be going to Iwo Jima to drop bombs and not deliver supplies. Yamada did not like the possibility of killing friendly troops.

Around 3:00 p.m., the entire K704th Squadron was called to a formation at which Admiral Kinpei Teraoka gave a speech to the aircrews of the four Bettys slated for the night time attack. The men were instructed to look for a line of blinking blue lights that would mark the front lines. They were to drop their twelve 60 kg bombs and then use the 20 mm tail gun to strafe as they departed. It wasn't called a suicide mission, but Yamada felt it was going to be a one-way trip.

That night, the Betty bombers left Kisarazu Airfield and passed the Izu Islands before making sight of Smith Island at 7:37 p.m.[104] In an attempt to confuse US radar operators, they headed to Torishima and then changed course for the Ogasawara Islands. As they neared Chichi Jima, searchlights pierced the darkness and then captured the plane. One, then another of the brilliant white rays stabbed the aircraft filling it with blinding light. Crack shot anti-aircraft crews were tracking the bombers, and were moments from firing when Ensign Nemoto used the handheld blinker light to flash the friendly code "*M.I.*" to the troops below. A moment later the brilliant lights went out.* Yamada Yamada prayed that they still had the element of surprise but was concerned that American night fighters had spotted the searchlights and would be on the alert. Even accounting for the curvature of the earth, the searchlights would have been visible for at least fifty miles. "Someone failed to inform Chichi Jima about our mission and it nearly got us killed," he said.

The Bettys then made a heading for the island of Kita Iwo Jima at the height of 9,000 feet. As the planes droned south, Ensign Nemoto set a new course in order to skirt the island of Haha Jima to avoid a similar mishap.

The silence was interrupted as the intercom crackled with the voice of the greenhorn gunner, Airman 1/c Tsunehara, whose young voice squeaked the urgent warning, "Enemy fighter!"

Dammit, they saw the searchlights. Airman 1/c Tsunehara was manning the top turret and had trained his 20 mm cannon towards a light in the distance. The other gunners scanned the sky and waited for enemy tracer rounds to tear through their thin-skinned bomber. But after several tense minutes, it was determined the jumpy dorsal gunner had mistaken the planet Mars for an enemy fighter's running light. Tsunehara's *snafu* put the entire crew on edge, but he was forgiven because it was his first combat mission. In an attempt to calm the men, Ensign Nemoto called out for an intercom check. One by one the men checked in. Then once again, silence.

At 8:00 p.m., the bombardier spotted Iwo Jima in the distance resembling a bed of glowing, writhing hot coals Yamada pushed forward in the cabin for a better view. The eerie beauty of countless lights, silent explosions, tongues of flame and sparks below captivated him. Yamada began to shiver but it wasn't

---

* The same Japanese AA gunners brought down several US aircraft, including Lt (jg) George Bush's TBF Avenger torpedo plane a few months earlier on September 2, 1944.

from the cold. "I saw streams of friendly tracer rounds pouring out from the northern half of the island towards the beaches, so I knew our boys were holding out," he said. The plane changed course as the crew tossed out bundles of chaff to confuse American radar operators and anti-aircraft gunners. Yamada said that the night sky behind them was filled with searchlights and colorful tracers as anti-aircraft guns from countless ships fired into the darkness. Streams of tracer shells arched upwards leaving glowing trails before exploding, which reminded Yamada of a fireworks show. Flashbulbs of light reflected off the Betty's wings and through its windows; the acrid smell of gunpowder filled the cabin as the explosions drew closer. He could hear shrapnel pinging and banging as it struck the aircraft. A near miss threw Yamada from his seat. *It was only a matter of time before they get us,* he thought. Ensign Nemoto described the fire as "thousands of brilliant arrows forming a curtain of light."

There was a Betty flying several miles in front of Yamada's plane that disintegrated in a bright explosion of light and color. Men and flaming debris tumbled to the ocean below. There were no survivors because Yamada said the bomber crews didn't wear parachutes.

Yamada has no explanation for why his plane was able to fly through the long brilliant streaks of light without being blown into pieces. The bombardier hunched over the bombsite as the target drew closer. The crew had their eyes fixed below, searching for the friendly blue lights. The bombardier did not want to release the payload on his countrymen. Yamada looked down to see American illumination rounds suspended above the battlefield by parachutes, casting a bluish-white ghostly light on the terrain. "It was what hell must look like," said Yamada. Here and there, long flames of fire stretched out and disappeared. "I see the lights!" shouted one of the crew. The blue lights marking the front lines weren't blinking but were solid and pointing straight up. The pilot made a course heading for the final bomb run while the gunners dumped more chaff. The bombardier flipped the switch at 8:20 p.m., taking less than one second to release twelve 60 kg bombs.

The pilot fishtailed and side slipped down and away from the target as the crew released more bundles of chaff. Ensign Nemoto wrote the time in his logbook noting that they had been under fire for eighteen minutes. He later said that it felt like three hours.

As the bomber fled from Iwo Jima, Radioman Iwao Yamada looked down and saw hundreds of ships under way, betrayed by luminescent wakes. Stunned at the number of vessels he saw, he says he knew that Iwo Jima was doomed.

Once the plane was at a safe distance, Ensign Nemoto checked on the crew, then cracked open a bottle of lemon soda to celebrate their survival. The Betty landed back at Kisarazu at 12:23 a.m., and turned out to be the first one back. Ensign Nemoto made his report to the squadron commander who who then made marks on a large map of Iwo Jima.

Admiral Teraoka appeared at the control center to proudly share the contents of a message he received from General Kuribayashi expressed gratitude for the bomb run and a desire for further support. The Admiral congratulated the crew on a job well done, and suggested they get to bed. However, due to the adrenaline rush of combat, and concern for the other Bettys, Ensign Nemoto, radioman Yamada and the rest of the crew elected to wait up until dawn, but no other planes returned.

Yamada had seen one plane go down over Iwo Jima but didn't immediately know the fate of the other two aircraft. He later learned that the second plane had taken flak in the left engine and diverted to Chichi Jima where it crash-landed. The remaining Betty took flak damage, jettisoned its bombs and managed to limp to Toyohashi Airfield. It turned out that Iwao Yamada's Betty was the only plane to drop their bombs on target.

One of those on the receiving end of this raid was Sergeant Cyril "Cy" O'Brien. A veteran of the Guadalcanal and Guam campaigns, O'Brien was a combat correspondent attached to the Third Marine Division. Although the division was held in reserve, O'Brien had "worked his bolt" and arranged for him and his bulky field typewriter to go in piggybacking with the Fifth Marine Division. On the night of February 24th, O'Brien was sleeping in a foxhole when the night came alive with anti-aircraft tracer fire from the ships. "It was like the Fourth of July, I tell ya," said O'Brien in a 2010 trip to Iwo Jima with the author.[*] "It looked like everyone in the Fleet was trying to bring him down. He dropped his bombs and got away. Don't ask me how he did it, but he got away," said O'Brien.

---

[*] The Iwo Jima Association of America works in connection with Military Historical Tours to bring veterans and their families to Iwo Jima for the annual Reunion of Honor ceremony held in March.

During the same 2010 visit, Cy O'Brien met Betty bomber gunner Hikōji Nozaki (K704[th] Attack Squadron). O'Brien shared what it was like to be on the receiving end of a Betty bomber attack. Typical of when WWII veterans meet their former foes, the pair of veterans traded honest smiles and handshakes. Through the author acting as interpreter, Nozaki joked to O'Brien, "If I would have known it was *you* down there, we wouldn't have dropped bombs on you."

Cy responded, "And if I'da known it was *you* up there, I would've told 'em not to shoot at you!"

In 1974, Ensign Masayoshi Nemoto was interviewed by NHK radio about the February 24th mission. During the course of the interview, Nemoto mentioned the blue lights marking the front lines. A man named Haruo Sakuma who had been a 12 cm AA gunner stationed at Iwo Jima's Osaka-yama, contacted Nemoto. Sakuma had survived the battle and was captured. According to Sakuma, the defenders had been promised a parachute resupply drop that night. Sakuma was ordered to hold a light with a blue filter to mark the drop zone, but the only Japanese supplies that fell on Iwo Jima were bombs. Sakuma was disappointed, but told Nemoto he was grateful that the Marines' attention was directed upward, which took pressure off the Japanese troops for a little while.[105]

Akikusa and the Tank

While the Americans owned the island by day, the Japanese defenders took temporary possession of the island at night. Despite the constant illumination flares, Japanese troops would take advantage of the darkness to conduct *kirikomi* (small scale banzai) raids and forage for enemy supplies. One night, Akikusa left Tamana-yama looking for supplies. He came across one of LtCol Nishi's tanks. "It was buried up to the turret, but it didn't look damaged so I guessed the crew had abandoned it when they ran out of ammunition," he said. The hope of finding something he could eat or drink drove him to explore the interior of the vehicle. "I waited until the illumination flare went out, and then crawled up to open the commander's hatch." Being a navy man, he'd never seen the interior of a tank before. The inside of the hatch was covered in a coating of white asbestos. Akikusa peeked down into the turret, and he was greeted by the horrible smell of decay. The next flare that blossomed overhead illuminated the smeared and broken remains of the crew. Akikusa quickly

Underwater Kamikaze

The Sixth Fleet commander, Admiral Shigeyoshi Miwa, had high hopes for his submarines and the *kaiten* pilots. But despite their best efforts, only the RO-43 was able to launch an attack using conventional torpedoes. On February 21st, the same day as the kamikaze attack, RO-43 damaged the destroyer USS *Renshaw* (DD-449), killing nineteen of her crew. On February 26th, aircraft from the escort carrier USS *Anzio* (CVE-57) sank RO-43 and I-368. That same day, the destroyer escort USS *Finnegan* (DE-307) located and sank I-370.

On March 1, a pair of *kaiten* laiden submarines, I-58 and I-36, were formed into the *Shinbu-tai* attack unit. They left Hikari submarine base for Iwo Jima to support the floundering *Chihaya-tai* attack unit.*

The submarine I-44, which also failed to launch any *kaiten*, was unable to maneuver for an attack due to aggressive US Navy anti-submarine warfare (ASW) forces. On March 6th, the I-44 and the newly arrived I-58 and I-36 were ordered to disengage.[106]

There were two other ocean-going Kamikaze units in the area; located 120 miles away at Haha Jima were the 3rd and 4th *Shinyō-tai* units. They were ordered to attack with their suicide speedboats loaded with 250 kg explosives. Haha Jima's *keibitai* commander stated that the fifteen-foot boats were intended for the defense of his own island, and besides, with a range of only 125 miles, Iwo Jima was too far away for them to operate effectively.†

Akikusa Wounded

On March 1, 1945, the Third and Fifth Marine Divisions moved up the center and west coast of the island. The Fourth Marine Division turned to the

---

* The submarine I-58 would gain notoriety for sinking the cruiser USS *Indianapolis* on July 30, 1945. The ship was sunk after delivering components of the atomic bomb that was dropped on Hiroshima.

† Airman 1/c Mikio Ōtsu was a *Yokaren* aviation course graduate that was assigned to the 130th *Shinyōtai* (under Captain Tsunezō Wachi's 5th Special Attack Fleet) in Kagoshima, Kyūshū. Ōtsu's accounts will be shared in an upcoming book by the author about Japan's Kamikaze units.

right to clear the area east of Motoyama Airfield and south of Hill 362C. Both Ōmagari and Akikusa found themselves located in a stout salient that included Nidan Iwa (Radar Hill or Hill 382), the Amphitheater, Charlie Dog Ridge, Tamana-yama Communications Bunker (Turkey Knob) and the destroyed former village of Minami. In this fantastically rugged area, the Japanese had strengthened the natural defenses by using cement, rebar, and boulders to transform the entire sector into a mighty fortress with interlocking fields of fire.

During the desperate fighting required for the Marines to seize and hold this strongpoint, those interlocking positions become known collectively as the "The Meat Grinder." Ōmagari said he could easily understand why the Marines called it that. He said, "Men didn't just die on Iwo Jima, they were ripped apart, torn to shreds and scattered. I saw torsos with no limbs, dismembered legs, arms and hands, and internal organs splashed onto the rocks."

Captain Fred Haynes (later MajGen), the Operations Officer for the 28th Combat Team, might have summed it up best when he said, "Each day we learned new ways to die."[107]

The shattered remains of a radar station, casemated field pieces and antitank weapons covered the top of Hill 382. Supporting machine-gun emplacements protected the concrete gun housings. In addition, LtCol Takeichi Nishi's light and medium tanks were dug in as pillboxes. From Hill 382, the land sloped to the south and east in a semicircular series of ridges and draws leading down from the plateau like giant steps. Roughly 600 yards to the south of Hill 382 rose a tough nut of a hill the Marines dubbed "Turkey Knob." It functioned as an observation post overlooking the entire southern end of the island. The high ground at Turkey Knob fell away to the southwest to form an exposed natural killing field known as "The Amphitheater." The Japanese strengthened the natural defenses in this area by constructing three tiers of heavy concrete emplacements in the south-sloping hill face. From these positions, 47 mm antitank guns and machine guns swept the southern approaches to Turkey Knob.[108]

Akikusa heard the rumbling of tanks and the terrifying whoosh of flames. "The flamethrower tanks were awful. I heard our troops screaming. The sounds combined to form a buzzing sound like radio static," said Akikusa. An officer told the men to be quiet because if they could hear the tanks, the Marines could hear them in the tunnels. "We talked in whispers," said Akikusa. "At night the Marines would pull back to consolidate and abandon their daytime fighting positions. We would crawl out to search those positions for discarded food," Akikusa said.

On the night of March 1st, with water and ammunition running low, the situation inside Tamana-yama was desperate. Akikusa explained, "Our orders were to defend our position to the death. But our communications equipment was down for lack of parts. Why did we have to protect broken equipment with our lives?"

An officer asked for volunteers to take a message to Captain Inoue's *Nanpō* HQ bunker. No one raised his hand. Akikusa felt he should set an example because unlike many of the others, he had volunteered for military service and was not a draftee. The officer asked again. Akikusa thrust his arm in the air. One by one, seven more hands went up. Akikusa was surprised to see his friend Shōji Kageyama's hand down at his side.

Each runner was given the same message orally and ordered to repeat it. They were to deliver the information to Captain Inoue's *Nanpō* bunker. As Akikusa moved towards the exit, Kageyama grabbed his arm and urged him to be extra cautious.

Akikusa said, "Don't worry, I'll be right back."

Akikusa recalled that the messengers' progress to the *Nanpō* bunker was hampered by the illumination rounds that made them freeze in their tracks countless times. They were almost to the bunker when Akikusa saw bright flashes of light. He dove to the ground as a shell screamed and exploded nearby. His ears were ringing. Akikusa and called out for the other messengers, but, if they responded, he couldn't hear them. *Were they all dead?*

Akikusa waited a few moments then crawled forward on his stomach. Then came another flash, and what felt like a baseball bat to his chest. Everything went black and silent. He couldn't tell if his eyes were open or shut, or if he was breathing or not. "I was cold. It felt like large blocks of ice were crushing me. I didn't feel any pain. I wanted to make sure I was in one piece, so I ran my hands across my shoulders and arms, and then touched my chest and stomach. My shirt and trousers were wet." He felt a bloody mess on his left thigh. "I tried to sit up but my legs were trapped. I called out for help, but no one answered," he said.

Akikusa twisted onto his side to free himself from the rocks and sand that held him captive. His eyesight slowly returned as an illumination flare floated down to earth and went out with a fizzle. He felt seasick.

Akikusa tried to get to his feet but his left leg collapsed, sending him down into a pile of jagged rubble. He decided to crawl on his hands and knees. Slowly, his hearing began to return. "I heard small arms fire whizzing and cracking so I stayed low," he said. He came across a shallow zigzag trench and rolled over the lip down into it, knowing it would lead to a bunker entrance. He crawled forward and found a partially sealed cave entrance. He summoned his last ounce of strength and screamed for help. But after hearing no response he laid his head down and closed his eyes and surrendered to the sleep.

His next sensation was being dragged across cragged rocks by unseen hands that pulled him down through a small cave opening. He found himself inside a tunnel, when a voice ordered him to get on his feet but he couldn't move.

In the dimly light tunnel a familiar voice said, "Is that Akikusa?" It was his pipe-smoking friend Yasuo Kumakura.

Kumakura and another man helped Akikusa down a sloping passageway to a room full of radio equipment where Lieutenant Honda and Warrant Officer Matsumoto came to their feet to receive Akikusa's message. Kumakura reached out to steady Akikusa as he crumpled to the ground. Akikusa recalled that the lieutenant yelled at him to stand and deliver his report, but the voice sounded like a dog barking down a long street. "I didn't care, I just wanted to go to sleep," said Akikusa.

Akikusa heard Kumakura shout directly in his ear, "Buck up, man, you can do it." Akikusa stood up couldn't salute because his right arm was stiff and his right hand was gnarled into a fist. With Kumakura supporting him, Akikusa felt something well up inside; he lifted his face and recited the message, "The Tamana-yama Communications Unit is low on food and water. Ammunition supply critical. It will defend to the last man. End of message." Akikusa added, "I was with several others. Please help them." Lieutenant Honda snapped an order to search for the other runners.

Akikusa was carried in a daze to the medical section. Kumakura helped gently roll him onto a wooden table where a corpsman and a doctor examined his injuries. Luckily, the shrapnel that tore through his thigh had missed the main artery and the bone. Akikusa was grateful they weren't going to amputate his leg. The doctor turned his attention to his smaller injuries and then to Akikusa's right hand. Without the benefit of anesthesia, the physician deftly cleaved off three of Akikusa's mangled fingertips at the first or second knuckle. After the bandaging was completed, Kumakura helped Akikusa hobble back to his cubbyhole to rest. They moved past hallways lined with 55-gallon barrels filled with kerosene or water, and crates of ammo and supplies. Akikusa noted that three of his fellow messengers had came in after him and suffered superficial wounds. No one made an effort to talk. Akikusa closed his eyes again and drifted off to sleep.

Akikusa woke up to throbbing pain and feeling disorientated. He was lying on a blanket atop a row of standing 55-gallon drums. *How long have I been asleep?* His mouth felt like it was full of cotton.

Yasuo Kumakura gently tapped him on the chest, "Sorry to wake you, your bandages need changing. I'll help you back to the aid station." Kumakura gingerly assisted Akikusa to his feet. His body was stiff, and he moved to the medical section like a squeaky tin man. Akikusa gratefully accepted a sip of warm, sulphur-tainted water from an aluminum cup

Sometime later, Akikusa was again awakened by the sound of Kumakura's voice, "Hey Aki, the other runners are returning to Tamana-yama." Akikusa's thoughts were of his buddy Shoji Kageyama who would be waiting for him to return. The pair had been through basic training, radio school, the shelling at Chichi Jima and now months of hell on Iwo Jima.

Akikusa said to one of the runners, "Tell Kageyama that I'm doing fine and will return to Tamana-yama soon." As the messengers climbed up through the narrow exit a kerosene lamp cast long shadows inside the bunker as they slipped out into the night.

Akikusa and the other sick and wounded men were packed tightly together like sardines on the tops of 55-gallon drums. Akikusa dozed off, and awoke to discover that his blood-soaked bandaged hand was stuck to a sleeping man's forehead. Akikusa carefully pulled his hand free, waking the man in the process. He apologized to the man, who then asked about Akikusa's accent. The man was named Miyashita and was from town of Takazaki which made them practically neighbors. Miyashita was a civilian postal worker who was conscripted into the military as a *gunzoku* civilian contractor. Miyashita was sent to Iwo Jima to work in the Motoyama Airfield Post Office and wasn't issued a weapon or given formal military training. Although wounded, he somehow managed to find refuge in the *Nanpō* bunker.

Miyashita asked Akikusa, "Do you think we'll make it home?" Akikusa reassured him that if anyone would make it home, it would be the lucky mailman. But Akikusa himself was losing hope.

Kumakura approached Akikusa and asked, "Hey Aki, how are you feeling?" Akikusa nodded an unspoken reply. "I brought you some food," Kumakura said as he extended his filthy hand in which rested a glistening ball of rice.

Akikusa choked back a tear of gratitude. He instinctively reached out for the rice ball with his dominant hand but it was bandaged into a tight fist. Akikusa rolled on to his right side and accepted the treasure with his left hand and a sincere expression of gratitude.

Over the next few days, thanks to a steady diet of a rice balls and pickled vegetables, Akikusa slowly regained his strength and was able to hobble around with the aid of a bamboo staff. It seems the supply of bamboo poles that Ōmagari rejected on the airfield had come in handy after all.

The following day on March 2nd, PFC Eric Ojerholm wrote a follow-up letter to his family, the first one since his missive dated February 9th. Out of respect, it is presented *exactly* as it was written:

March 2, 1945
"Iwo Jima"
750 miles from Tokyo

Dear Folks –
Hope you don't mind this V-Mail letter, it is the only thing available.

I'm very happy to be able to write this letter, and grateful to God that I'm alive and happy.
Hope you're all fine and well. I hope you received my pre-invasion letter as it should clarify matters some.
Was aboard ship quite some time. Landed Hr 12 on D"day, the 19th.
Just got relieved from the front lines yesterday, and it was hell! I consider myself luck to be safe.

I have very much to say but will tell you all later. Undoubtebly you at home know more about this "push" and the Tokyo bombings, etc. than any of us just from the radio and papers.

I have seen plenty of Japs, dead and alive and likewise Marines. It really is a shame to see such destruction of life, especially when it is the fellows you've lived with. Luckily, none of my real close friends were killed, although some were wounded. Lived off K rations for most of the time and didn't mind it a bit.

This afternoon was the first time I washed in 11 days, and it was in salt water! In fact, even got a letter from you dated Feb. 7th. I prayed and dug plenty all the time. I dope we don't have to go up again. We were the assault battalion of the 27th, and up on the front too long. Have only one good souvenir, a Jap rifle, and have neither the time nor the stomach for anything else.

Will try to write soon again.

With love to all,
/s/ Sonny

The Imperial Mum

Ōmagari's aircraft maintenance bunker was about 100 yards from the *Nanpō* HQ bunker where Akikusa was convalescing from his wounds. On March 5th, Captain Inoue called Ensign Ōmagari and the other junior officers for a briefing. Captain Inoue said there was to be a "General Attack" (*Sōkōgeki*). *Had Kuribayashi changed direction and now wanted a banzai attack?*

Ōmagari didn't yet know that Captain Samaji Inoue and MajGen Sadasue Senda conspired to stage an unauthorized mass banzai attack. Despite direct orders from Kuribayashi, this pair of high-ranking officers put aside their Army vs. Navy differences and decided to do things their own way.

Ōmagari recalled disagreement on what day to conduct the attack, March 8th or March 10th. For the Navy, the number 8 was an auspicious number because the Pearl Harbor attack took place on December 8th (due to the International Date Line). Others suggested that March 10th would be better because it was Army Commemoration Day (*Rikugun Kinenbi*).*

---

* Celebrating the fall of the city of Mukden, China, during the Russo-Japan War.

Traditionally, the term "general attack" meant that a unit had a plan of action with a timetable to complete specific objectives. On the islands of Saipan, Guam, Anguar, Tinian, and now on Iwo Jima, the words "general attack" came to mean that the commanders had declared, "*We are no longer able to conduct organized warfare so you must chose your own method of death.*"

Kuribayashi had expressly forbidden banzai charges, but this was technically not a banzai charge, but a general attack. Ōmagari said that it was mere semantics, but it was clear that it meant mass suicide.

For the attack, Lieutenant Hideo Koshi planned to lead Ensign Ōmagari and the 3rd Company of aircraft maintenance men. The password was *Kesshi* (do-or-die); the countersign was *Kantō* (fight bravely). Lieutenant Koshi would take a route past the wreckage of the Iwo Jima Shrine, through the *Uguisu* area to the western shore, and then south past Chidori Airfield. From there, they would continue south to assault Mount Suribachi.

Rather than risk capture, the injured men who were unable to participate in the attack were to be given grenades with which to kill themselves. Lieutenant Koshi ordered Ensign Ōmagari and three other junior officers to return to their bunkers and pass the word to their petty officers. There was no need to tell the wounded men until the last minute.

The sixteen-petal imperial mum crest, called *kiku no gomonshō*, was considered holy and could not be allowed to fall into enemy hands. Everything bearing the crest had to be defaced or destroyed. In addition to burning documents, codebooks and personal correspondence, the men also burned paper money because it bore the imperial mum. Ōmagari said they were using files to deface or remove the imperial crests on the tops of their rifles.

The activity didn't go unnoticed by Akikusa. Shortly after this flurry of activity, Nakamura came to pay Akikusa a visit with a few pieces of hardtack. Akikusa asked, "Please tell me what is happening."

Nakamura led Akikusa to a secluded alcove and whispered, "There will be a general attack in a couple of days. You and the other wounded won't be allowed to join us. Don't tell anyone, it hasn't been announced yet."

Akikusa returned to his steel drum bed and squeezed in next to the mailman who asked, "What did he say?" Akikusa hemmed and hawed, trying to find the right white lie to tell the hopeful postman. In the end, he claimed no new word had come. This seemed to calm the worried letter carrier.

On March 7th, some of the wounded men heard about the General Attack. Bad news travels fast. The men pieced together that the Americans had cut off the bastion, creating two separate defensive zones. A banzai charge involving all units in the Tamana-yama area would commence on March 8th, at 6:00 p.m. That night, someone spread the word that US Marines had fought to within a dozen yards of the Tamanya-yama Communication Unit's bunker's main entrance. Akikusa grew worried about his buddy Shōji Kageyama who was still there deep inside. Akikusa knew that Kageyama would be going out on the general attack with the men from the Tamana-yama Communications Unit and wished to die alongside him. But there was no way for Akikusa to make it back to join his old friend.

On the same day, the third platoon from PFC Eric Ojerholm's D Company, 2nd Battalion, 27th Marine Regiment was having a tough time. According to Ojerholm's platoon leader, the third platoon was trapped between a small hill and a heavily battle-scarred sandstone cliff, caught in a deadly crossfire and pelted with hand grenades. The Marines were in an untenable position and needed covering fire so they could escape. Ojerholm attempted to move in to position to take over for a wounded machine gunner, but was shot in the head and killed instantly.

While the battle raged above them, the Japanese officers deep inside Captain Inoue's bunker issued water to the troops so the men could conduct a traditional farewell water toast. Akikusa said, "I begged them to take me with them. I even showed them how I could walk with the aid of my bamboo stick." Akikusa witnessed men smashing radio equipment, desks and tables, and burning documents. Akikusa said at 6:00 p.m., scouts in groups of six left the southern, northern and central exits to seek out weak spots in the American lines. Captain Inoue was in charge of the group that left through the central exit. The others were lined up in the hallways waiting their turn. A phone message for Captain Inoue came in from Kuribayashi's HQ stating, "A general attack is not approved. Control yourself." But it came too late; the arrow had left the bow.

Captain Inoue and MajGen Senda and had ordered the General Attack to commence shortly after midnight on March 8th, which was early morning on March 9th. There was no turning back.

Akikusa stood by a group of radiomen in the back of a line waiting to depart on their final mission. He looked at the faces of those he had served with; Suzuki, Kumakura, and the kindly Nakamura who brought him food every day. The radiomen shuffled forward, greeting Akikusa as they passed. As Kumakura passed Akikusa he pleaded, "Take me with you."

Kumakura replied, "Not with that leg, you'd only slow us down. I promised my parents I'd come home with a Golden Kite medal. I can't do it with you hanging on to me."

As Nakamura moved passed Akikusa he said, "Listen closely. The units in the north are not taking part in this attack. Don't follow us. Stay behind in the bunker." And with that, Nakamura handed Akikusa a grenade saying, "Take this as a keepsake. And remember to take care of that leg."

The others' farewell greetings became a blur as they disappeared up the rabbit hole into the star-shell illuminated night. They were followed by a request from Akikusa, "I'll be right behind you, be sure to wait for me at the *Sanzu* River."*

Akikusa felt useless and ashamed. "I tried to get up and follow them but didn't have the strength," he explained.

There was now an eerie emptiness inside the bunker. Where there had been shouts, movement of materials, and the clacking of rifle bolts, there were only the muffled sounds of gunfire slipping in through the small entrances. Akikusa crawled up to take a peek out of the exit and saw a hellish, smoke-filled landscape illuminated by ghostly flares and criss-crossed by red and green tracer fire. High-pitched shrieks and whistles accented the large and small explosions that echoed across the terrain.

From Ensign Ōmagari's viewpoint, he and Lieutenant Koshi broke out the last remaining stores of water to share with the men. Each man received a single hardtack biscuit and a piece of dried bonito as a last meal. Ōmagari's fellow "90-day wonders" Ensign Yutaka Nakamura and Ensign Kenichi Yoshida would lead their own platoons. Ōmagari and the other officers removed their rank insignia. He said, "When the attack started I left our bunker with my sword in hand for my last night on earth. I pondered how I would meet my end. Would it be a bullet or an explosion? Would it hurt much? Would my father

---

* The River *Sanzu*, which separates the world of the living from the dead, is the Japanese Buddhist equivalent to the River Styx in Greek mythology.

know where I died?"

The Marines facing them were the Fourth Division's 23rd and 24th Marine Regiments, which had spent March 7th assaulting the area known as Turkey Knob. Despite all efforts by the Marines, the Japanese strongpoint held out, so the Leathernecks consolidated their lines for the night. In many places it was too rocky to dig in so they piled up rocks for cover. Company E, 2/23 and Company I, 3/24 manned long lines containing the Japanese bulge.[109] They were on edge due to a noticeable increase in Japanese activity during the early evening. Something was brewing.

Lieutenant Koshi led Ensign Ōmagari and his men out into the open, right on schedule, but it was a struggle for them to stay together in the darkness. After advancing roughly 200 yards they were pinned down by an angry mortar barrage. *Was it theirs or ours? Did it matter?* Star shells then lit the night. There were several close calls as mortar rounds whistled, cracked and ka-rumped around him. Ōmagari pushed his body into the jagged rocks and waited for the end. After only a short time the barrage began to slacken so Ōmagari crawled to Lieutenant Koshi and shouted in his ear a request for orders. An illumination round revealed that Lieutenant Koshi's legs were horribly mangled. Koshi used feeble hand gestures to issue the order to continue the attack. Ōmagari acknowledged and stood up to relay the command to those around him. Ōmagari took over the group, which by now had become a jagged conga line that stretched hopelessly into the darkness through craters and gullies.

The advance was slow because the men had to drop to the ground whenever a flare erupted overhead. Each man in the long line of creeping figures had to watch the man directly in front of him to get the signal to drop. However, by the time the last man hit the deck, the front man was up and moving again. Crossing unfamiliar crater-filled terrain, Ensign Ōmagari kept looking back for his men but was unable to keep them together. It would be meaningless to yell out, so he pushed on.

When they had progressed about 500 yards from where Lieutenant Koshi lie dying, a machine gun opened up and scattered the group like startled sparrows. After the firing slowed down, Ōmagari made an oral roll call but came up with only twenty men. He had no idea where the others were, or if they were still alive. Ōmagari moved his men forward and came across a different group of naval troops, and then another. Instead of the separate units taking different routes to the airfield, they had all been instructed to assemble at the shrine using the same general route. Japanese Army and Navy units were mixed together in chaos, and it wasn't long before this group of about 400 men drew fire. The Americans fired mortars and machine guns for about two hours while the confused mass of troops huddled in bomb craters for protection.

According to US records, at 11:00 p.m., the 2nd Battalion 23rd Marines, and the 3rd Battalion 24th Marines, reported large-scale infiltration attempts along the regimental boundary. Then at 11:30 p.m., a full-scale counterattack (which Ōmagari claimed was an unintentional encounter) hit Company E, 2/23. Shortly after midnight, Company E reported a severe ammunition shortage. This company alone expended 20 cases of grenades, 200 high-explosive 60 mm mortar shells, 200 60 mm mortar illumination shells, and uncounted quantities of .30-caliber ammunition. The Navy's support ships expended 193 star shells during the night.[110]

Ōmagari and his men hunkered down under the glow of illumination flares wafting overhead and waited as the Marines fired seemingly endless amounts of tracer fire over their heads. *This is suicide; perhaps I should take them back to the bunker.* Ōmagari said that he pitied the men who looked to him for guidance. He knew nothing of ground combat, and his men were grossly out-gunned and out-numbered. Ōmagari tried to get his bearings by lifting his head to look for the dark shadow of Mount Suribachi, but didn't know in which direction to look. "I was totally lost," he said. During a lull in the firing, he was tempted to crawl up a small berm for a better look. But a few near misses convinced him it was a bad idea. He and his men were in a pickle the Japanese refer to as, "A carp on a cutting board." Just then, a large group of Japanese Army troops filtered silently through the area. Ōmagari didn't know where the troops were heading but decided to take his men and follow after them.

The entire group stumbled into relatively quiet area that contained a cluster of bunkers belonging to Baron Takeichi Nishi's 26th Tank Regiment. It was located in the Maruman area, which became known to the US Marines as "Cushman's Pocket."* At the entrance to one of the bunkers a tanker soldier

---

* Named for LtCol Robert E. Cushman Jr., commanding officer of 2nd Batt, 9th Marine Regt who received the Legion of Merit for his actions. He later became Commandant of the Marine Corps.

questioned Ōmagari about why he was not at his post. Ōmagari paused, *I can't tell him we're lost,* "We are on the General Attack," he answered.

The tanker asked, "What attack? No such attack has been authorized. You must return to your post at once."

Ōmagari and the man argued, each claiming to be in the right. In response to what sounded like a drunken bar fight, an army officer thrust his head out of the bunker and bellowed at the men to get inside because their squabbling would draw unwanted attention.

Once underground, the heated argument continued between the tankers and the newcomers, some of whom accused Baron Nishi's tankers of cowardice for not joining the attack. Ōmagari was equally puzzled to find so many soldiers buttoned up inside the bunkers while their comrades were dying all around them. A few of the tanker officers began to side with the navy personnel, and talked of joining the banzai charge.

Two of Ōmagari's classmates, Ensign Yutaka Nakamura and Ensign Kenichi Yoshida, arrived at the bunker in the middle of the discussion. The trio of college boys were happy to see that the others had made it thus far unharmed. There was disagreement among the junior naval officers as to whether or not to follow the final order given by Captain Inoue, or listen to Baron Nishi who was adamant that all troops must stay in position.

Baron Nishi said that although Captain Inoue and MajGen Senda had informed Division Headquarters of their general attack order, they had done so ex post facto, and that Geneal Kuribayashi countermanded the general attack However, Ōmagari was suspicious that the Olympic medalist was lying so he could commandeer the navy troops. Ōmagari felt conflicted because he knew Kuribayashi's standing orders were to defend one's own position to the death. Baron Nishi ended the discussion with a written message that proved that Kuribayashi had countermanded the banzai order.

Baron Nishi explained that since he had lost so many men, he had enough food and water to accommodate the newcomers. Eventually, both the army and navy officers who had led their men into Nishi's bunker complex agreed it would be foolhardy to grope their way through streams of machine gun fire to return to their original bunkers. Ōmagari reluctantly turned over his sailors to Baron Nishi and his Executive Officer Major Matsunaga.[111] The tankers gave each newcomer a quart of water and five hardtack biscuits.

Ōmagari noticed American weapons inside the bunker and examined what he called a "repeating rifle" (M-1 Garand Rifle) and a "machine pistol" (Thompson sub-machine gun, or possibly an M-3 'Grease Gun'). The Japanese had no qualms about taking weapons, water, food or cigarettes from dead Americans. A seaman named Okoshi said, "We lost our humanity. When we found a dead man we didn't feel sorry for him, we checked his pockets."[112] There was no respect for the dead, either friend or foe. During his subsequent movements around the island, Ōmagari said that debris fields usually marked where skirmishes had occurred. The Marines and US Army soldiers discarded cans of food, boxes of rations, canteens, bandages, helmets, grenades, webbed gear, clothing, ammunition and sometimes weapons, too. Firefights resembled the aftermath of a tornado. "Whether the Americans were advancing or retreating, they left a trail of trash that was treasure to us," Ōmagari said.

Shortly after Ōmagari found refuge in Baron Nishi's bunker complex, the General Attack fizzled and stalled. Back inside the *Nanpō* HQ Bunker, tattered men staggered back inside. "No one was talking, but it was obvious the General Attack had been a failure," Akikusa said.* The attack had died out, but the Americans continued mopping up until noon. Subsequent Fourth Marine Division advances uncovered large numbers of dead Japanese that were caught in the artillery barrages cast by the Marines. Captured documents revealed that in addition to the *Nanpō* Naval Air Group and Navy *keibitai*, in the attack there were elements from the 310th Independent Infantry Battalion, 3rd Battalion, 145th Infantry Regiment, 314th Independent Infantry Battalion, and an engineer unit. The Americans tallied 784 Japanese bodies. The Americans suffered 347 casualties, 90 of which were killed-in-action.[113]

As the sun rose following the general attack, a small group of heavily armed naval officers and petty officers, men who were unknown to Akikusa, entered the *Nanpō* bunker. Their leader was Lieutenant Commander Sonosuke Tachikawa, an Etajima Naval Academy graduate and dive-bomber pilot.[114] Commander Tachikawa addressed the survivors in a booming voice saying, "The Japanese military has been rendered ineffective. To ensure that proper discipline is maintained, I assume command of all remaining forces in this

---

*   MajGen Senda and some of his staff made that to Kuribayashi's HQ are reported to have killed themselves on March 17th.

sector. You will follow my orders with no deviation." Akikusa said that it was through intimidation of force that the officer, who bragged often that he was a pilot, took control of the bunker.

Lieutenant Commander Sosonosuke Tachikawa landed on Iwo Jima in December 1944, as a passenger in a Tabby transport aircraft. Tachikawa once commanded the Navy's 4th Reconnaissance Squadron in the central Philippines. When the squadron's aircraft were destroyed, he was forced to march north with the other naval aviators to Tugeugarao. He was evacuated to Taiwan, and then ordered to Iwo Jima.[115][116] Tachikawa was assigned to Captain Inoue's *Nanpō Shotō* Naval Air Group bunker after Akikusa was transferred to the Tamana-yama bunker, which explained why Akikusa didn't recognize him. One of the men with Tachikawa was PO2/c Riichi Koyatsu, who told a similar story. Koyatsu had been one of Captain Inoue's orderlies; but claimed that Tachikawa returned to the bunker only after Captain Inoue was killed.[117]

Akikusa said that the cantankerous Tachikawa took command of the survivors, but displayed few qualities that were typically associated with leaders. Tachikawa didn't take inventory of weapons or supplies, never took a roll call, nor inquired about the wounded. From their lack of wounds, and uniforms that bore no suggestion of having crawled across rocks and dirt, Akikusa suspected that Tachikawa's group didn't participate in the General Attack, but hid in one of the side tunnels until it was over. While the others that returned from the attack wore bloody and tattered uniforms, on the contrary, Commander Tachikawa's band of men looked out of place with their fresh appearance.

Akikusa and another man decided to fend for themselves and set out in search of water in the tunnels. The pair picked up a length of hollow rubber tubing and moved along the many corridors searching for 55-gallon drums that might still contain some water. There were about 500 barrels so it was only a matter of time before they found one that still had water in it. They pushed over the nearly empty barrel at an angle, revealing its reflective contents. With anticipation, Akikusa lowered the hose into the liquid, took a deep breath, and sucked the contents into his dry mouth. It was water mixed with kerosene. There was sand in it, too, that created a gritty feeling in his mouth. He coughed as he spat out the oily fluid.

They moved along to the Aid Station section of the cave. Akikusa held his grenade firmly in his left hand as he limped along with his bamboo pole. They checked more barrels but had similar results. In the darkness, Akikusa made a wrong turn and ended up alone in a dead-end tunnel. The smell emanating from the inky darkness told him that he was at the morgue pit. This wasn't intended to be their final resting place, but the loss of the island had ensured that it would be.

The Japanese require a Buddhist funeral ceremony in which they believe chanting will cleave the spirit from the body and send it into the joyous afterlife. Failure to conduct the ceremony, and ensuing cremation, would cause the spirits of the dead to wander the earth in an unholy form of limbo. Akikusa stared at the bodies of men who would receive no funeral rites. He could make out the ghastly pale glow of their mummified hands and faces peering back at him from the mound on the floor that had once been a deep pit. Small bits of luminescent light, resembling candle flames, drifted as if on their own volition. He remembered the tales of ghosts visiting the dead during the summer *obon* season, but this was no campfire ghost story, this was real. The tiny orbs hovered up and down, coming from all directions at once. He backed away, never taking his eyes off the pile of dead men. He began to panic. He recalled a Buddhist chant his grandmother taught him as a boy, and softly recited it as he moved away. He realized he had lost his hand grenade somewhere along the way. Like one searching for a contact lens, he kneeled and felt the dirt around him but had no luck in finding his one-way ticket off the island.

Akikusa set down to rest in a large anteroom that had once been the Battle Operations Planning Center. The desks, chairs and shelves had been smashed, but thankfully the officers hadn't set the room on fire when they left. There were others in the room, too. He witnessed one of them lose his grip on reality as a man asked no one in particular, "Are my parents here yet? They said they were coming to visit me today. We should all go home." A muffled shot echoed out from the next passageway; it was a sign of something sinister.

Even the Dead are Called to Fight

At Baron Nishi's tanker complex, Ōmagari said that Baron Nishi's tank crews were obsessed with destroying American tanks. The Japanese tanker crews had no more operational tanks, so they utilized suicide attacks using explosives.

On that first evening, the tanker officers gathered to pore over a well-used map. They deduced in which areas the Marine tanks would be operating, and assigned "tank-killer teams" to fan out and destroy them. Each member of the tank-killer team carried on his back a 10-kg plastic explosives charge in a wooden box. The four and five-man tank-killer teams would leave the bunker after midnight and were to reach the ambush areas by 3:00 a.m. The tank-killers were to lie in wait until a tank lumbered past, then hurl the explosive. The device could be detonated by pulling a cord, or by being crushed under a tank tread. If the tank-killer was lucky, he could survive the blast by ducking into a hole. If no Sherman tanks appeared, the teams were to return and try again the next night.

Ōmagari felt conflicted as his friend Ensign Yutaka Nakamura joined a tank-killer team and exited into the night. In the morning, the various teams returned without any of their naval troops. An army officer said that Ensign Nakamura and a few others had been gunned down, and the rest of the sailors deserted. Ōmagari couldn't believe it because his men had performed admirably during the previous General Attack. His men were not cowards. The next day produced the same results, so Ōmagari volunteered to accompany one of the tank-killer teams. He wanted to know why his sailors were deserting, and thought, *if I die destroying an enemy tank, so much the better.* He said, "I welcomed a quick end to my suffering."

At 10:00 p.m., a salty army corporal led his four-man tank-killer team made up of Ōmagari and two sailors. They kept to the shallow trenches as they moved slowly towards the ambush zone. Ōmagari admired the NCO's ability to keep them together in the darkness. Around 4:00 a.m., they arrived at the ambush site to the smell of decay. Dead bodies, in various stages of decay and dismemberment, carpeted the ground. The moonlit area was a killing field. Some of the dead were felled by flamethrowers that burnt off their flesh to expose glistening bones. The corporal whispered for the men to lie down amidst them. Ōmagari was numb inside, so had little trouble dragging bloated corpses by the feet. He sat down and leaned back into the pile of shattered men.

Before getting into his own position, the NCO crawled over piles of the dead to check on each man. He squirmed up next to Ōmagari and whispered, "You stand out like a sore thumb, sir. You don't look dead." Ōmagari wasn't selling it as a corpse. If the flamethrower tanks spotted him they would torch the whole group. The corporal instructed Ōmagari to smear blood on his face, and cover himself with intestines and organs. Ōmagari balked at coating his body in the guts of his countrymen. The NCO spoke through clenched teeth that if Ōmagari didn't convince the Marines he was dead, the flamethrower tanks would burn him and the others alive.

The NCO pulled his bayonet from its metal sheath and brought it down hard against a dead man's torso, splitting the belly open. He pulled out a slippery mass of viscera. He handed the bayonet to Ōmagari and pointed to another corpse. With the fate of the mission at stake, Ōmagari accepted the glistening bayonet. Ōmagari tried to open the buttons of a dead man's jacket, but the corpse was too bloated so he sat up on his knees and swung the bayonet down into the dead man's abdomen, hacking through the uniform and exposing the dead man's organs. Ōmagari used the tip of the bayonet to fish out a long string of intestines. Ōmagari unbuttoned his own jacket and stuffed the entrails inside. He hacked off a large section and inserted it into a tear in his pant leg. Seeing this, the NCO was satisfied and crawled away. "The dead were no longer seen as human beings, but as objects. Even the dead were called to fight," Ōmagari said.

Ōmagari lay on the cold rocky ground, intertwined with several corpses as he waited for the Sherman tanks to arrive.[118] He sensed the unseeing eyes of the dead and thought, *Will someone be wearing my guts tomorrow?* He looked at the twisted face of a dead man whose mouth was open as if caught in a silent scream. The man's mouth was filled with what first appeared to be rice, but was a pile of fly larvae.

This was going to be Ōmagari's final sunrise, and he hoped the end would be quick. The sun slowly warmed the ground, stirring the satiated blowflies. Some were too boated to fly and simply walked around on the corpses. Any sudden movement might alert the Marines, so the tank-killers fought to remain still as the flies wandered across their bodies. The sounds of distant gunfire and whining aircraft engines morphed into a macabre lullaby that caused Ōmagari to momentarily nod off. He awoke to the tickling sensation of maggots crawling on his throat, and for a moment wondered if he wasn't already dead. The stiffness in his back forced him to roll over on his side for relief, and as he slowly lifted his head he saw a group of Sherman tanks with 100 or more Marines trailing behind them. The lead tank was belching long, oily flames at a hillside. *This is insane. It would be impossible for us to do anything if they came this way.*

In one of the Zippo tanks was Alabama native First Lieutenant James Short, in command of a platoon of five tanks in Company C, 5th Tank Battalion, 5th Marine Division.[119] He was recommended for the Silver Star almost as soon he came ashore on February 19th.

The day wore on for Ōmagari, but the Zippo tanks never came within range of his killer team. The sun dipped into the horizon, which was the cue for the Leathernecks to consolidate their lines for the night. Ōmagari heard the corporal moving towards him so he tried to sit up. But like in a ghoulish version of *Gulliver's Travels*, Ōmagari was pinned down by the strings of intestines that had shriveled and hardened in the sun. Ōmagari's uniform crackled as he rolled to his knees, breaking the corpse's grip. The tank-killer team silently returned to the bunker under cover of darkness. Ōmagari understood why his troops had deserted. *Who could survive that and possibly bear to go out again?*

Ōmagari bitterly complained to the Army officers who justified it by citing two previous successes. Ōmagari defiantly asked how many of the officers had gone out on such a mission. The room fell silent as a tanker officer gripped his sword and cursed for an apology. Ōmagari didn't budge. Another officer moved between the belligerents and the situation simmered down.

Ōmagari feels that Baron Nishi, like many officers on Iwo Jima, didn't have a clear understanding of the battle because he conducted his operations from deep inside his bunker complex.

Despite Ōmagari's complaints, the tank killer teams continued their activities. Ōmagari's classmate, Ensign Kenichi Yoshida, was sent out with a tank-killer team and torched alive by a flamethrower tank the following day on March 11th.[120]

On March 12th, Lieutenant James Short's Zippo tank was attacking enemy bunkers when he was hit in the face by a Japanese machine gun round that shattered one of the vision ports in the commander's hatch. Lt Short was temporarily blinded and left with a scar, but was able to eventually return home to his wife and four-year-old daughter Paula Jean.

Kuribayashi's Farewell Message

Radioman Shōichi Kawai and his four-man communication unit were ordered to move to the hospital cave adjacent to LtGen Kuribayashi's 109th Division HQ bunker complex on March 7th. On the morning of March 15th, 1st Lt Inada informed Shōichi Kawai of his promotion to Sergeant. The lieutenant removed a metal star from his own rank insignia and handed it to Kawai saying, "Congratulations on your promotion. Add this to your cap rank." Kawai removed his rank insignia, added the small metal star (bringing the total of stars to two) and sewed it back on to his cap. Kawai wrote that he was deeply moved by the lieutenant's gesture.[121] The lieutenant then told Sgt Kawai to report to Colonel Tadashi Takaishi, Kuribayashi's Chief-of-Staff, in the "battle operations center," a natural occurring high-ceiling cave inside Kuribayashi's HQ bunker. Humbled by the honor of meeting the Chief-of-Staff, Sgt Kawai did as instructed and then returned to 1st Lt Inada's bunker.

At 5:25 p.m., on March 16th, Kuribayashi sent his final farewell message to Imperial General Headquarters in Tōkyō via the radio relay station at Chichi Jima. The end of his message contained his *jisei* three-stanza death poem. It become famous in post-war Japan, even sparking a book bearing the title of one of the lines.

So sad to fall (in battle*), our ammunition is exhausted, we are unable to fulfill this heavy duty for the Nation.

I will pick up my sword, though my body lay decaying in the field, I shall reincarnate seven times to seek revenge. My earnest thoughts will go to the Empire long after this island is overgrown with ugly vines.

(Signed) LtGen Kuribayashi, End.[122]

The Japanese High Command released his statement to the public after revising it to "How regretful to fall." It seems those in charge didn't want the public to think that soldiers "felt sad" about dying for the Emperor, so they changed Kuribayashi's final message. The following day he was promoted,

---

*   The words "in battle" do not appear in the message but are implied by the word chiru (散る) which is the kanji characters used to describe both the falling of cherry blossoms and warriors. Chiru is also used to describe kamikaze pilots who "fell like cherry blossoms," and evokes an image of the cherry trees at the Yasukuni War Shrine in Tōkyō, a place where dead soldiers' and sailors' spirits were said to gather in the after life.

making the 53-year-old Japan's youngest full General.[123]

Lieutenant Inada told Sergeant Kawai that the entire 109th Division staff was moving that night to link up with the remnants of the 145th Infantry Regiment. "You and your team will remain here under the command of Major (Kazumi) Oka to transmit messages so the enemy will think the Division is still in place," Inada said.* Major Oka was the officer in charge of preparing food for the men in Kuribayashi's bunker.

The Division HQ officers would leave behind ninety wounded men and a squad of five radio operators. Those left behind, and those who were leaving, each received two *Onshi Tabako* cigarettes bearing the Imperial mum seal; these were gifts from the Emperor to be smoked with reverence. They were smoked with the golden printed mum seal facing upwards out of respect.

The Olympian

After the deaths of his friends Ensigns Nakamura and Yoshida, Satoru Ōmagari considered taking his small band of Navy survivors back to the *Nanpō* HQ bunker. However, Baron Nishi disbanded the tank-killer teams, so Ōmagari decided to stay for a while. Baron Nishi's group was running low on water. A week earlier, General Kuribayashi had ordered Captain Yoshinobu Hakuta and newly promoted 1st Lt Yasuhiko Murai to move their 314th Infantry Battalion from Higashiyama to reinforce Kuribayashi's 109th Division HQ in the north. Baron Nishi deduced that Captain Yoshinobu Hakuta couldn't have transported his remaining barrels of water and food supplies without the use of motorized vehicles. Captain Hakuta's bunker would be perfect for Baron Nishi's horseless cavalry and the mixed bag of stragglers.

At 9:30 a.m. on March 14th, the Marine Corps conducted an official flag raising in the north at Kitano Point. With a great deal of handshaking and saluting, the American brass declared the island secure. Command and control was now to be transferred to the US Army. As a result, large numbers of US Army troops commenced landing on March 21st.[124] As many Army veterans will attest, "No one told the Japanese the island was secure!" While the bulk

---

* Major Kazumi Oka (岡和三少佐) was a silver-haired officer from the Independent 312th Infantry Battalion who was transferred to Kuribayashi's HQ to command the kitchen/galley unit.

of the Marines left the island, the 9th Marine Regiment stayed behind for two more weeks to help the US Army's 147th Infantry Regiment with their mopping up operations. The US Army fully took over from the Marines on April 4th.[125]

Thanks to the hardworking Seabees, Iwo Jima's central and southern airfields were operational by the end of March.[126] US Army P-51 fighter escorts arrived to give protection to the B-29s on their long missions to Japan. The US Navy Seabees and Army Pioneer units were often called upon to seal caves with their heavy equipment. Floodlights, trip flares, dogs, day patrols and night ambushes were effective, but it would take another two months to eradicate the stubborn Japanese.

On the same day as Kuribayashi's farewell message, Baron Nishi's men headed for their new bunker at Higashiyama. Perhaps not impressed with Ōmagari's aircraft maintenance troops' lack of combat experience and recent desertions, Nishi ordered Ōmagari and twelve of his armed petty officers to the rear. Due to the effects of the American illumination flares and detours needed to avoid American positions, it took the entire night to move to the area where Captain Hakuta's abandoned bunker complex was *supposed* to be located. The bombing and naval shelling had changed the terrain dramatically, so much so that the exhausted troops were unable to locate any of the sealed entrances. Panic started to creep in; there wasn't time to make it back before the sunrise, and being caught in the open would mean a death sentence. Baron Nishi made the decision to move down to the rocky shoreline until dusk to avoid American patrols.

At around 8:00 a.m., the Americans discovered Nishi's group and started a lop-sided firefight. Ōmagari was paralyzed with fear, and was unable to issue a single command. "I stayed hidden in the rocks. Every so often, one of our men would fire back at the Americans. It was a one-sided engagement. Our bolt action rifles made a pitiful 'pop' sound, while the enemy had automatic weapons and plenty of ammunition," Ōmagari said. The rugged terrain prevented the Americans from advancing. The standoff sputtered when the Americans pulled back as night fell. In the darkness, Baron Nishi sent a squad to reconnoiter north towards Kuribayashi's Division HQ. The scouts returned three hours later reporting that there was no way to make it through. And with that, Baron Nishi led the unit back to the original bunker complex. As the Japanese trudged through the night, Ōmagari's spirits were lifted when he picked up a few cans of discarded American rations. "I could not imagine carelessly dropping food like the Americans did," he said.

When the group returned to the 26th Tank Regiment bunker complex around 6:00 a.m., March 18th, they were shy about fifty men who had been either killed or inadvertently left behind on the rocky coastline. The Americans had blown the main entrance shut, but the soldiers quickly dug out a smaller side entrance. Inside were some of the wounded that were left behind. Baron Nishi believed the Americans would be back at first light, and told his men it is better to die out in the open than inside the tunnels. He posted skirmishers in foxholes around the area in preparation for a Japanese version of "Custer's Last Stand." As the sun climbed out of the sea, Ōmagari saw transport aircraft flying overhead bearing "big white stars." But for reasons unknown, there was no American activity around Baron Nishi's bunker. Ōmagari guessed that since the Americans had blown the bunker shut, they must have crossed it off their checklist. "They had no idea that we had reoccupied it so they left us alone," he said.

Perhaps encouraged by a lack of aggressive enemy contact, Baron Nishi decided to head north to link up with Kuribayashi after dark. The group should have arrived before midnight, but Ōmagari said that the entire group went in circles until they came to a spot called *Ginmeisui* east of the 3rd airfield, at the cliff line near the shore.* At 3:00 a.m. or 4:00 a.m., the point guard walked into trip wires near a US machine gun nest. The Americans lit the area with flares and tracer fire. It became a grenade-duel as the Japanese conducted a fighting retreat to escape the kill zone. Ōmagari and his rear guard stayed with Baron Nishi's staff as they descended the cliffs, but became separated in the chaos.

Ōmagari found himself alone, wedged into a tiny cave on the edge of the cliffs. The sun rose to the sound of waves pounding against the jagged shoreline below. Between 10:00 a.m. and 11:00 a.m., Ōmagari heard machine gun fire from the area above him. Sometime after the firefight ended he heard dogs barking. Ōmagari was not afraid of dying, but was terrified of being ripped apart by dogs. He made the decision that if the dogs found him, he

---

* In many English language books, it is listed incorrectly as *Ginmyōsui*, the correct pronunciation is "*Ginmeisui*." This was confirmed directly with the Iwo Jima Association of Japan.

would take his own life with his pistol. Ōmagari drew his pistol and rotated the safety lever forward. He struggled to rack the semi-automatic pistol but it was frozen solid from months of neglect. He listened as the sound of the yelping dogs grew fainter, and then disappeared. "I had never once cleaned my pistol since coming to Iwo Jima," wrote Ōmagari.

He waited until dark before climbing up from the cliff line where he encountered several friendly army and navy troops hiding in the little caves that dotted the cliffs. They grouped together and started for Baron Nishi's bunker complex. The survivors moved along the shoreline staying low in the water to avoid American patrols. It was too dangerous to head straight for the bunker, so it took them almost two days. He expected to meet up with LtCol Takeichi Nishi and the others, but neither he or anyone else had seen the Baron after the firefight. Ōmagari didn't actually witness Nishi's death, but is certain that he heard the firefight that ended his life.*

On a historical note, Baron Takeichi Nishi wasn't the only Japanese Olympian to die on Iwo Jima. Thirty-three-year old Tatsugo Kawaishi was a swimmer who took the silver medal in the men's 100-meter freestyle at the Los Angeles Olympic games in 1932. Before the Pacific War, Kawaishi was an enlisted man who qualified for the Army's Officer Candidate Course (like Shinjirō Nishi). After completing his tour of duty in the late 1930's, Kawaishi was discharged, got married and started a family. When the war worsened for Japan, Kawaishi was recalled and given a commission. And just like Corporal Tadashi Abe and Lieutenant Genichi Hattori, Tatsugo Kawaishi left his young family and headed to Iwo Jima. The silver medalist was in the 3rd Battalion, 17th Mixed Independent Regiment. Actual details of his death are vague.

The Americans also had an Olympic medalist on Iwo Jima; 28th Marine Regimental commander LtCol Harry Liversedge (later BrigGen) won the Bronze Medal in the shot put competition at the 1920 Olympics in Antwerp, Belgium.

Buttoned up inside Baron Nishi's bunker, Ōmagari and the other stragglers remained in need of sustenance. US soldiers and Marines patrolling the area would fire at anything that moved, so the Japanese snuck out only late at night

---

    *   Ōmagari admits that Japanese historians and other Iwo Jima survivors are in disagreement as to the date of Takeichi Nishi's death.

to forage for dropped boxes of American C and K rations. During one of these searches for food, Ōmagari found something glorious, a box hidden in a crevice. Inside were twenty slender, olive drab colored cans labeled "Beer." None of the men knew what exactly what to make of the cans of liquid because in Japan beer was only available in bottles. There was some discussion as to what the contents could be. It was decided the contents must be vegetables pickled in beer. The consensus was that since it was customary in Japan to make *tsukemono* (pickled vegetables) using *sake* rice wine, the Americans, who don't drink rice wine, must must use beer to pickle their vegetables.

Using the tip of a bayonet, Ōmagari stabbed the top of one of the cans and sniffed cautiously at the contents. His nose told him all he needed to know. He held the can of liquid gold between trembling hands and pressed it to his lips. "The beer was fantastic! We all got drunk and had a wonderful time," Ōmagari said. He kept his eyes peeled for another windfall, but that was the only time they found any beer.*

Inside the tanker bunker, the troops separated into army and navy groups that foraged independently and generally didn't mix with each other. The men obtained a few M-1 carbines, Thompson sub-machine guns, M-1 Garand rifles, BAR automatic rifles and various types of grenades. Some of the American weapons they discovered were damaged, but they were able to scavenge enough undamaged weapons to arm themselves. The M-1 Carbine and the Thompson sub-machine gun were the favorites due to their compact design and high-capacity magazines.

Ōmagari warned his navy troops about growing careless and failing to cover their tracks. It didn't take long for the Americans to figure out there were stragglers in the area. The US Army's 147th Infantry Regiment systematically investigated the caves, making it dangerous to linger in any area for long. At the end of March, Ōmagari decided to take a handful of petty officers with him back to his original combat station at Captain Inoue's *Nanpō* HQ bunker. He reasoned there would be ample food and water, as well as friendlier naval personnel at the bunker.

Ōmagari and his men moved quietly during the night. They lost their

---

* Beer provided for the troops during WWII included brands such as Schaefer, Pabst, Budweiser, and Iron City.

way time and time again. Many of the landmarks such as hills and terraces were leveled flat by the Seabees. He saw Motoyama Airfield at night. "It was illuminated and lined with countless shiny aircraft," Ōmagari said. His heart dropped into the pit of his stomach. The Iwo Jima he once knew was no more. He was amazed how quickly the Seabees had graded and enlarged the airfield. Ōmagari encountered Marsden matting, interlocking steel strips that could transform uneven fields into flat parking lots. The matting minimized enemy bomb damage and allowed for quick repair. "It would have taken us a year or more to do what the Seabees did in that single month," Ōmagari said. The Marsden matting would eventually be replaced by asphalt.

No time for gawking - they needed to get underground before sunrise. The men located the bunker entrance area and crawled on their hands and knees, sniffing the ground like bloodhounds. They were searching for traces of human decay. "We could smell the tunnels, so knew we were in the right spot, but we had no tools so we couldn't dig out the entrance." The group reluctantly moved on in search of shelter.

In the pre-dawn darkness, Ōmagari's men came across his former Naval Reserve classmate Ensign Kōhei Kikuta foraging along with two enlisted men. Both officers thought the other was killed when the invasion began. Ōmagari asked if his group could spend the night in Ensign Kikuta's bunker. Kikuta agreed, and took them to the bunker where an Army lieutenant in charge agreed to let Ōmagari's well-armed men enter the bunker. But upon entering, Ōmagari had second thoughts. Inside were about forty naked men and stacks of dead bodies.

After a couple of days, the emotional and physical atmosphere of the bunker was deemed unhealthy, so Ōmagari suggested that Ensign Kikuta and his two sailors join his men in search of a new bunker. Ōmagari's group had canteens so they were able to negotiate admittance into another bunker by using sips of water as bargaining chips, "a sip was the price of admission," Ōmagari said. There were fifty or so men in the new bunker where the men formed tribes based on personal preference or home prefectures, and refused to acknowledge rank or protocol. Ōmagari described them as "undisciplined rabble." The troops were sloppy when they foraged for food and failed to properly cover their tracks. For safety reasons, Ōmagari and Kikuta decided to leave.[127]

Ensign Satoru Ōmagari experienced several different bunkers and classified them into two categories; disciplined, and tribal. He concluded that one would live longer in a bunker ruled by discipline. During his time wandering, Ōmagari had witnessed unspeakable acts of violence as Japanese killed each other to survive. He said that without discipline and leadership, even good men reverted to a primeval state of kill-or-be-killed. Ōmagari witnessed men get strangled over something as trivial as a half-empty canteen of stale water, a cigarette or a few hardtack biscuits. Once, a lone straggler asked for permission to enter the bunker but gate guards demanded that the newcomer shake his canteen before they would let him in. The swishing sound proved the stranger's canteen was half full, so they invited him in and strangled him with a bootlace. The murdered man was a member of the Japanese military and a fellow human being, but it didn't matter. "I was numb. I did nothing to stop it, so I am just as guilty," Ōmagari said.

"When men lose their minds, they turn into something much worse than animals," Ōmagari said. "A normal person would willing give a dying man a drink of water, but we wouldn't waste a drop of water on a dying man. We thought only of preserving our own lives." he said.[128]

The US Marines, soldiers and seabees weren't the only enemy on the island. And it wasn't the age-old Japanese *Army vs. Navy* feud; it was "Japanese vs. Japanese." If one were inside the cave, one was a member of the "inside tribe," if one were trying to get into the cave, one was a member of the "outside tribe." Ōmagari said that water, food and, in particular, acts of mercy were in critically short supply. "My experiences changed me fundamentally. I lost faith in humanity. I tried to write about my experiences after the war but no publishers would work with me. They wanted uplifting tales of courage, not the shameful disgusting truth. I encountered no glory on Iwo Jima," he said.

One night, Ōmagari's men happened upon one of Iwo Jima's rare freshwater puddles. They would sneak down at night to fill their canteens with the stagnant water. The Americans soon caught on and threw phosphorous grenades in the shallow water in order to make it unfit to drink. The stragglers had no choice but to choke down the bitter water. One night, the Americans set up an ambush at the watering hole but a few of the Japanese escaped the ensuing firefight and managed to make it back to the bunker to warn the others. A few nights later, Ōmagari and a few men investigated to see if the Americans were still guarding the water source. The ambush team was gone, but they had left behind the corpses of several Japanese soldiers that were rotting in the shallow water. Having no choice, the thirst-craved men knelt and filled their canteens with the foul slurry. One man took a swig and spat out a bit of human tissue, which quickly ended the use of the puddle as a source of drinking water.

The Doctor's Dilemma

At one of the underground field hospitals, army doctor 1st Lt Kazuyoshi Morimoto wrestled with a moral dilemma. As a physician, he was sworn to protect human life, but the Japanese military code of ethics forbade surrender. He wrote that his hospital cave had three weeks worth of water when the Marines landed. But by the end of February, the steady flow of wounded who arrived at the hospital had depleted the water supply. Those in the hospital cave were reduced to a half-cup of stale water per day. Men were reduced to squeezing muddy water through a dirty cloth. The troops wanted to leave the field hospital in search of water but Dr. Morimoto refused to let anyone leave the cave, saying, "We are all going to die eventually, so why not die together?"[129] Dr. Morimoto wrote, "We were taught that duty was heavier than a mountain, and death was lighter than a feather."[130]

The US Army troops flooded the hospital cave with seawater, then with diesel fuel, which they set on fire. As a countermeasure, the Japanese erected a barrier, complete with blankets to keep grenades and smoke grenades from being thrown in. For a short time it worked.[131] After a dozen more of his men lost their lives, Dr. Morimoto suggested surrendering to the survivors. Despite protests from three of his orderlies who worried about not being able to ever return to Japan, Dr. Morimoto surrendered his surviving patients and men.[132]

In February 1985, Dr. Kazuyoshi Morimoto attended the first joint US-Japan "Reunion of Honor" held on Iwo Jima and is quoted as having said, "I survived and returned to Japan, but for forty years my heart has been here on Iwo Jima."[133]

The Final Days

On March 21st, Japanese Imperial General Headquarters announced that the defenders of Iwo Jima had perished on March 17th in a glorious general attack. Newspapers announced the selfless samurai-like end of the island's brave defenders.

Akikusa's father never got a letter from his son, but received word through his connections that his son left on a ship for Iwo Jima. He read the newspaper account of the *gyokusai* and initially feared the worst. However, Akikusa's mother insisted her son was alive. In April, Akikusa's father visited a soothsayer to see what, if anything, the spirits would say. The psychic-medium claimed she could see visions in her dreams. The following day she told them she had dreamed of their son hiding underground. Akikusa's parents clung to that bit of hope and continued to pray for his safe return.

Months later, a letter arrived from the Japanese Department of the Navy informing the Akikusa family of their son's death on Iwo Jima. There was also a voucher to cover his funeral expenses, as well as a stipend for their loss. The letter stated the family could retrieve his *ikotsu bako* (cremated remains box) at the town hall. The symbolic, but empty, cardboard box would be used at the funeral. Akikusa's parents took the box but refused to cash-in the funeral expense voucher because his mother just knew her son was still among the living.*

By March 25th, even though Iwo Jima was written-off by the Japanese High Command, Vice-Admiral Kinpei Teraoka wanted to get in the last word. He ordered eight Betty bombers from the K704th Squadron to set out for Iwo Jima on a night mission to seek revenge for the souls of the fallen. The planes would fly from Kisarazu Airfield in two echelons of four planes each and drop their payloads from 24,000 feet. Iwao Yamada recalled the heavy volume of accurate AA fire that they encountered during the previous bombing raid, and didn't expect to make it back a second time.

Vice-Admiral Teraoka gave the Betty crews a rousing speech to send them on their way. The first group of bombers left at 3:05 p.m., and Yamada's second group took off at 3:20 p.m.[134] Teraoka sent two separate groups in case roving American night fighters destroyed one of them.

There was trouble from the start. One of the planes in the first group immediately developed engine trouble and returned to Kisarazu, leaving only

---

* The boxes were traditionally made from wood. The cremated remains of the soldier/sailor were placed inside and presented to his parents. Wartime shortages, and the inability to send back the remains of the dead, resulted in empty boxes made of thin cardboard being delivered to bereaved families.

three planes to carry on in the first group. The number of bombers was down to seven.

The Gremlins were busy with the second echelon as well. High winds caused two of the bombers in Yamada's second group to collide, forcing both planes to limp home. This left only five planes.[135] At 5:45 p.m., when Yamada's two-plane echelon reached a pre-determined navigational turning point that required a 6-degree turn to port, inexplicably, the lead plane turned 6-degrees to starboard. Due to radio silence, Yamada could only watch the errant craft slowly drift off course into the purple haze of the setting sun. It was never seen again. Yamada thinks the navigational error was caused by a combination of exhaustion and freezing cold temperatures. Yamada's Betty bomber was now alone, about twenty minutes behind the first group of planes. Admiral Teraoka's "Last Word Attack" was down from eight to only four planes.

Roughly two hours later, Yamada was startled to see the tiny island bathed in brilliant lights. *Was it a trap? Why weren't they under blackout conditions?* Ensign Nemoto ordered the crew to drop some chaff and then changed course. The on-board radar operator reported no enemy air-to-air contacts. Far in the distance, Ensign Nemoto could see that the bombers in the lead group were taking heavy fire from US ships, which confirmed there were no night fighters nearby.

The first group of three Bettys dropped their bombs at 8:50 p.m., and headed back to Kisarazu, but only one actually made it back, the other two vanished without a trace.

There would be a twenty-seven minute gap between the first group of bombers and Yamada's lone Betty bomber.

Amidst a spider web of AA fire, Yamada's bombardier released the payload over the island at 9:19 p.m. The crew claimed to have visually confirmed eight bomb strikes that resulted in starting six fires. As the Betty fled, Yamada said he could see the glow from Iwo Jima all the way to the island of Kita Iwo Jima. Yamada's plane safely returned to Kisarazu at 1:15 a.m. "I can't explain how none of us were wounded," said Yamada.

Three-and-a-half hours later, General Kuribayashi ordered, or even possibly led, roughly 300-400 officers and men to their own "Battle of Little Big Horn" at Motoyama Airfield. Kuribayashi orchestrated the attack to occur at a secure aviation bivouac to cause the most damage possible to airmen who were asleep in their tents. The confused hand-to-hand fighting continued until dawn and left 44 American dead and 88 wounded.[136] Among the casualties were four wounded Black Marines and two that lost their lives.* Two of the Afro-American troops, Privates James Whitlock and James Davis of the 36th Depot Company, earned bronze stars that night.[137]

To date, Kuribayashi's remains have not been identified, and there is debate in Japan as to where and how he died. Japanese survivors paint various pictures of Kuribayashi's final moments: Kuribayashi personally led the banzai charge; Kuribayashi shot himself and was buried inside his bunker; Kuribayashi fell apart mentally and leadership fell to another officer; Kuribayashi was shot by another officer when he suggested surrendering.

The destruction of Kuribayashi's command was the proverbial singing of the fat lady. There were still thousands of Japanese scattered across the island, but organized resistance would prove to be over.

Ōmagari, Akikusa and the others had no way of knowing that the island's supreme commander was dead. They received no new orders, so they followed the directive to "hold at all cost." Harunori Okoshi, the 17-year-old said, "We couldn't surrender, and were forbidden to retreat. The standing order was to defend our positions with our lives. What else could we do?"[138]

The Seabees

Ōmagari and Akikusa both separately remarked on the incredible transformation they witnessed due to the efforts of the American Seabees. Ōmagari, who had previously worked his men to the bone filling in bomb craters, was shocked at how quickly the Seabees graded, leveled and widened the airfields. He had never seen a bulldozer before and marveled at its simple design and brute strength. The amount of mechanical equipment the Americans were able to transport across the ocean was staggering. Ōmagari was angry with his own government for starting a war with a nation that had such industrial capabilities.

American bombers and fighters required vast amounts of aviation fuel. In order to more efficiently feed the thirsty planes, the Seabees built a ship-

---

*   KIA: PFC Harold Smith, 8th Ammunition Company, and Private Vardell Donaldson 36th Depot Company.

to-shore underwater pipeline. It was buoyed at its seaward end and brought ashore south of Tachikawa Point. In addition, Seabees built four 1,000-gallon gasoline storage tanks that also helped regulate the temperature of the high-octane aviation gas. The aircraft fuel for Iwo's fighters could now be delivered directly from tankers anchored off shore instead of being manually hauled ashore in 55-gallon drums. A second pipeline was later established on the west side of the island.[139] On April 3rd, the beaver-like Seabees began work on the North Field (unfinished airfield No. 3). They also worked on improving the Japanese water catch basins to help meet the demand for water. In addition to building the airfield, fuel tanks and buildings, the Seabees made life more comfortable for the pilots. Army Captain Jerry Yellin was a P-51 pilot (78th Fighter Squadron, 21st Fighter Group) assigned to escort B-29s targeting Japan. On April 7th, he participated in his first eight-hour roundtrip escort mission. "When I got back to Iwo, my back and legs were so stiff I needed help getting out of the cramped cockpit. The Seabees quickly built tubs for us to soak in, complete with hot water on demand. Those Seabees were a great bunch of guys," said Yellin.[140]

Captain Jerry Yellin arrived on Iwo Jima on April 6th, and set about dropping napalm in the northern sector.[141] "Napalm is horribly effective stuff. I pity anyone on the receiving end," Yellin said. Akikusa, Ōmagari and many other survivors shared the sentiment. "When I first saw liquid fire I was terrified," said Ōmagari. Akikusa said, "The rocks and sand were on fire. There was nothing for the fire to consume, yet it burned." Iwo Jima's Japanese survivors agree that napalm and flamethrowers were the two most dreaded weapons they encountered. The Japanese had flamethrowers too, but it was a weapon not suited for the defensive battle in which the Japanese found themselves.*

---

* During the 2012 trip to Iwo Jima, the author discovered a rusted, and nearly complete, Japanese flamethrower rig in the weeds near a concrete bunker.

PART 4
The Holdouts

The Field Hospital Surrenders

On Tuesday, April 10th, US soldiers from the US Army's 1st Battalion approached the Japanese 2nd Mixed Brigade's Field Hospital Bunker and sent in a POW to parlay with the occupants. PFC Shūji Ishii said that one of the hospital's lieutenants left the bunker with the POW to talk to the Americans. The officer returned and went straight to Captain Iwao Noguchi without saying a word. Rumors flew among the enlisted men about what would happen next. The following morning, Ishii asked his *hanchō* if he had heard anything. The man replied, "There was talk among the officers that we will be giving ourselves up to the protection of the Americans soon."

Upon hearing this, Ishii recalled a discussion he had with an NCO several days before; the man was examining the medic's field book. The NCO noted that according to the International Red Cross, medical personnel fell under a different category than combatants and would therefore not technically be considered prisoners-of-war. The man reasoned, that as a result, there would be no shame in exiting the bunker.

On the evening of April 15th, Captain Iwao Noguchi issued orders that all hands would exit the bunker the following morning to "accept the protection of the US Army." Captain Noguchi assured the men that he would take responsibility and asked that his men place their lives in his hands.[142]

Ishii said that he felt conflicted; he didn't want to bear the shame of surrender, yet desperately wanted to see his wife and two little girls. On the morning of April 16th, Captain Noguchi and the other officers pushed and coerced the others towards the one remaining entrance that hadn't been sealed shut. Ishii stated that several men refused to surrender and stayed inside the bunker. Army medic PFC Shūji Ishii joined seventy-five other Japanese who exited the bunker en masse to become the largest single group of Japanese to surrender on Iwo Jima. Ishii stated that even as the Japanese were surrendering, several US soldiers smiled and offered cigarettes and chocolate bars. He thought, "We were lied to about Americans being evil, cruel beasts."

The Americans proudly posed for photographs holding a large Japanese national flag and a hospital flag bearing a red cross.

The hospital POWs were trucked to a holding compound near the beach on the western side of the island and questioned by a Nisei interpreter. After a thorough medical examination by a US Army doctor, the holdouts were provided the opportunity to bathe with seawater. They were issued American uniforms with the letters "PW" painted on them, and then sprayed with DDT.

The POW compound that Ishii was in was home to roughly 300 Japanese who were awaiting transport to Guam. During the ensuing roll call, Ishii vomited and passed out. A US Army doctor re-examined him and sent him in a marked ambulance to a smaller compound for sick and injured POWs. There were about sixty other patients at the POW field hospital, which was comprised of tents surrounded by barbed wire.

Ishii said that he was given a bar of Lux soap and allowed to take a shower with fresh water, the first time he had washed with fresh water in over a year. He was then given a comfortable set of flannel pajamas. At 5:30 p.m., an orderly brought him a stainless steel tray. He looked at the tray in wonderment. "They gave me two slices of bread, a serving of corned beef, mashed potatoes, spinach, slices of pineapples and a cup of coffee. I could not believe my eyes, such a banquet of food! I had forgotten the taste of pineapple and coffee and felt like I was tasting them for the first time," wrote Ishii.[143]

The Naval Construction Battalion Bunker

In mid-April, Ōmagari decided to leave the undisciplined Army bunker and make for the 204th Naval Construction Battalion (*Setsuei tai*) bunkers. He reasoned that the naval engineers would welcome him and his men. Ōmagari had previously seen their exceptionally well-crafted shelters and was impressed with the quality of workmanship. Ōmagari and ten others traveled through the night to one of the Naval Construction Battalion bunkers but were disappointed when the engineers refused their request for asylum. Ōmagari and his men returned to the Army bunker. Several day later, Ōmagari came back to the Japanese Construction Battalion bunker to ask again for permission to enter, only to discover it was partially flooded, and most of the occupants were dead. Ōmagari thought, *if the engineers would have let us in we'd be dead, too.* This was one of countless "what if" scenarios he experienced on Iwo Jima.

Over the next week, the Americans began to surround the air raid shelter where Ōmagari was hiding. During the day there were calls to surrender made by Japanese POWs, while during the night, American machine gun positions sprouted up. The Americans threatened to dynamite the shelter if the Japanese didn't surrender.

Corporal Edward Mervich was trained as an artilleryman with the US Army 147th Regimental Combat Team. He came ashore on March 20, 1945, but due to the nature of the terrain in the assigned area, the 147th Regiment couldn't use their cannons. As a result, he was made a rifleman.[144] Corporal Edward Mervich said that he was involved in daytime patrols and dangerous night ambushes. "The Japanese stayed hidden during the day and came out at night to forage for food," Mervich said. The US soldiers were often on edge and exhausted from the combination of day patrols and night ambushes.

Mervich said that his men would set up trip wires and place empty cans filled with pebbles on the wires that would rattle if disturbed. They also rigged trip flares that would shoot off if a trip wire were tugged. Mervich said that one night while on an ambush patrol, the trip flare went off and a few nervous men began shooting at shadows. Mervich chuckled saying that he saw a cat scampering away, "Why a cat was out there, I'll never know."

The men from the US Army's 147th Regimental Combat Team worked hard to walk a fine line between providing security and convincing the stragglers to give up. "Whenever we found them in the caves, we tried to get them to surrender. Our superiors told us that the enemy was more valuable alive because they could write letters home to their families and tell them how good we were treating them. The plan was to convince the Japanese not to resist our invasion of their homeland," said 90-year-old Edward Mervich.

Mervich explained the use of POWs in convincing the stragglers to surrender, "We got the POWs to write notes to their friends that were hiding out. They told their friends that we'd give them water, food and medical care."

Ōmagari saw similar notes from captured Japanese and didn't believe the so-called "propaganda." Ōmagari decided that they needed to escape from their current spot and make another attempt at the Naval Construction Battalion bunker. Even if it was half-flooded and full of dead men, it was better than staying where they were. Ōmagari and a few others crawled out through a gap in the perimeter after midnight.

Once Ōmagari reached the Navy Construction Battalion bunker, he noted the seawater had receded to reveal only a few wounded men who offered no protest. Within a day or two, some Army stragglers arrived, and soon, there were fifty people inside. Ōmagari thinks the food-scroungers weren't careful in hiding their tracks, or were greedy in their pilfering, because the Americans returned threatening to flood the bunker.

The following day, the Americans gave the stragglers another chance to surrender. When none came out, men from the 147th Infantry Regiment's Pioneer Unit ran a hose down into the entrance and began pumping seawater into the bunker. Ōmagari said that the men bumped into each other in the darkness as they tried to get away from the frigid rising tide. Within less than an hour, the waist-high water drowned several who were unable to get to a high spot due to their injuries. The salt water carried lifeless bodies down the corridors. The Americans then poured in oil mixed with diesel fuel, which they then ignited with explosive charges. Ōmagari and a few moved to upward-sloping side tunnels and were spared the flames that raced along the surface of the water. The black fumes that rose from the ventilation ports proved that the bunker was larger than the Americans had thought. Those who crawled out of the bunker's various exits were mowed down.

After the flames died out, the Americans didn't attempt to enter the bunker. However, fearing the Americans might flood the cave again, Ōmagari snuck out late that night using a connecting tunnel with several men in tow, including Ensign Kōhei Kikuta.[145]

The *Nanpō* Bunker

Ōmagari, Kikuta and the handful of enlisted men found a new hiding place. They squeezed into a small air raid shelter where they spent the next few days. One night, while scrounging for food, Ōmagari ran into three sailors who had been ejected from the *Nanpō* bunker. Each man was armed with only a hand grenade. They were told to kill an American and take his weapon. Ōmagari was surprised that an officer could send men out on *kirikomi* attacks at this stage in the battle. The trio said there were about 100 personnel inside the *Nanpō* bunker, with water and limited rations. Ōmagari asked the men to take him to the hidden bunker entrance, but they claimed they would be shot on sight. All they would do was point to the general area before they departed.

Ōmagari returned to the small shelter and had a discussion with Kikuta. They were determined to get into the *Nanpō* bunker; after all, it was Ōmagari's original combat station.

Deep inside the *Nanpō* HQ bunker was the wounded radioman Tsuruji Akikusa. LtCdr Tachikawa would not permit anyone to leave the bunker, even to forage for food. LtCdr Tachikawa's solution to the dwindling water and food supply was to send small numbers of enlisted men to their deaths in *kirikomi* attacks. Men were regularly ejected from the bunker armed with nothing but a grenade and told to kill as many enemy troops as they could. They were ordered not to return to the bunker, or face charges of "cowardice in the face of the enemy" and receive a summary execution. This was a legal way for LtCdr Sosonosuke Tachikawa to conserve food and water by reducing the number of mouths to feed. Tachikawa could claim he was following orders by holding out to the last man, even if it that last man turned out to be himself.

After two months of constant contact with US Marines and Army troops, Ōmagari's little band of men had become experts at evading detection. Ōmagari had seen many things: beaches packed with landing craft; cranes, bulldozers and steam shovels that chewed away at the earth like hungry termites; floodlit airfields lined with aircraft; and floodlights mountains of supplies. He was in awe of the transformation. Although Ōmagari's small group was well-armed with American weapons, their purpose was not to kill, but to survive. On the second or third night of May, Ensign Satoru Ōmagari led Ensign Kikuta and a handful of armed men through barbed wire and trip flares to the *Nanpō* bunker.* In order to detect the trip wires in the dark, the Japanese walked slowly bent over with their hands out in front of them like crawdads. There were American tents, machine gun nests, and vehicles on the roads to avoid.

Ōmagari and the others reached the bunker area but couldn't find the entrance so they crawled on their hands and knees, sniffing at the ground like bloodhounds. They happened upon a man huddled up in a small space in the rocks and asked if he was from the *Nanpō* bunker. The man pointed to an area in the dark and quickly scampered away. Ōmagari and his men spent the next

---

* This is where the stories of Tsuruji Akikusa and Satoru Ōmagari briefly converge. Each told similar but slightly different viewpoints of the same experiences from May 2nd – until their capture. The author has done his best to accurately depict each man's experiences as told by the former POWs.

several hours trying to find an entrance.

Finally, one of them happened upon a small opening to the Navy Accounting Storekeeper bunker, which was connect by a tunnel to the *Nanpō* bunker. After some digging, Ōmagari approached the tiny opening and was met with bayonet points. He figured that once he officially announced himself, he would be recognized and welcomed back into the bunker complex. After all, there should still be a few men inside that he had previously commanded during the airfield work.

He said, "This is Ensign Ōmagari of the *Nanpō* bunker. I am returning to my combat post." He was met with silence. Several of Ōmagari's men shouted confirmation to those inside guarding the entrance with fixed bayonets. The guards refused to allow him in but instead sent for a runner who listened to Ōmagari's story, and then disappeared for quite some time. The runner returned to relay a message from Commander Tachikawa who not only denied the request, but ordered the intruders to leave. Ōmagari asked the runner to speak with the commander again, but the runner refused saying, "I am sorry, sir. These are his direct orders." Ōmagari looked at the faces of the guards aiming their rifles at him and made the decision to take his party back to the small bunker to talk things over.

Over the next two days, the men in Ōmagari's group discussed the situation. There had to be food and water in the *Nanpō* bunker, or else why would the occupants defend it? The occupants had no right to hoard the supplies that were intended for fellow naval personnel. One of the petty officers suggested barging their way past the guards and if there was violence and shooting, so be it. "Either they die, or we die," the man said. The others agreed.

Ōmagari's eight armed men returned to the entrance determined to enter or die in the attempt. An armed sentry tried to stop the group but they brushed him aside. Another guard raised his rifle and warned them to halt. In response, one of Ōmagari's men fired a burst from his Thompson sub-machine gun into the ceiling and shouted, "How dare you aim your weapon at a naval officer!" Thinking the Americans were assaulting the entrance, more armed guards appeared with rifles at the ready.

Ōmagari demanded to be readmitted into the bunker, but the guards countered saying that Commander Tachikawa had ordered that those who left the bunker were forbidden to re-enter. Ōmagari refused to back down, stating he had the legal right to return to his original battle station. The guards claimed that the island's military command structure was disbanded after the general attack, so Ōmagari was not recognized as a member of the late Captain Inoue's former *Nanpō* unit. Captain Inoue was dead and the bunker was under the control of Tachikawa, therefore Ōmagari was no longer part of the *Nanpō Shotō* Naval Air Group command structure. As a result, Ōmagari and his men would not be permitted to enter. Ōmagari's men continued to declare themselves to be lawful occupants, and held their ground. As neither side would back down, the men were on the brink of a friendly-fire disaster.

In the midst of the shouting, a runner from deep inside the tunnel arrived with a message from Commander Tachikawa stating that he had granted Ōmagari's request to re-enter the bunker.

Ōmagari said there were some men inside the *Nanpō* bunker who warmly welcomed him, but there were others who did not. One of those unhappy with the forced entry was radioman Tsuruji Akikusa, who hadn't heard of Ōmagari until the day he bullied his way into the bunker. Akikusa commented, "The outsiders were heavily armed, and threatened to shoot anyone who opposed them. They had no right to enter our bunker, but did so by force."

Ōmagari soon found a flight suit to replace his filthy uniform. He was satisfied with getting a daily ration of food and water without having to risk his life stealing it.

Surprise in the Tunnel

Ivan Prall was a US Army combat photographer who landed on Iwo Jima on March 4, 1945, and stayed until October 1945. When the war broke out, Prall was a student at Northern Illinois University. He had studied photography as an elective. He enlisted in the US Army on August 7, 1942. Prall went through boot camp at Camp Roberts in California, before serving in the 78th Infantry Regiment in North Carolina. He volunteered for duty overseas and traveled through California's Port of Chicago (north of San Francisco), then to the Dutch East Indies, to New Caledonia, and then to Fiji. It was on Fiji that he learned that aerial photographers were in high demand. Ivan Prall volunteered, and found himself in Hawaii taking a photography course. He was then sent to Saipan where he was assigned to VII Fighter Command as a flying photographer. He was then sent to Iwo Jima.

On Iwo Jima, Ivan Prall spent much of his time with the Seabees "because they had better chow," he said. Ivan exchanged his Army-issued uniform for the more comfortable cotton shirts worn by the Seabees. The Seabees built Prall a small water tower so he could take showers, and a dark room to develop his negatives. Ivan was an admitted souvenir hunter and brought back an assortment of trophies; rifles, helmets, fans, a pistol, ammo pouches, flags and a sword. He traveled around the island, documenting Japanese fortifications, bunkers and weapons. He took photos of heavy mortars, AA guns, tanks and other vehicles.

Prall experienced a couple of close calls with Japanese combatants in April and May, 1945. One of his missions was to photograph Japanese installations. He once looked down a nearly vertical cave shaft and spotted a sword. Despite being duly warned about booby traps, he tied a rope around his waist and scampered down the incline. Further down the tunnel he saw a barricade of rocks and sandbags. As Prall picked up the sword, he heard snoring from inside the cave and scrambled out as fast as he could. One of his buddies begged him for the sword saying he could sell it for $10, which would get him into "the big poker game." Prall gave the man the sword and warned the others about the dozing enemy inside. A few days later, a Seabee spotted a rifle down in the same hole and climbed down to retrieve it. He was shot and died the next day. "That incident made me a lot more cautious," wrote Prall.[146]

While most Marines and soldiers on Iwo Jima never saw a living, breathing enemy soldier, Ivan Prall encountered three of them. On one occasion, Prall and another man went to photograph what was classified as a headquarters cave. They discovered it was not a simple cave, but a maze of tunnels and connected chambers. Prall found an army enlisted pith helmet resting on a shelf carved out of the wall. Prall pushed the flexible cloth-covered split-bamboo pith helmet into his pack.* He also found some photographs in an officer's trunk. He and the other man continued to explore the cave. They shined their flashlights down the passageway and were startled by a rustling sound. The explorers doused their lights and made a beeline through the pitch darkness for

---

* This particular pith helmet belonged to Private Shinji Ehara of the Shibuya *Butai* Battalion Headquarters. Ivan Prall gave the pith helmet to the author in 1994. In 2011, the author was able to finally locate and present the helmet to Shōzō Ehara, the dead soldier's younger brother.

the exit. Prall said that a souvenir-hunter was between him and the exit. In a panic, Prall punched and shoved the man ahead of him, all the while the other photographer was pushing Prall from behind. "We wanted nothing more than to get out of that tunnel!" said Prall.

At the sunlit entrance, the three men piled on top of each other under a chorus of shouts and gunfire as American soldiers fired their M-1 rifles down into the cave and tossed in grenades. Prall untangled himself from the dog pile to discover the "souvenir-hunter" was an emaciated Japanese soldier. "I don't know who was more surprised, me or him!" said Prall. The sickly Japanese straggler offered no resistance and was turned over to the MPs.

The second incident occurred while Prall was photographing caves on the western shore of the island. He had a few men with him and was carrying two cameras and a .45 pistol. "A Jap came running out of a small cave with a rifle. He was pointing that bayonet right at me so I turned and ran. I yelled, 'shoot him, somebody shoot him'. One guy's carbine jammed so he scattered, too. Someone else got the Jap in the top of the helmet," said Prall. The Japanese soldier dropped his weapon and ripped off his helmet before scrambling back into the cave. Other Americans rushed to the entrance to toss in grenades. Prall crawled up to the Japanese helmet and picked it up. It had a net on it with bits of dried leaves and grass woven in. The bullet had grazed the top of the Japanese soldier's head and exited the back of the helmet, leaving a blood splatter inside the crown. If the Japanese soldier didn't die immediately, it is doubtful he lasted long with such a horrific head wound.*

The third incident occurred during a card game in one of the Seabee six-man tents about a mile north of Suribachi. Without warning, the center tent pole and the ground around it collapsed, revealing a tunnel. Exposed in the hole at their feet were a thin Japanese man and another who retreated back into the tunnel. The Japanese soldier was hauled out and taken to the field hospital. Eager to get the tent set back up and the game going, the Seabees trucked in a load of gravel and dumped it in the hole.

Prall said that the Japanese would sometimes hide in wrecked ships along

---

* Ivan Prall also gave this steel helmet to the author, but there was no identifying information inside. In 2011, Ivan Prall's grandson Tom asked for the helmet as a family keepsake, so the author gave it to him.

the western shore. Prall explained that during the search for stragglers he observed a Japanese LST with some tanks still on deck. The Japanese couldn't get them unloaded because the ships were too badly damaged or had listed too far.

The Great Escape

One day, an enlisted man approached Ensign Ōmagari with a request. The man said that LtCdr Sosonosuke Tachikawa had announced a plan to steal an American plane and fly back to Japan. The man reasoned that Ōmagari knew the outside terrain and could help Tachikawa achieve his goal. Ōmagari was stunned at the absurdity of this idea, but understood the underlying message, *Help us get rid of this madman.* Ōmagari agreed to do what he could.

Radioman Akikusa heard about the plan as well and recalled how foolish it seemed.

Several days later, Ōmagari had almost forgotten about the harebrained scheme when Commander Tachikawa called for him. Tachikawa asked Ōmagari what he knew about the status of the island's Japanese defenses. Without letting on that he already knew of Tachikawa's plan, Ōmagari explained truthfully that the surviving troops were scattered into disorganized pockets, and the Americans had built a small city above them. The airfields were filled with transport and fighter aircraft. The runways were lined with trucks, jeeps, earthmovers, rows of tents, and pallets of supplies.

This sounded preposterous to Tachikawa, who had not exited the bunker since the battle began. Tachikawa had been sending his men out on one-way *kirikomi* attacks, but denied himself any intelligence they could have provided by refusing to let them back in. Ōmagari was able to finally convince Tachikawa that the airfield was indeed occupied. This seems to have further watered the seedling that grew into a plan. Ōmagari claimed he didn't talk Tachikawa into believing there were aircraft *just for the taking*, but merely told him what he wanted to hear.

Ōmagari and Akikusa independently described another half-baked plan to escape. A group of petty officers talked of sneaking to the rocky shoreline north of the landing beaches. There they would rip wooden planks from the decks of wrecked Japanese ships to construct crude single-man rafts onto which they could cling to as they swam out to sea. One of the local residents, who had been drafted into the defense of the island, had shared with them details about the unique ocean currents that ran counter-clockwise around the island.

The men thought they could paddle out at night to thread the American ships. Then drift north on the current to Kitano Point. The ocean currents would then carry them safely to Minami Iwo Jima Island by morning. The challenge was getting to the coastline without being turned into a bloody smudge. It was desperate men that dreamed up this "Kon Tiki" plan. Men who had never exited the bunker so had no clue as to what awaited them aboveground.

On May 5th, Commander Tachikawa shared the details of his own "Great Escape" plan with Ensign Ōmagari. Despite having never seen the airfield since the invasion began, nor (unlike Ōmagari) having never personally witnessed the transformation of the island, Tachikawa said that under cover of darkness he would lead a group of seven men to the airfield to steal a cargo plane and return to Japan. It was an audacious stunt that would have made Steve McQueen blush with envy. In essence, Tachikawa was talking about committing a court martial offense by abandoning his post in the face of the enemy. This was the same crime for which he had threatened to personally execute the surviving members of the destroyed Kamiyama 5-inch naval gun.

Despite the overwhelming odds, if Commander Tachikawa did somehow sneak his team inside a C-47 transport aircraft, he faced more than a few obstacles: Would the plane be gassed and ready?; Would he know how to start it, let alone fly it?; Would the American AA gunners not shoot him down as he flew away?; Would the P-61 Black Widow radar-equipped night fighters not pursue him in the air?; Could he navigate all the way back to Japan in the dark with no charts?; Would he be shot down by friendly AA gun crews if he actually reached Japan?; Tachikawa couldn't expect that any plane he managed to commandeer would be stocked with seven parachutes, so he would have to locate and land on a friendly airfield in the dark. But could he do so unmolested?

On top of those challenges, if the band of optimists did somehow make it back to Japan, they could expect a court martial followed by a short walk to a firing squad. Ōmagari wondered if Tachikawa was a madman, or was his daring scheme merely a cunning ploy to arrange for him and his followers to fall into American hands with honor.

On the night of May 8th, dive-bomber pilot Tachikawa left the bunker with six men in tow; a naval physician, a naval reconnaissance pilot, an army 2nd Lieutenant, a naval reserve officer named Lt (jg) Morinaka, and a pair of naval enlisted orderlies. After Tachikawa and his group crawled out of the narrow tunnel into the night, the armed gate guards quickly sealed it behind them with rocks and sandbags. This left Ensign Satoru Ōmagari as the senior ranking officer in the bunker.

Two hours later, a ruckus echoed through the normally silent tunnels, which drew Ōmagari to the sealed entrance. Commander Tachikawa and his band of dreamers had returned and were demanding to be allowed back in. The same stone-hearted officer who sent others on one-way suicidal *kirikomi* attacks, had the gall to order the guards to let him back in. The enraged gate guards pointed their weapons at the entrance and swore to shoot anyone who tried to push through. Ōmagari heard Tachikawa asking him to come out and talk. Ōmagari instructed the guards to open the seal so he could listen to what Tachikawa had to say. However, as Ōmagari stepped towards the entrance, the guards pointed their weapons at him. The iron-fisted rule of Tachikawa had created a pressure cooker that was about to explode.

Thinking quickly, Ōmagari reminded the guards of a samurai expression, "The warrior must show mercy." But it didn't work. Ōmagari then tried a different approach saying, "The longer they are out there, the higher the risk of them being spotted. Then the enemy will be coming for all of us." With that, an agreement was reached where Ensign Ōmagari promised to take full responsibility for the "deserters" who would be permitted access for one night only. If they refused to leave the next night they would be forced out along with Ōmagari. On these conditions, Tachikawa and the others were allowed to re-enter.

The following night, Commander Sosonosuke Tachikawa and his band of followers quietly left as promised. Neither Ōmagari nor Akikusa has any idea of what became of the group.

Tachikawa's departure created a power vacuum. Ōmagari knew what would happen if the troops in the bunker were allowed to fall into tribal law. So he assumed command and made a 180-degree policy change. There would be no more *kirikomi* attacks, and foraging for food was now permitted. Ōmagari and his men shared their experiences with the hermits who had been sealed in the tunnels. Ōmagari's men held informal lectures: US landmines; defeating trip flares; how to locate water; and how to cover one's tracks when stealing from the enemy, etc. Ōmagari stressed three important rules on foraging; only two to a team, cover your tracks, and never take so much that the Americans would notice it.

Akikusa said that in his opinion, Ōmagari was an outsider who bossed the survivors around, but he admitted that Ōmagari's petty officers shared valuable tips on scrounging that helped keep him alive.

Scrounging for Food

By now, Akikusa's leg had healed to the point where he could join the scavenging efforts. One of Ōmagari's petty officers gave Akikusa the lower half of a rusted, broken sword. The man had removed the tiny bamboo peg in the middle of the cloth-wrapped handle in order to remove the handle and hand guard. As he rotated the blade in his hands, Akikusa noted it resembled more of a tool than a weapon. It could be used to pry open wooden crates, or cut through cardboard boxes or canvas tents. The older sailor warned Akikusa about empty ration cans with rocks in them that the Americans strung on strands of wire. The man was specific, "The Americans start shooting the moment they hear a sound so be careful." It was risky, but Ōmagari's men were living proof that the foraging could be done. Akikusa said, "If I was going to die I wanted to do so on a full belly."

The scavengers exited the bunkers late at night to carefully pick through trash dumps or steal directly from the massive stockpiles of American supplies. Akikusa said, "I didn't want to hurt anyone. I just wanted something to eat." During one of his foraging expeditions Akikusa was surprised to see Black troops. "We were encouraged by this because we thought it meant that the enemy was getting desperate enough to send in his second-tier troops," said Akikusa. It is possible that Akikusa saw African-Americans of the 8th Field Depot (8th Ammunition Company, 33rd, 34th, and 36th Marine Depot Companies), the 43rd Amphibian Truck Battalion, or the 476th Amphibian Truck Company.

Akikusa's confidence grew with each successful foraging trip. One night, he ventured out with his bamboo stick and makeshift sword-tool. He made steady progress as he crawled towards a row of pallets that were covered with canvas tarps. He froze when he heard slight metallic clinking sound. He moved and heard the sound again. His realized his sleeve was caught on some barbed wire. Akikusa was a victim of the American's cheap but effective early-warning system. As he struggled to free himself, a loud pop went off overhead bringing the midnight sun. As a steady stream of tracers buzzed overhead, sounding like a flock of angry bees. Another illumination round lit the entire area. Akikusa pressed his body against the earth knowing his only chance was to remain perfectly still. A flare landed about fifty feet away and sputtered out.

Perhaps because there was no return fire, the machine gun fire waned and stopped. Akikusa gingerly slid on his belly and tried to turn around, but his right sleeve was still hooked. He gently twisted his arm, which caused a chain reaction of rustling barbed wire. He couldn't make any sudden moves or it might set off the cans again. He remained still while he tried to figure out what to do, he then remembered the parable of a pheasant that had escaped a trapper's snare by plucking out its own tail feathers. With his left hand he slowly unbuttoned his shirt and then carefully wriggled free.

He crawled forward, playing a deadly version of the children's game "red-light, green-light." Just as the second flare died, a bullet struck the tip of Akikusa's bamboo crutch with a distinct *thrang*. The pole flew out of his grip and bounced across the rocks. "My stick!" he almost shouted as he reached forward. The sound of the bamboo dancing across the rocks confirmed the gunners' suspicions and they began firing again. Akikusa remained motionless through a third and fourth flare, hoping the gunners would think they had got him.

After the gunners grew bored, Akikusa slowly slithered back to the bunker entrance leaving his shirt hanging on the barbed wire.

As he crawled down into the bunker, he heard Americans shouting in the direction from which he had come. He thinks that a patrol sent out to examine the wire must have discovered his uniform. It had been his closest call yet.

Several nights later, Akikusa, along with a sailor named Andō, and two others worked their way south along the shore. They spotted stacks of unguarded supplies under tarpaulin sheets. Akikusa ducked under one of the canvas sheets and found crates of ammunition, which was something useless to him. He crawled under another tarpaulin and found crates and cardboard boxes. He used his pry bar to open a crate of what turned out to be bottles of soda pop. Careful not to make a sound, he pulled one out, pried off the cap, and took a sip. He said, "The sweet, carbonated beverage was the most delicious thing I have ever tasted in my life.'"* He quickly gulped the rest of the contents of the bottle, and although tempted to grab as many bottles as he could carry, he recalled the petty officer's advice about not taking too much at once. He took just one soda bottle and two cans of food, then started back to the bunker in the darkness.

After twenty minutes of trying to find his way, Akikusa realized he was lost. The sky was turning from dark to gray. *If I don't get underground by the time the sun comes up I'm a dead man*, he said to himself. He was unable to find the *Nanpō* bunker so he crawled into a shallow crevice for the time being. The sun rose to the sound of barking dogs. His heart skipped a beat as he heard shouting in English. Akikusa tucked himself into a tight ball and squeezed his eyes shut. He was startled by a voice speaking in his native tongue booming from a bullhorn, "To the officers and men in the bunkers. The war is over. The Americans have control over the entire island." *They must know about the tunnel.* It wasn't a trick; the voice was definitely that of a Japanese. The unknown man using the bullhorn continued, "The Americans mean you no harm. I am proof they will guarantee your safety and give you food and water. Those who are wounded will received medical treatment. I will be back tomorrow, but after that, they will flatten this entire area with heavy machinery and the tunnels and caves will be sealed forever."

The group of dogs and soldiers moved on to another spot and repeated the same speech. It was the end of the first week of May. When Akikusa made it back to the bunker that night, he discovered that Andō and the two others hadn't returned. After Akikusa was captured in May, he learned that Andō had been caught that night while hiding under a tarp. Andō wouldn't admit it, but Akikusa thinks it was Andō who spilled the beans about the bunker, which sent the dogs and American soldiers out to look for it.

The defenders knew the battle was lost, but talk of surrender was illegal under military law, and instigators risked having their skulls cracked, or worse, ventilated by a pistol round. The goal was to hold out until the tides of war turned and the Japanese Navy could retake the island. One survivor, Harunori Okoshi, claimed that a POW entered his cave bearing American chocolate

---

* Mr. Akikusa demonstrated the act of downing that refreshing beverage with a satisfying sigh.

bars, cigarettes, a canteen of fresh water and food. "He tried to convince us to surrender. Without warning, someone shot him in the back," Okoshi said. A man with a pistol justified the murder by claiming, "It was for his own good, and for the honor of his family."[147]

Calls to Surrender

The US Army's 147th Infantry Regiment and 724th Military Police Battalion were enjoying success using dog patrols to sniff out the Japanese, but were having difficulty in getting the holdouts to surrender. In hopes of talking the Japanese stragglers into giving up, the Americans used a combination of Caucasian and Nisei soldiers that had received Japanese language training that was conducted by the Military Intelligence Service (MIS).

They also utilized POWs who were often enthusiastic participants in identifying bunkers and convincing their comrades to surrender. Ensign Satoru Ōmagari said that he and the other holdouts viewed the POWs as traitors who could not be trusted.[148]

US Army Corporal Edward Mervich said that the POWs tried hard to get their comrades to surrender, and some even went down into the caves with cigarettes, water and chocolate bars. Sometimes the POWs were killed by those they were trying to rescue. Mervich explained that one time as a POW were calling out to the stragglers to surrender, a grenade came hurtling out of the small cave entrance and struck Mervich in the leg. "I thought it was a rock. Lucky for me it was a dud," said Mervich. The stragglers didn't appreciate the US Army's sincere attempts to get them to surrender.

Mervich said that on another occasion, a pair of POWs volunteered to climb down into a tunnel to talk their friends into surrendering. The two men emerged from the cave unharmed saying that there were twenty-two die hards inside. Following repeated calls to surrender, Mervich heard muffled gunfire coming from inside the cave. "We backed up a weasel weapons carrier with a couple of 55-gallon drums full of diesel fuel, and poured them into the cave. Well, then we set it on fire with a phosphorus grenade. And that was the end of that," said Mervich.

While patrolling the northern end of the island, Mervich said that he observed dozens of corpses floating in the ocean below the cliffs. "The Japanese jumped off the cliffs rather than surrender," said Mervich.

One of the US Army Caucasian language officers that worked hard to get the Japanese to surrender was Second Lieutenant Manny Goldberg. Goldberg had spent two years in Japan as a teenager and commanded a detachment of Nisei interpreters on Iwo Jima. One of Goldberg's Nisei soldiers, TechSgt Terry Doi, would take off his shirt to show he was unarmed, and carrying only a flashlight, would enter cave after cave convincing many to surrender. Perhaps several dozen Japanese were saved due to his daring actions that earned him the Silver Star.*

One of the Japanese who surrendered to Lt Goldberg's team on April 9, 1945, was First Lieutenant Yasuhiko Murai, the army infantry school instructor who had been hastily sent to Iwo Jima. Goldberg and Murai met again long after the war and became good friends.

A day or so after the "raft group" left the *Nanpō* bunker, there was a commotion at one of the guarded entrances. Someone was calling out to Ensign Satoru Ōmagari by name. Ōmagari went to the entrance and listened; a shiver ran down his spine as he recognized the voice of his friend Ensign Yamamoto. Ōmagari surmised that Yamamoto must have been captured earlier, because he was not with the raft group. Although Ōmagari wanted to meet with Yamamoto, the sentries refused to let anyone in or out, so the call to surrender went unanswered.

The following day, the Americans presented another chance to surrender, or risk being flooded. Ōmagari was one of the few who had survived a flooding attack and was deeply concerned. Like before, Ōmagari heard the sound of jazz music coming over a loudspeaker before the attack began.

Radioman Akikusa heard men shouting "Gas!" as a fog resembling dry ice rolled in from the southern entrance. As Akikusa hobbled away from the smoke, his hand struck a gas mask hanging on the wall. *What a stroke of good luck.* He donned the mask but after only a few breaths his eyes began to sting. *Damn, it's broken.* He dashed it to the ground. He pressed his face into his sleeve and continued past the morgue pit to the eastern entrance. He crawled up a steep narrow stairway into an observation post to get above the creeping

---

* Although not trained at MIS Language School, PFC Guy Gabaldon (2nd MarDiv) used his positive childhood experiences with a Nisei family to help him conduct similar work on a grander scale on Saipan.

fog.

Akikusa heard shouting near the central entrance as canisters dropped in from ventilation shafts. The canisters popped and hissed, producing yellow smoke that rose to the ceiling. Akikusa panicked, *It's poison gas. I'm trapped.* He saw a wisp of yellow smoke rush past him up into the ceiling behind his head. It escaped through a finger-sized hole that had not been sealed when the lookout-post had been closed. Akikusa clawed at the dirt to scratch out a space large enough to press his face up against the hole and pressed his lips into the small hole. While he sucked in fresh cool air from the outside, men below him on the tunnel floor coughed and wheezed. Like a goldfish stuck in a dirty fish tank, Akikusa found himself gulping air through a tiny hole in the ceiling as screams echoed through the tunnel. The gas eventually dissipated and Akikusa slid down from his perch. Others had survived too, so he reasoned it wasn't poison gas.

Akikusa hoped the Americans had given up but he was wrong. The US Army called upon the Seabees to help with the straggler problem. The Seabees flooded the underground bunkers with a mixture of seawater and gasoline, and then ignited the mixture to force the Japanese out or kill them in the process. The Seabees has access to gasoline-powered pumps, hoses and the know-how to draw water from the shore to flood the caves and tunnels. It was organized and methodical. If the water didn't drown the Japanese, the fire would burn them to death. If the fire didn't burn them, the ensuing lack of oxygen would result in death by asphyxiation.

Ōmagari said the US Army never lied about their intentions, "They offered us many chances to surrender." He heard the familiar sound of water splashing down like a waterfall as it entered the cave entrance. *Oh no, not again.* The water seeped and moved to the lowest points picking up human waste and debris as it traveled.

Radioman Akikusa noticed men emerging from the various side rooms and tunnels to see what was going on. He was startled at how many people were still alive. It took a couple of hours for the water to reach waist-high. Some men splashed around like kids in the cool refreshing water. Akikusa climbed to a higher point away from the water because it smelled like the sewage water used to irrigate the fields back home. The water created a rancid outhouse smell.

Ōmagari and the others who had been through a flooding attack needed no encouragement to move further into the complex to escape the water. What Akikusa didn't notice was that the Americans had also pumped fuel or oil into the complex. It floated on the surface of the water coating anything and anyone it touched. Then the waterfall stopped. It was except for the sound of men splashing through the water.

Akikusa moved back up into his cubbyhole to get closer to the "goldfish hole." As he crawled up and away from the water he heard an explosion; flames raced across the surface of the water engulfing those who had moments before been reveling in its cool touch. Screams reverberated through the tunnels, which were momentarily brightened by the fire. The skin on the faces of some of the burn victims peeled and hung down like old wallpaper. Those on fire would drop down into the water to put out the flames, only to come up and catch fire again. Akikusa said it was like seeing ghosts bobbing up and down in the water. The wounded were screaming, thrashing and splashing around crying out, "Help me, Help me!" Others yelled at them to be quiet. "Don't scream! They'll know we are in here!" Some of the injured who screeched in agony and were shot by their comrades. Akikusa said, "Bam, Bam. One after another, the burning men where killed." He recalled one man who was yelling, "Help me, Mother, Help me!" and was quickly shot in the head.

Another survivor claims, "We killed the wounded out of mercy. They were badly burned; we had no way of caring for them. The men were going to die anyways so we helped them," said Harunori Okoshi as he gestured putting a gun to his own temple.[149] Ensign Ōmagari admitted to killing some of those who were severely injured, saying it was done out of mercy.[150]

After the flames died out there were still a few oil-soaked bits of rubbish that burned like torches floating on the water; it created a ghoulish glow inside the smoky tunnels. The smoke began to escape through the ventilation holes, and Akikusa observed charred bodies slowly bobbing along a watery hallway. One man splashed towards Akikusa and climbed up into the cubbyhole with him. He didn't recognize the man who was badly burned, but whispered to him, "Shhh, stay quiet and don't draw attention to yourself." He gently patted the man's arm to reassure him but the man winced in pain. After some time, Akikusa gently tapped the man's hand for a response but he was dead.

Captured

It seems the Americans assumed the flooding had done the trick since there was no follow-up attack. Akikusa, Kumakura, Okoshi, Ōmagari and the others were trapped in the flooded, smoky cave system. They were waist deep in dead bodies, filth and excrement. It was perhaps one or two days later that a POW approached the bunker entrance and began to shout his own name. "It is I, Chief Petty Officer Mizawa." He had previously been in the *Nanpō* bunker and wanted permission to re-enter to talk. *Was it a trick?* No one inside the bunker responded. A figure wearing an American uniform and shining a flashlight scrambled down into the bunker. The holdouts raised their rifles to shoot, but Mizawa quickly shined the flashlight in his own face so they could confirm his identity. Mizawa handed over several packs of American cigarettes, chocolate bars, and a canteen filled with fresh water to prove that the Americans meant no harm.

"The act of surrender was not the problem. The worry was being executed once the Americans sent us home," said Ōmagari. Although Mizawa assured the holdouts that they wouldn't be killed by the Americans, he could not guarantee they wouldn't be given court martial trials when they returned to Japan.

CPO Mizawa was allowed to exit the cave, and promised to return the following day.

Late that night, Ensign Satoru Ōmagari led his small group of men through a connecting tunnel to an outlying air raid shelter. Akikusa, Kumakura and several others stayed behind. Akikusa remembers Ōmagari and his men exiting the *Nanpō* HQ bunker and believed they were giving up.

Without warning, Yasuo Kumakura moved down the tunnel to the radio communications room where he and Akikusa had worked. Akikusa tried to follow, but Kumakura moved too quickly. As Akikusa turned the corner he heard a blast. Kumakura had taken his own life with a hand grenade. Akikusa's last memory of Iwo Jima was crawling up a carved rock stairway to a ventilation hole.

100 bullets

Another man who was in the *Nanpo* bunker was Seaman 1/c Haruji Mita, a naval aircraft armorer with the 316th Fighter Squadron (301st Naval Air Group).

Half of his unit's fighters were dispatched to Truk Lagoon, but were caught up and destroyed in the Marianas Turkey Shoot when they reached Saipan to refuel.

The remaining half of the Zero fighters were then sent to Iwo Jima. Seaman Mita was among the support troops that were scheduled to follow the Zeros to Truk Lagoon aboard the transport vessel *Shozui Maru*. After the Turkey Shoot, the *Shozui Maru* was diverted to Chichi Jima.* Mita's unit spent ten days on Chichi Jima before being shuttled via four small wooden boats to Iwo Jima. He discovered that the remaining Zeros from the 316th Fighter Squadron had been destroyed in the July 4th US naval barrage. "There were no aircraft left to work on, so I was assigned to Captain Inoue's *Nanpō* Naval Air Group," he wrote.[151] Seaman 1/c Mita spent the next six months armed with only a pair of binoculars on the western shoreline at "Brown Beach 2" as part of an 8-man squad tasked with scanning the horizon for friendly and enemy vessels.[152]

Two days before the Marines landed, Seaman 1/c Haruji Mita was issued a Type-99 Arisaka rifle and 100 rounds of 7.7 mm ammunition, and was told there would be no resupply. "I was a terrible marksman. I had only been to the firing range once during basic training at Suzaki (Suzaki Naval Air Group Ordinance Maintenance School)," wrote Mita.

After the Marines landed, Seaman 1/c Haruji Mita hid in various bunkers surviving by taking water and rations from the dead. By the end of April 1945, Mita found himself in a bunker at Tamana-yama. Haruji Mita said that he heard US Army Nisei soldiers calling out over loudspeakers saying, "Think of your parents. Think of your wives and children back home. We won't harm you. Please come out so you can return safely to your families." Mita said that the call to surrender had an effect on the older men who had wives and children.

One of his fellow stragglers was an army corporal named Hiroshi Kurihara who could speak English and claimed that he was familiar with America. Mita wrote, "Corporal Kurihara told us that the Americans would never torture or kill POWs." On April 13th, Corporal Kurihara tried to convince the others to join him in surrendering, but he exited the bunker alone.

"Even in elementary school we were told that the Americans were *kichiku*

---

* The *Shozui Maru* was sunk on July 4, 1944, while anchored at Tokinoura Bay on neighboring Ani Jima by aircraft from Admiral Joseph Clark's task force.

(cruel beasts). We heard of the things our own soldiers did to Chinese prisoners so was afraid of what the Americans might do to us," wrote Mita.

In the end of April, Haruji Mita and a few others tried to make their way to the eastern shoreline in hopes of escaping on a raft. They were discovered and attacked moments after leaving their bunker at Tamana-yama. Haruji Mita was hit in the left buttocks and barely made it back into the cave.

Ten days passed and Mita's left leg became infected and swollen. After another round of surrender calls, Mita and seven survivors decided to surrender. Mita passed out as he crawled from the cave into the bright sunlight. He woke up in a tent, feeling disorientated. An American medic treated him to a smile and a pack of cigarettes. A Nisei soldier named Inoue told Haruji Mita that after he fainted he was put on a stretcher, loaded onto a jeep, and taken to the field hospital where a surgeon removed two grenade fragments from his buttocks. Mita even received a blood transfusion from an American donor. In the process of being nursed back to health, Haruji Mita felt ashamed for believing the wartime propaganda about the Americans. "Was this the behavior of cruel beasts?" he wondered.

Haruji Mita's leg was put in a cast and later he was able to walk with crutches and spent two months in the field hospital. When it came time to board the ship to Guam, an American medic named "Sergeant Bocha" (a man from St Louis, Missouri, who told Mita that his fiancé was a school teacher) said through a Nisei interpreter, "I hope you get better soon and can return to your family in Japan. I want to go home, too." Mita said that those words were forever etched on his heart. After another month in a field hospital on Guam, Haruji Mita was shipped to a detention center on Oahu.

"The only war medals I ever got were the scars on my backside," wrote Mita.

Saved by a Dog

Tsuruji Akikusa says he came to his senses in a US Army field hospital on Guam on June 1, 1945. He says that he was awakened by Miyashita, the mailman who had been in the bunker with him. Miyashita explained that Akikusa had been discovered by a war dog and taken to the US Army field hospital on Iwo Jima, and then shipped to Guam. Try as he might, Akikusa says he can't remember anything for the two week period after Kumakura's suicide. "I owe my life to that American soldier and his dog who rescued me," he says.

Another POW with a similar experience is Private Kiichi Abe, the combat engineer that was sent to the island to dig tunnels in April 1944. Kiichi Abe's bunker was under attack by a flamethrower when he blacked out.[153] He woke up in the US Army field hospital tent on Iwo Jima with no recollection of being captured.*

The Anguish of Surrender

Ensign Satoru Ōmagari and his naval aircraft maintenance men were able to hold out a little longer. One night, their air raid shelter began to fill with water. Ōmagari was confused because there had been no standard pre-attack warning from the Americans. In addition, it was the middle of the night, and from his experiences he understood that American soldiers never attacked in the dark. The stragglers choked and coughed, *was it poison gas?* Ōmagari joined the others in clawing their way out for fresh air; they were armed to the teeth and ready for a fight. But when they reached the surface it was dark and absolutely quiet. *Where were the Americans?*

The ground was sopping wet, which was evidence that a heavy rainstorm had recently passed over the island. The hard-packed airfield must have been unable to absorb the runoff that flowed down into the air raid shelter. Mud had clogged some of the small ventilation shafts that normally permitted the noxious fumes (from human waste and naturally occurring sulfur) to escape.

The men decided to wait until dawn before re-entering the air raid shelter. Later that morning, the Americans discovered the tracks in the mud left by the Japanese, and realized that there were more holdouts underground. The US Army troops sent in a POW to relay a message of surrender.

After talking to the POW, the occupants reached a decision following two hours of deliberations. The men would agree to surrender only if Ensign Ōmagari, as an officer, issued them a direct order. The enlisted men and petty officers felt that if they were following direct orders, they could not be executed

---

* The amnesic experiences of Akikusa and Abe are not rare, but closely mirror those had by other Japanese POWs that Urlich Straus interviewed for his book, *The Anguish of Surrender*.

once they returned to Japan. Ōmagari told the stragglers that he would take full responsibility. With that assurance, thirty-six holdouts emerged from the air raid shelter, leaving twenty or so behind. Most of those who emerged were in their underwear except Ōmagari who says he was wearing a flight suit. The time was 4:00 p.m., May 17, 1945. Ōmagari said he didn't know for certain what became of the twenty men who chose to stay behind.

Ōmagari's group of POWs was taken to a flimsy stockade of tents enclosed in barbed wire and ordered to bathe with seawater. "They gave us American uniforms with the letters "PW" painted on the back," Ōmagari said. He spent two weeks in a temporary camp with about eighty other POWs gorging on a steady diet of freshly baked bread, canned rations, crackers and cola. They watched B-29s come and go, living with the guilt that their failure to hold the island meant that bombs were falling on their native soil.

Roughly two weeks after Ōmagari surrendered his men, a PO2/c Koyatsu and three other stragglers made a late night break for the shoreline hoping to build a raft and float to freedom. They made it as far as a cave on the water's edge where they were discovered in the morning and captured by a US Army Corporal.[154]

Ōmagari, Akikusa, Higuchi, Mita, Koshi, Ishii, Koyatsu and the others were shipped to Guam. Ōmagari said, "On Guam, the interrogaters asked me about our so-called 'new secret weapon'. I didn't know what they were talking about. During one interrogation by a Japanese-speaking Caucasian intelligence officer, Ōmagari answered all his questions honestly, but the American angrily accused him of lying.[155] After several more interrogations about "a new fireball weapon that flew slowly," Ōmagari put two-and-two together and realized they were referring to the "foolish contraption" he mocked during the testing phase.

"To me, the rocket-bombs were not a 'new secret weapon' but a desperate field expedient." Ōmagari believes that during the first four days of the invasion when the rocket-bombs made their debut, the Japanese launched between fifty and sixty of the 60 kg rocket-bombs, and between twenty and forty of the 250 kg rocket-bombs.*

The average Japanese serviceman was not familiar with the Prisoner of

---

* The Yokosuka Naval Air Technical branch also invented the *Ohka* (Baka Bomb) manned suicide rocket, and the *Kikka* jet-powered fighter.

War Convention of the Geneva Accords of 1929; neither Japan nor the United States had ratified it. The War Department furnished Japanese POWs with a translation of the "Geneva Convention Relative to Treatment of Prisoners of War, July 21, 1929." As the days passed with no abuse or torture, the Japanese POWs' fears of torture and execution subsided. "They fed us well. We were treated by both American and Japanese medical personnel," said Akikusa.

The POWs were transported from Guam to Oahu for formal processing. On June 30, 1945, at a naval detention center on the island of Oahu in the Territory of Hawaii, Akikusa received his "Basic Personnel Record" with POW serial number 41J-4561-MI. The document states he was captured on May 15, 1945. The fingerprints on the document show that Akikusa was missing three fingertips. Akikusa signed the second page of the document that had the following disclaimer: "I have been fully advised of my rights under the Geneva Convention, and hereby declare of my own volition that I do not desire to have either my government or my family notified of my capture." As a result, Akikusa's name was not submitted to the International Red Cross Prisoner Information Bureau.

Akikusa, Ishii and Ōmagari all said they were held at a US Navy detention center near Pearl Harbor, near the beach, then transferred to a US Army facility located in the mountains about thirty minutes away by truck.* Both Shūji Ishii and Haruji Mita wrote that the US Army camp held about 800 POWs including recent arrivals from Okinawa, many of them teenagers. Some of the POWs were Koreans who had volunteered or were drafted into the Japanese military and were held in a separate part of the facility away from the Japanese.

Both Shūji Ishii and Satoru Ōmagari described meeting a warm-hearted Japanese-speaking US naval intelligence officer in Oahu; Lieutenant Otis Carey, whose parents and grandparents had worked as missionaries in Japan. Lieutenant Carey was born in Hokkaido and attended elementary school in Japan, which explained his oral language proficiency.[156]

Another bi-lingual naval intelligence officer that they spoke highly of was Lieutenant William "Billy" H. Gorham III. Lieutenant Gorham's father was William R. Gorham II; an American engineer who first brought his wife and sons to Japan in 1918. William R. Gorham II was an engineer for Nissan Motors

---

* Iroquois Point POW Camp located at Ewa Beach, Oahu.

in the early 1930's, and eventually rose to the position of plant manager at Hitachi's Kameari military tank factory in Tōkyō.* He also conducted research on the highly classified area of jet aircraft engines.[157]

Young Billy Gorham went to the Unites States to attend high school, and was enrolled at Caltech when the Japanese attacked Pearl Harbor in 1941. He entered the US Navy in 1943, after his college deferment ended, and worked for the Office of Naval Intelligence in Pearl Harbor as an interrogator.

About a half year before the Pearl Harbor attack, due to restrictions on foreigners living in Japan, and faced with possible deportation, Mr. and Mrs. William R Gorham II renounced their US citizenship and become naturalized Japanese citizens. William R. Gorham II legally changed his name to "Katsundo Gōhamu."†

Ishii wrote that since B-29s were bombing military production facilities across Japan, naval intelligence officer Lieutenant Billy Gorham asked every POW if they knew if his father's tank factory was still standing. One day, a POW told Lieutenant Gorham that he had worked at his father's tank factory in the fall of 1943, and reassured him that he had seen the lieutenant's father.[158]

Akikusa's POW records show he left Oahu on June 27, 1945, on a ship bound for San Francisco. Ōmagari would be sent the following month to Seattle, Washington. After arriving in San Francisco Bay on July 5th, Akikusa transferred to a ferry that took him to the Prisoner of War Processing Center at Fort McDowell on Angel Island; it is here that Japanese POWs received immunizations and were tested for various diseases before being sent to POW camps across the United States.

The food continued to be plentiful, and in short time "I began to worry about getting fat," said Akikusa. A typical day of meals at Angel Island: Breakfast: sausages, rice, apples, coffee, milk and sugar; Lunch: sukiyaki, cabbage salad, rice, caramel pudding; Dinner: Spaghetti and hash, baked tomatoes, lettuce and tomato salad, rice, cake and hot cocoa.[159] Akikusa claimed he took in more calories in a single meal as a POW than he received in several days as a

---

* This factory produced the Type-97 *Chi-Ha* and *Shin-Hoto* medium tanks for the Japanese Army. Other companies such as Mitsubishi and Hino produced tanks, too.

† Katsundo Gōham wasn't prosecuted as a traitor by the US Government since he had renounced his US citizenship prior to the outbreak of the Pacific War.

straggler on Iwo Jima.

Life in the USA

On August 3rd, naval radioman Tsuruji Akikusa, aircraft maintenance crew man Haruji Mita, and army medic Shūji Ishii were among the enlisted POWs that took an eye-opening train ride across the continent with stops of various durations in Ogden, Utah; Omaha, Nebraska; and Chicago, Illinois. "I could not believe the scale and beauty of North America," said Akikusa. The POWs ate C-rations, but the escorting MPs made sure the POWs received coffee and donuts when they were made available. They eventually arrived at Camp Michaux, also known as Pine Grove Furnace POW Interrogation Center, near Harrisburg, Pennsylvania on August 6, 1945; the same day the Americans dropped the Atomic bomb on Hiroshima.

The 100-acre Pine Grove Furnace Camp was used to house German U-Boat crews and naval officers. It was expanded to include prisoners from Field Marshall Erwin Rommel's Afrika Korps. Pine Grove Furnace POW camp was primarily utilized by the Provost Marshal General as an interrogation camp for enemy officers, but Akikusa's records prove that Japanese enlisted men were also housed at the installation. Akikusa and Ishii were just two of the 161 Japanese that passed through the gates during the war.[160]

Dictaphones hidden in the ceiling could record the high-value German POWs' conversations (The inventor of the German Buzz Bomb was held here). The camp was under supervision of the Intelligence Department of the Army with a private telephone line to Washington, D.C. It was home to 1,500 prisoners and 150 American personnel. To maintain secrecy, if questioned, guards were instructed to say they were stationed at Carlisle Barracks located thirty minutes away. Pine Grove Furnace POW Camp was also known as Camp Michaux, 3300 SCU, and Camp S-51-PA.[161]

Ishii wrote that the enlisted POWs had been separated from their officers for a long time. He noticed an air of resentment at Pine Grove Furnace POW Camp when a few Japanese officers were brought back into the mix. He wrote, "They still had an air of authority. They ordered us to heat up their water so they could take hot showers!" The enlisted POWs had been watching how the American enlisted men interacted with their officers and had grown accustomed to the comparative informality and mutual respect.

Every morning and evening the Japanese POWs would form up for "colors" and "retreat" and render honors to the stars and stripes. "The Americans didn't force us to salute their flag, we did so naturally," Ishii wrote.

Ishii said that there was even a piano in the chow hall, which was unthinkable in the Japanese Army. The POWs watched a film once a week. Ishii recalled one film in particular that was so popular they requested an encore showing the following week; the 1940 comedy, *The Road to Singapore* starring Bob Hope, Bing Crosby and Dorothy Lamour. "Even though we didn't understand, what we couldn't stop laughing at the sexy comedy."[162]

Tsuruji Akikusa said the hills surrounding the camp in Pennsylvania were filled with beautiful deciduous trees. Some POWs went on work details at a lumber mill. However, the injuries to Akikusa's right hand kept him inside the camp on grass cutting detail. Akikusa was surprised to learn that POWs were paid for their labor. Enlisted men received roughly 80 cents a day, and officers received $1.00 per day. Just like in the military, the officers were charged for food, clothing, and laundry.[163] The money was placed in a US Treasury Trust Fund, and distributed in the form of coupons that could be redeemed at the camp canteen. POW camps were required by the Geneva Convention to operate a canteen where POWs could purchase item such as cigarettes, candy, soft drinks, crackers, toothpaste, shoe polish, handkerchiefs, and local produce.[164] "I didn't smoke back then, so I bought cigarettes to use as poker chips when we played card games like *Hanafuda*," said Akikusa.

In regards to the canteen system, Ishii wrote that he felt that while his countrymen back home were suffering under strict rationing, POWs could buy almost anything they wanted from the canteen with the money they "earned." He said a bar of Lux soap cost 4 cents, and a pack of cigarettes was 9 cents. Ishii wrote, "There was a friendly camp guard named George who used to joke saying, 'I can't wait for you boys to leave so I can get out of the Army and go home, too.'"

About a month after Akikusa left Hawaii, Ensign Satoru Ōmagari was sent to the Port of Seattle, Washington. "When I stepped off the ship I thought I was in the middle of a giant automobile factory. There were so many cars!" said Ōmagari. He and other officers were put on a train bound for Oakland California, which is where he learned of Japan's capitulation. At one of the stops, three black soldiers boarded Ōmagari's railway car holding up a newspaper with the bold headline, "JAPS SURRENDER." The men danced and mocked the POWs. Ōmagari knew it was an inevitable, but wished he could have learned of it in a more dignified manner. The date was August 15, 1945, exactly one year after Ōmagari first set foot on Iwo Jima. It seemed like an eternity had passed.

Later that day, he arrived in Oakland where MPs and a Nisei interpreter escorted the POWs to trucks that took them to a wharf. The POWs took a ferry and headed north passing under the Oakland Bay Bridge, past Treasure Island and Alcatraz to Angel Island POW Processing Center. It was on the ferry that Ōmagari experienced the wonder of the Golden Gate Bridge. Ōmagari said, "Its enormous size and graceful design were strikingly beautiful;" for a moment he forgot about the war.

The ferry passed a white hospital ship anchored near the bridge; it had crosses painted on all sides. The Nisei soldier said, "That's one of your disguised military ships. We captured it transporting troops and ammunition to the Philippines. What kind of cowardly nation does this?" The Nisei said that his parents taught him that Japan followed the *Bushidō* code of honor. "But my parents were wrong," he said. Unable to respond, Ōmagari's face flushed hot with shame.

One such wolf in sheep's clothing was *Tachibana Maru*, captured August 2, 1945, by destroyers USS *Conner* (DD-582) and USS *Charrette* (DD-581) in the Banda Sea, north of Timor. It was carrying 1,500 healthy troops from the 11th Infantry Regiment who were disguised as medical patients. The ship had left the New Guinea area bound for Singapore loaded with crates marked "medical supplies" containing rifles and machine guns, mortars, and ammunition. The entire incident was caught on film.[165] Among other things, the footage shows US sailors opening wooden crates marked with red crosses and pulling out helmets, leather belts with ammunition pouches, rifles and light machine guns. The cameraman caught stacks of bundled rifles, 75 mm artillery shells, and "patients" dressed in hospital robes marked with red crosses on their sleeves. Yuji Nishihama was one of the soldiers that were captured on this ship. He described how the Japanese created false medical records for the troops, and confirmed that they packed their gear in wooden crates marked with crosses. The soldiers were told the ship would be scuttled if it were hailed by an Allied vessel. Nishihama attributed his survival of the war to this event.[166] The taking of the *Tachibana Maru* marked the largest single capture of Japanese troops during the war.*

After leaving Angel Island, Ōmagari's group of POWs took a train to Texas. Tunnel engineer Kiichi Abe was placed in a POW camp south of San Antonio called Camp Kenedy (Kenedy Alien Detention Camp), which experimented in the re-education of pro-democratic Japanese POWs. "We were treated well and had plenty of good food to eat," Kiichi Abe said. He added, "After the war, the Americans offered us the chance to stay in Texas and apply for US citizenship. Some of us considered it because we were ashamed to return to Japan." Abe didn't say if anyone took advantage of the offer.

Another POW who was housed at Camp Kenedy was an army reservist corporal named Toshiharu Takahashi, an older man who had been with the Independent Combat Engineers, 1st Mixed Brigade, on Iwo Jima. Takahashi had completed two tours of duty when he was recalled and sent to Iwo Jima, leaving behind a wife and daughter. He was wounded and captured on March 18, 1945, following Kuribayashi's banzai attack. Takahashi said he met Ensign Kazuo Sakamaki, the two-man "midget sub" commander who was captured during the Pearl Harbor raid. Ensign Sakamaki was the very first POW (from any country) taken during the Pacific War.[167]

Still another POW who found himself in southern Texas was radioman Sergeant Shōichi Kawai, the man who was tasked with sending false radio messages from LtGen Kuribayashi's HQ bunker. He said he arrived at Camp Kenedy on July 30, 1945. Kawai learned about the end of the war at a special assembly. The following day, the Americans began playing Japanese folk songs over the loudspeakers. The highest-ranking POW, Captain Moriji Yamaga, gave an encouraging speech about returning to Japan to rebuild their homeland. The music and speech were coordinated by camp officials to discourage suicides. Captain Yamaga was chief of the 4th Weather Observation Section, 4th Fleet, stationed at Truk Lagoon. The 4th Weather Observation Section was transferred to Guam in April 1944, because Truk Lagoon was considered too dangerous due to US Naval air attacks. Captain Yamaga and a few of his technicians were

---

* As a historical sidenote, in September 1942, *Tachibana Maru* carried 265 POWs (civilian employees of the Morrison-Knudson construction company) from Wake Island to Yokohama.

captured on Guam on September 2, 1944. Ironically, Truk Lagoon was never invaded, and had Captain Yamaga remained there he would have been able to continue his work.

Sergeant Kawai wrote that in addition to POW #1, he also met Commander Kanjirō Ono who was Vice-Admiral Chūichi Nagumo's communications staff officer of 1st Mobile Force (*Dai ichi Kidōbutai*). Commander Ono was aboard the aircraft carrier *Akagi* when it was sunk at Midway. Sergeant Kawai also claimed that there were three staff officers that held the rank of either Lieutenant Commander or Commander, and thirty officers with the rank of Lieutenant or Lieutenant (jg). In addition to the thirty-five or so officers, there were 140 – 150 non-commissioned officers in the camp when Sergeant Kawai was held there. It seems that the Americans concentrated their high ranking Japanese POWs at Camp Kenedy.

After passing through Texas, Ensign Satoru Ōmagari's journey continued on to Pine Grove Furnace POW Camp in Pennsylvania.[168] Ōmagari spoke little about this camp and seems to have been there for a short while before being driven to Fort Eustis POW Camp on a bus with blacked-out windows. According to Ōmagari, when they got off the bus, the exhausted Japanese fell onto the grassy lawn like cats in a sun puddle. Ōmagari heard manly voices singing and looked up to see a row of German POWs behind a wire fence clad in dark uniforms with the letters PW on the sleeves, back, and pant legs.[169] "The Germans knew we were coming and serenaded us in an act of friendship. The Germans tossed things through the wire fence: bars of soap, toothbrushes, and cigarettes." Ōmagari watched his countrymen scramble for the items like kids under a broken piñata, and recalled the looks of disdain from the Germans.[170]

Fort Eustis was home to an experiment set up by the Special Projects Division of the US Army's Provost Marshal General. The Americans gathered German POWs who displayed anti-fascist views to undergo a re-education process before being repatriated. The goal was to seed post-war Germany with "pro-Democracy" Germans.

While these re-educational activities were offered to the Germans at Fort Eustis, they were not offered to the Japanese. However, there was a re-education program for the Japanese POWs held in Texas at Camps Huntsville, Kenedy, and Hearne.

According to Professor of History Arnold Krammer of Texas A & M

University,

"The program was directed by Lt. Colonel Boude C. Moore, born in Japan to missionary parents, educated in the United States, and resident of Japan from 1924 until 1941. He was assisted by Dr. Charles W. Hepner, a luminary from the Far Eastern Branch of the Office of War Information, who had spent some thirty years in Japan. Together they organized a dazzling program of lectures by the faculty of Sam Houston State Teachers College, with simultaneous translation into Japanese; study of the English language and literature; comparisons of American and Japanese newspapers, books, and magazines; and the translation of material for distribution to the Japanese prisoners not participating in the program. The most important activity was the assignment every two weeks of a new "study topic" which required group and individual research and discussion. The topics ranged from an assessment of Japan's civilian and military morale to the comparison of various segments of Japanese and American ways of life. Moore and Hepner hoped that these exercises would cause the prisoners to consider the nuances of the subjects and require some measure of democratic input by all members. They also believe[d] that the reports would serve as a barometer of the POWs' morale and allegiance to the Emperor. Augmenting these pursuits was a heavy dose of American music, newspapers, movies and cartoons, and such recreational activities as softball, table tennis, and baseball. The prisoners were also encouraged to attend Sunday religious services in an effort 'to replace their traditional Emperor-worship with a more positive philosophy, and to show them the close relationship between democracy and Christian principles.' When the program ended in December 1945 .... the authorities believed that a significant, if unknown, number of the prisoners had embraced the principles of the American dream. Unfortunately, no follow-up investigation traced the careers of the Japanese "graduates" and their impact, if any, on postwar politics."[171]

Satoru Ōmagari recalled that only eight of the 120 – 130 Japanese servicemen that were confined at Fort Eustis POW camp were officers. Japanese officers had separate quarters and didn't associate with the enlisted ranks, not even in the mess hall.

Soon after arriving at Fort Eustis, a guard handed Satoru Ōmagari a mop and bucket and escorted him to one of the German officers' barracks. He was met with icy stares as he quietly put down his tin bucket and dipped the mop into the water. Ōmagari looked around and noted stacks of books on the shelves. A German startled him by shouting and kicking over the bucket. The man pointed to the door. The message was clear, *you are an officer, and are not to clean anyone's barracks.* Ōmagari gathered up his things and quickly left.

Ōmagari said he learned that the American Red Cross had donated German-language books and other materials to the former Nazis who gathered in groups to study law, medicine, art, architecture and other lofty subjects. Ōmagari said, "The Germans studied while the happy-go-lucky Italian POWs played soccer all day. We Japanese frittered away our time gambling for cigarettes playing *go*, *hanafuda* and mahjong."* Looking back at the way the different groups used their free time, Ōmagari said, "We were like country bumpkins. We should have done more to educate ourselves like the Germans were doing."

One of Akikusa's first impressions of Fort Eustis POW Camp was of the American guard in charge of his enlisted barracks. He was shorter and much older than the other guards so Akikusa secretly nicknamed him "Gramps." The day after the Japanese POWs arrived, Gramps instructed the enlisted POWs to form into teams of three for work party assignments. He assigned Akikusa and two other men to the mess hall for KP (Kitchen Police) duty. The three Axis nations' POW barracks were segregated, but shared at least one mess hall and laundry duties. Akikusa said KP duty was shared by all three Axis nations with a German cook in charge; "Hans" had been a chef before the war. Hans examined Akikusa's mutilated hand and assigned him to busboy duty in the dining hall. The other two Japanese went into the kitchen to peel potatoes.

The three Japanese POWs on KP duty arrived at the mess hall early in the morning, and stayed until post-dinner cleanup. The Axis POW groups ate separately; first the Germans, then the Italians, followed by the Japanese.† Akikusa said the Germans and Italians bussed their own tables, and pushed

---

* Similar to the card game rummy, mahjong is a game of skill and calculation with a degree of chance.

† It would seem there were multiple mess halls due to the large number of POWs. Perhaps this particular mess hall was shared with the relatively small number of Japanese.

in their chairs as they left. However, he was unhappy with the behavior of his own countrymen. They left their metal trays out, didn't clean their spills, and left the tables and chairs in disarray.

As the Japanese KP team headed back to the barracks after the third day of work, a disgruntled Hans told them, using gestures, not to come back. Akikusa asked an Italian KP what was wrong, and the man replied in gestures saying, "Hans thinks the Japanese are stupid."

On day four, Akikusa was put on grass-cutting duty. The men on this detail were given small sickles with which to trim the grass. "Some men put their hearts into it, while others hunched over and mindlessly hacked at the dirt," Akikusa said.

Two days later, Gramps called Akikusa into his office saying that Hans had submitted a request for only one Japanese POW to work in the mess hall. Gramps asked Akikusa if he could handle it. The following morning, Akikusa reported to Hans to prove that Japanese were indeed not "stupid."

One day, Hans was in a good mood, and asked the KP crew if they had any special requests for a special meal. Akikusa replied that he would enjoy some Japanese-style curry rice. However, he felt Hans couldn't possibly know how to make it, or acquire the necessary ingredients, so quickly felt bad for even mentioning it.

One evening after Akikusa's shift in the mess hall, Hans called him back into the kitchen. The stoic German grinned as he presented him with a plate of curry rice. Tears filled Akikusa's eyes as he blurted out a stream of "thank you's" in Japanese, German, Italian and English. *How did Hans do it? It tasted just like what Mother used to make.* Tears of joy rolled down Akikusa's cheeks as he ate the nostalgic delicacy that he had not tasted in almost two years.

As the KP crew enjoyed the rare treat, an Italian man asked Akikusa if he had seen the latest American movies. Akikusa stated he had not seen *any* movies since coming to Fort Eustis. The surprised Italian said that the Americans would provide the Japanese with a projector and movies if they merely requested them. Akikusa later spoke with a senior Japanese POW who talked to Gramps about the issue. Soon, the Americans agreed to allow a one-time "movie night." The Japanese requested that event be held on Sunday afternoon. The Americans provided two films, a 16 mm projector and a German POW to operate it. The camp movie theater was unavailable, so the Japanese created one in the barracks by standing the beds and tables up against the walls and hanging a bed sheet.*

"The films were in English but we got the gist," Akikusa said. He recalled seeing John Ford's *Stagecoach*, followed by a newsreel featuring the Pacific War. One by one, the Japanese audience began to utter complaints as they watched Japanese aircraft go down in flames. The disgruntled catcalls grew louder as images of Japanese corpses filled the screen. The second movie was *Tarzan*, which the men enjoyed. After the double feature, Gramps turned on the lights and announced through a Nisei interpreter that since they had behaved, they could have another movie night the following weekend. The POWs applauded the welcome news.

The following Sunday, Gramps kept his promise. Akikusa can't remember what two films they saw, but the newsreel showed the battles for Guam, Saipan and the bombing of Tōkyō. On the third movie night, the opening film was *Dracula*. The newsreel that played before the second feature included scenes from the battles of Iwo Jima, Okinawa, air raids over Japan, and the September 2nd surrender ceremony aboard the battleship USS *Missouri*. Akikusa was reminded of the deaths of Kageyama and Kumakura and became depressed. Akikusa now understood why the Italians wanted the Japanese to see this footage for themselves; images don't lie. After the newsreel, the German projectionist set up the second movie, which was a shoot-em-up gangster film.

Akikusa recalled seeing several movies: Charlie Chaplain's *The Gold Rush*; a Buster Keaton silent comedy; an action film starring Tyrone Powers; and a western movie featuring John Wayne. The most memorable film he saw was *Gone with the Wind*. Akikusa still enjoys watching old American movies and is a fan of John Wayne.

Although there was no popcorn served during the films, the Japanese did enjoy something that their comrades back in Japan could never dream of. Satoru Ōmagari said, "We had cake for dessert at lunch and dinner. But against Japanese (and US) military regulations, the greedy types would sneak pieces of cake into their barracks. The guards repeatedly told them to eat only in the mess hall, but they didn't listen. Finally, the Americans had no choice but to

---

* Presumably the camp theater was in constant use in the re-education of German POWs.

cancel dessert for everyone. That was a big disappointment."

The hoarding mentality extended even into the laundry system. Germans, Italians and Japanese POWs shared the laundry duty. In addition to the roughly 130 Japanese POWs, Ōmagari estimated there were 3,000 Germans and 1,000 Italians at the camp, which meant a mountain of laundry each week. Ōmagari said, "For some reason, the Japanese were able to get far more than our fair share of socks and underwear. The Americans told us not to take more than three pair of underwear per man per week. But, no matter how many times the guards scolded us it didn't matter," said Ōmagari.

When asked if he or anyone at Fort Eustis POW camp attempted to escape, both Akikusa and Ōmagari said they had not heard of any escape attempts or even of plans to escape.

As the leaves began to change color in Virginia, Akikusa watched the German and Italian POWs depart for their home countries. Akikusa knew that his time would come soon. During their time as POWs, although provided ample opportunity and the means, neither Ōmagari nor Akikusa wrote home to their families. They worried how they would be received when they returned. They wondered if they would be ostracized.

Shūji Ishii said that shortly before the Japanese were repatriated, a new POW arrived; "a Japanese Army major by the name of Yoshida who claimed to have been an information officer on Saipan." Shūji Ishii wrote, in his book published in 1946, that the POWs treated Major Yoshida with respect since he was the senior ranking man in the camp. However, it wasn't long before rumors began to circulate that Yoshida was not who he claimed to be. A couple of the enlisted POWs recognized him as Lieutenant Colonel Takashi Hirakushi, former Chief-of-Staff of the 43rd Division on Saipan. Colonel Hirakushi maintained the charade until after the war. He went on to write several books and articles about his experiences on Saipan, which included witnessing the ritual suicides of Major General Keiji Igeta, Lieutenant General Yoshitsugu Saitō, and Vice-Admiral Chūichi Nagumo on the night of July 6, 1944.[172] Colonel Hirakushi was captured the following day after the July 7th banzai attack.[173]

Homeward Bound and Beyond

On December 13, 1945, the former POWs walked over snow-dusted ground to board trucks headed to Washington D.C. where they would catch a train to Seattle, Washington. Unlike the POWs in Texas, who were given the chance to stay in the USA, Ōmagari said the offer was not extended to the Japanese held at Fort Eustis, Virginia.

At the same time that hundreds of Japanese former POWs were transiting to the West Coast for repatriation, the Japanese Government was sending official death notices to grieving families. Ōmagari and Akikusa both said their parents received notices that their sons died honorably on March 17, 1945. This was the day that was recognized as Iwo Jima's official final day, and the blanket date of death for all of Iwo Jima's defenders.

On December 16, 1945, beneath a typically overcast Seattle sky, Satoru Ōmagari, Tsuruji Akikusa, Shūji Ishii, Haruji Mita, and Kiichi Abe were five of the 200 or so former POWs that boarded a US naval transport vessel for Japan.*

Ōmagari said, "There was a storm that hit the Aleutian Islands that delayed our return by about a week. During the voyage we ate the same food as the ship's crew and our MP guards; steaks, stew, fresh bread and lots of cake. We had coffee, juice and cola, too."

The former POWs arrived at the port of Uraga at Yokosuka late on the night of January 7, 1946.† It happened to be Akikusa's nineteenth birthday. The Naval port of Yokosuka was full of American warships and transport vessels. There were American MPs, SPs (Shore Patrol) and servicemen everywhere. The former POWs would spend one last night on the ship before disembarking. The following morning during roll call, one of the POWs was missing. An inspection revealed he had jumped to his death from an upper deck. The tunnel engineer Kiichi Abe said, "He was my friend. I think he was too ashamed to face his family."[174]

The former POWs went through a US Army inspection process for contraband items, and then were examined at the Japanese Naval Hospital. The POWs took a walk down to the Army's Yokosuka Coastal Artillery Battery

---

* Shoichi Kawai stated that his POW ship pulled into the port of Uraga at 10:00 a.m., on January 4, 1945. It is possible that Kawai left Seattle a few days prior to the others who stated they arrived on January 7, 1945.

† Historical Note: On July 8, 1853, Commodore Matthew Perry's ships arrived at this same area with the goal of opening Japan to trade.

where the Japanese Government's Department of Returning Veterans (*Fukuin Kyoku*) had set up shop to assist citizens and veterans returning from POW camps and far-flung islands across the Pacific. The *Fukuin Kyoku* issued new uniforms to the veterans from stocks of war surplus.

During the demobilization process, Ōmagari and Akikusa both learned that on May 1, 1945, they had been given a "posthumous" promotion. Ōmagari was now a Lieutenant junior grade, and Akikusa held the rank of Petty Officer 2nd Class. It didn't seem to matter to Akikusa, other than he was issued a petty officer cap instead of a sailor's cap. Although many of the men had been promoted, they didn't receive rank insignia because the Japanese military was legally defunct.

Akikusa received 500 yen in cash (not a small sum of money in postwar Japan), and a small booklet that identified him as a "returnee" with free train travel privileges.

Kiichi Abe was also grateful to receive such a handsome sum of money, but said that the port of Uraga was full of displaced people and beggars, and that the shops were barren. Prices were outrageously high and he quickly feared running out of money. Kiichi Abe wondered if he shouldn't have stayed in southern Texas where food was plentiful.

Even after reaching Uraga, neither Tsuruji Akikusa nor Satoru Ōmagari contacted their families with the news of their arrival. They wanted to tell them in person.

After completing his discharge paperwork, Akikusa walked down to a certain photo studio in Kurihama to pose for a commemorative photo in his newly issued petty officer uniform. It was the same photo studio where he took his first portrait in his sailor uniform in 1943.

He then visited the *geshuku* (Sunday home) where he and his comrades had spent many a pleasant afternoon during their training. The family was surprised and happy to see that he had returned safely.

Akikusa wanted to tell his parents in person but his plan was foiled when he bumped into someone from his hometown in Kurihama. His dramatic return was blown.

To his relief, Akikusa's parents were waiting to greet him when he walked down the gravel path to the family home in Yabegawa. His parents had heard that he had been spotted, but were afraid to believe it could really be true.

They hadn't told anyone in case it had been a mistake. His mother cried as she touched her son's arms and shoulders. His father told him to rush to Yabegawa Elementary School because the town was holding a joint funeral for the village war dead that very day.

Akikusa jogged and walked the four miles to the school. As he approached the gymnasium, he could tell that the air was thick with funeral incense. He quietly stepped in to see most of the townspeople kneeling on the floor waiting for the ceremony to begin. Akikusa's black framed portrait rested on a table behind a box wrapped in white cloth along with a dozen other estuary boxes and photos of dead soldiers and sailors. Akikusa recognized most of the faces of the dead men. He bowed, removed his photo and box, and retreated to the back of the room. "I attended my own funeral service," he said.

That evening, his parents told him about the psychic's vision of seeing him hiding underground. "There are many mysteries in life that defy explanation," said Akikusa.

After arriving in Uraga, Satoru Ōmagari traveled all day to reach his mother's home in Fukushima. He arrived after midnight on January 9, 1946. He tried to open the front sliding door but it was locked, so he knocked softly. After a few moments, his mother cautiously appeared with a candle. She slid open the door just enough to see Ōmagari in his uniform and thought she was seeing her son's ghost.

Once inside his home, Ōmagari saw a black-framed photo of himself inside the family Buddhist *butsudan* altar. Due to the official death notification from the Japanese Government, the family had already conducted his funeral service.

Tsuruji Akikusa married his childhood sweetheart Ayako in his parents' home on Christmas Day, 1946. Like millions of other Japanese, the couple struggled to make ends meet in postwar Japan. Akikusa's injuries to his hand hampered his ability to work and required several operations over the next three years. In September 1948, he was able to get a job with Tōbu Tetsudō Railways working 18-hour shifts as an apprentice. He later transferred to the company's Electrical Division in 1960. He retired in 1982, and started his own business as an electrician under the auspices of the Tōkyō Electricity Management Engineer Association. Akikusa still works as a part-time electrician, and manages properties that his decades of hard work have permitted him to acquire.

Akikusa and his wife were blessed with two daughters; Sanae and Yoshiko, but have tragically outlived both of them. Their only son, Shigeyuki, gave them a grandchild.

Akikusa has avoided veteran associations because they tend to glorify the war. He was unable to talk about Iwo Jima war for decades, and never shared his experiences with his parents. Immediately after the war, he began a journal that grew into dozens of notebooks. The writing helped him deal with the horrible memories that haunted him. "We Japanese did horrible things to each other on Iwo Jima," he said.

Some Iwo Jima survivors have contacted the families of their fallen friends. Often times, they were met with angry comments, "How were you able to come back when my husband (brother, father, uncle) didn't? How is it that you are still alive?" Others would ask if the returnees knew how their loved one died. Most of the survivors only knew the men in their own bunker so were unable to provide answers. One returnee tried to pay his respects at the grave of his battalion commander but was turned away by the dead man's family.[175]

When asked if he had seen Clint Eastwood movies *Flags of our Fathers* and *Letters from Iwo Jima*, Akikusa said, "I deeply appreciate director Eastwood's depiction of the battle. Until his movies came out, Iwo Jima was passing into oblivion in Japan. Iwo might have been a heroic battle for you Americans, but it was a crushing defeat to us. We survivors didn't talk about it. These movies brought Iwo Jima back into the public eye and a new generation started talking about our sacrifices. The positive effects of Mr. Eastwood's movies are far reaching. Maybe more than he could ever imagine. I would like him to read my story someday. I would like to thank him in person."

In appreciation for addressing the Japanese side of the battle, the Emperor of Japan awarded Clint Eastwood the Order of the Rising Sun Gold Rays with Neck Ribbon, (aka Rising Sun 3rd Class) at the Japanese Consul General in Los Angeles on July 22, 2009.

Satoru Ōmagari, like millions of other Japanese, struggled to find work in a land that was devastated by war. Eventually, a friend employed him as a magazine reporter. Following this, Ōmagari worked at a small publishing company where he met and fell in love with Tokiko Onoda, a woman ten years his junior. Tokiko was a well-heeled graduate from Japan Women's University. They got married in 1952, and were blessed with a daughter that they named Yoko. In 1955, Ōmagari took at job in Tōkyō as a sales rep for "*Matsuura Koatsu Kikaisakusho,*" a chemical fertilizer company that did business with large conglomerates such as Mitsubishi, Nissan and Sumitomo. Ōmagari's wife Tokiko took a job as a middle school language teacher. She passed away in 1980. Ōmagari retired in 1992 and resides with his daughter Yoko.

Ōmagari used to meet with former Iwo Jima POWs, and was an early member of the Iwo Jima Association that was founded by Tsunezō Wachi. However, Ōmagari parted ways with the group in the 1970's over a dispute regarding the recovery of the mortal remains of the Iwo Jima's dead. Wachi sought to recover, cremate, and bring the remains back to Tōkyō. Ōmagari strongly opposed the idea saying, "Iwo Jima is part of Japan, it is not a foreign country. We defenders said if we died we would become the soil of Iwo Jima." Ōmagari felt it would go against the dead men's wishes to be exhumed from their battle stations. Ōmagari said that visiting Iwo Jima to chant Buddhist mantras and lay flowers is one thing, but taking the dead off the island was wrong. Ōmagari has no desire to ever set foot on Iwo Jima, "Why in the world would I want to dredge up those horrible experiences?" he said. Ōmagari used to go on day trips to hot springs with a handful of other former POWs, but Father Time put an end to those days.

When asked if he had seen Clint Eastwood's pair of movies about Iwo Jima, Ōmagari said that he deeply appreciated Mr. Eastwood's praiseworthy efforts to portray the battle from both sides. He said, "No movie studio would permit a director to portray the actual realities of war. Audiences would be repulsed and walk out. Any film that showed what it was really like in any war would be a financial disaster. It is in the nature of the entertainment industry to make war seem glorious and honorable, but I experienced nothing honorable on Iwo Jima."

Shinjirō Nishi "We were doing our patriotic duty as red-blooded Japanese citizens. We thought we were protecting our homeland." His mother, Hata Nishi, was killed in a B-29 bombing raid on April 12, 1945. Nishi blames her death on the Japanese political and military leaders who started the war. Following the war, Shinjirō Nishi's famous uncle, former Vice-Minister of Foreign Affairs Haruhiko Nishi, acted as defense counsel for accused A-Class war criminal Foreign Minister Shigenori Tōgō. Although Tōgō escaped the hangman's noose, he died in 1950 after serving only a portion of his twenty-year sentence. Haruhiko Nishi later served as the Japanese Ambassador to Australia and then to England.

During the postwar occupation, Nishi got a job doing KP duty for a US Army engineering battalion that was headquartered on the 6th floor of a department store in Tōkyō called "Isetan." The concrete building was one of just a few in Shinjuku that was still standing after the B-29 fire bombings left the city in ashes.

In 1970, Shinjirō Nishi spent six months studying English at Georgetown University in Washington D.C. He said, "I was the oldest student on campus, older than some of the faculty members, too." He enjoyed touring the area's museums, monuments, and magnificent public buildings. He said, "Through my interactions with American soldiers, and later with students at Georgetown, I learned that Americans are wonderful people."

Nishi came to Guam in 2012, where the author introduced him to some former US Marines who participated in the battles of Guam and Iwo Jima. The governor of Guam, the Honorable Eddie Baza Calvo, presented the Marines, as well as Mr. Nishi, with peace medals during a special ceremony the night before the old Marines flew to Iwo Jima for the Reunion of Honor ceremony with the Japanese.

To make sure that future generations learn the truth about the horrors of war, and thus the importance of peace, Shinjirō Nishi speaks to Japanese civic groups and Japanese Self Defense Force units about his wartime experiences. Nishi wants to visit Iwo Jima someday to say prayers for his friend Hirō Hachiya. "The Japanese Government says I'm too old to visit Iwo Jima so I couldn't fly to Iwo Jima with the American veterans in 2012," he said. He is alive and well as of February 2014 when the author visited him in Kagoshima.

Iwao Yamada "We lost too many intelligent young men in that war. I'm sure it was the same for the Americans. We must never allow our government or military leaders to drag us into another war, especially with people who have proven themselves to be such good friends." Mr. Iwao Yamada went on to own an elevator installation and maintenance company that his grandson now runs. Yamada's experiences on Iwo Jima were depicted in a Japanese docudrama "*Iō Jima Senjō Yūbin no Haitatsu*" (Delivering Mail to the Battlefield on Iwo Jima). Mr. Yamada is alive and well.

Teruko Abe sent letters to her husband during the war using the military address code for his unit (similar to an APO address). She received a postcard from him in September 1944. In it, her husband asked if she was getting enough baby formula, and if there was sufficient coal to heat their home. In October 1944, Corporal Abe replied to another letter containing a photo of their second daughter Michiko, who was born after he deployed. Teruko Abe's next letter to her husband was returned stamped "undeliverable."

With the surrender announcement on August 15th, Mrs. Teruko Abe, and her two daughters Yoshiko and Michiko, became refugees in northern Korea. The Russians arrived, causing widespread fears of mistreatment among the Japanese civilians who had called Korea home. Teruko Abe made her way south to Pusan to escape the Russians' well-earned reputation for cruelty. At Pusan, there were Japanese soldiers and civilians waiting for repatriation. The Americans landed in Korea in early September 1945, and quickly worked to stabilize a line between North and South at the 38th Parallel. The Koreans wanted the former Japanese occupiers out of their country, and luckily for Teruko Abe, the US government provided US and captured Japanese ships to transport them home.

Teruko Abe was born and raised in Korea, so Japan was a foreign country to her. She decided to make her way to her husband's parents' home in Niigata, the logical place to meet up with him. Perhaps he was already safe and sound, waiting for her and the girls to arrive. When she arrived in December, she received the worst news possible. Her husband had been declared dead by the Japanese Government.

Her late husband's family had no room for her and her girls, for they were housing relatives whose homes were destroyed in the B-29 raids. Teruko Abe stayed with her brother Tadashi Kageyama for a brief period. Ironically, her brother served as a Betty bomber crewman with the K704th Naval Air Group and had once delivered a supply of water to Iwo Jima.

Teruko and her two girls moved into a group home for widows of the 20th Heavy Mortar Battalion where she operated a sewing machine to earn a living, and then later worked at a department store. She never remarried and holds no resentment towards the Americans who killed her husband on Iwo Jima, and her brother on Wake Island. "It was the war that destroyed my family. Both sides suffered great losses and unspeakable tragedies," she said. Her nephew, Sachio Kageyama, has visited Iwo Jima dozens of times in search of the remains of the war dead. Mrs. Abe says of her late husband, "We were married less than three years and I have only happy memories of him. He was a good man and a good father."

Teruko Abe makes peace bell amulets for the Americans who visit Iwo Jima to attend the Reunion of Honor ceremony. To date, she has made and handed out over 800 amulets as a symbol of friendship. Mrs. Abe is alive and well.

Tsunezō Wachi, Rose Ogawa-Wachi said of her late father, "After the war, my father dedicated his life to pray for the souls of both the Japanese and Americans who lost their lives on Iwo Jima. He went to America many times and truly liked and respected the American veterans."

After Captain Wachi left Iwo Jima in October 1944, he was assigned to the South Western Fleet Headquarters. He was later involved in organizing the *Shinyō* kamikaze speedboats units located in southern Kyūshū.

At the war's end, Captain Wachi was arrested and held at Sugamo prison in Tōkyō for five months and interrogated. On November 10, 1945, while incarcerated, Wachi submitted a letter to LtCol Richard Hayward, commander of the 1st Battalion, 8th Marine Regiment, requesting permission to return to Iwo Jima. In the letter (his daughter sent the author a photocopy of the original letter) Wachi stated his intention to become a Buddhist priest in order to conduct religious ceremonies on Iwo Jima for the dead.[176]

Wachi testified at the war crimes trials and was eventually released. He quickly entered the Buddhist priesthood and later founded the Iwo Jima Association of Japan (*Iōjima Kyōkai*) with the aim of promoting world peace, and recovering the mortal remains of those who died on Iwo Jima. He visited the US many times seeking to reconcile with his former enemies whom he expressed respect and admiration. Tsunezō Wachi passed away on February 2, 1990.

Epilogue

Sitting on a *tatami* straw mat floor in Tsuruji Akikusa's home, surrounded by piles of WWII documents, the veteran's journals and aging photos, the author asked Akikusa if he had any thoughts that he would like to pass on. This is what he said:

"The United States and Japan are have become good friends. In the end, did my fellow countrymen suffer and die needlessly on Iwo Jima? That is a difficult question. I don't know what to say about that. It is much too sad to think that it might be so.

People speak of a glorious death in battle, but what mother would rather have a telegram announcing her son's death than see his smiling face?

Peace is beautiful and should be guarded and protected. There is no life that is meaningless on this planet. The war taught me the value of life, of everyone's life."

Appendix I: Casualties

US Casualties:
6,775 Killed
19,217 Wounded
2,648 Combat Fatigue
49 Missing in Action (USMC and US Navy)

Source: Report by Lieutenant Colonel Whitman Bartly, Division of Public Affairs, Historical Section, USMC Headquarters Section. The KIA number includes Army personnel attached to the Marines during the initial 36-day phase of the battle but not Army personnel who were engaged in the post-battle mop-up activities.

US Army Casualties during the mopping up phase:
24 Killed (16 from US Army's 147th Infantry Regiment)
54 Wounded
6 Missing in Action (US Army, 147th Regiment)

Source: *Always Ready, The Story of the US 147th Infantry Regiment*, by Tom Mcleod.

Japanese Deaths in Battle and Casualties:

The question of how many Japanese died at Iwo Jima finds no simple answer. In 2004, the Japanese Ministry of Labor, Health and Welfare, *Kosei Rōdō Shō, Shakai Ōenkyoku,* provided the following data to the Iwo Jima Association of Japan. The official Japanese Government numbers indicate the deaths of *military personnel only* in relation to the Iwo Jima area of operations occurring from December 8, 1941, to August 15, 1945. The figures include deaths at sea and of aircraft personnel, but does *not* civilians. The number also does *not* include those who were medically evacuated and may have died. Nor does it include those who were captured.

14,661 Army
7,264 Navy
21,925 Total Military Dead from 12/8/41 - 8/15/45

The following are the military casualties as calculated by the Iwo Jima Association of Japan. The casualty numbers do *not* include men who were medically evacuated prior to the landing (some of whom died in Japanese military hospitals). Those who were medically evacuated would normally be counted as casualties (in the West) but they have fallen off the radar in the official Japanese numbers.

19,900   Military Deaths
 1,033   Military Casualties, (POWs)
20,933   Total does not include civilians, airmen, or sailors lost at sea.

The figure of 20,933 casualties has long been the accepted number. However, in digging deeper, the Iwo Jima Association of Japan later provided the author with figures that *included* civilian deaths and civilian casualties in the battle.

20,129   Military and Civilian Deaths
 1,041   Casualties (Military and Civilian POWs)
21,170   Total number of Military and Civilian Deaths, and POWs

The above number of 21,170 does not include anyone who was evacuated due to wounds or illness. Perhaps we will never know the true number of casualities suffered by the Japanese in the battle.

Appendix II:
Records from the 147th Infantry, US Army

A report dated June 4, 1945 submitted to 1st Battalion Headquarters by First Lieutenant William M. MacArthur lists twenty large caves and installations in the 1st Battalion sector that were engaged and investigated. The report covers activities until May 31, 1945. In the report are five of the cave installations that appear in this book. "TA" means "Target Area" and refers to a grid map used by the US during the war to target and control the island.

No. 1 Yasenbyouin cave – Army Field Hospital – TA 185-A

Was closed by battalion Pioneer Section after equipment had been salvaged by Island Command Salvage detail, principally medical supplies, although a large quantity of ammunition, grenades and rifles, plus swords and pistols was [sic] taken. Many dead bodies reported in burial section of cave. 73 Prisoners – 7 killed.

No. 3 Setsueitai Caves – Construction Battalion Caves – TA 185-K

Caves were closed by Marines, then reopened by Japs, closed again by battalion Pioneer Section. Considerable foodstuffs and water, personal equipment. 10 prisoners – 2 dead in cave, 20 killed in area.

No. 7 Setsueitai Cave – Construction Battalion Cave – TA 202-P

Cave was closed by battalion Pioneer Section when repeated efforts to induce the Japs to surrender failed. Investigation prior to closing resulted in finding of 12 bodies. Further advancement into the cave was prevented by occupants throwing grenades. A large store of provisions was found and reported to the Salvage Officer, Island Command. Six prisoners were taken from the cave and the others were gathered up in nearby hiding places. 53 Prisoners – 8 dead.

No. 9 Nishi Tank Regiment Caves – TA 201-C & D

These caves are now almost entirely under the air strip. Twelve prisoners were taken from various entrances, and six dead were counted in one cave. The caves are not thoroughly investigated because of the clinging smoke and terrific heat within. They were blasted and covered completely with bulldozers. A large quantity of food and personal equipment was recovered. There are believed to be more dead in the caves. 12 Prisoners – 6 dead.

No. 13 *Nanpō* Cave – South Area Air Base Cave – TA 201 – R

Twelve Japs captured near beach disclosed the location of the others. After a week's work, 51 were captured in and near the cave, 1 blew himself up and 19 were killed by burning gasoline. The cave was spoken of as the third largest on the island, and contained 3 AA guns, 2 machine guns, 2 knee mortars, thousands of rounds of ammunition, rifles, grenades, explosives, radios, food, water and a large amount of personal belongings. Most of the material was very badly burned, and the ammunition exploded. 63 prisoners – 20 dead.

A seven page report dated June 6, 1945 by the Office of the S-2, HQ 147th Infantry Regiment describes general cave conditions on Iwo Jima.[177] It also specifically addresses the *Nanpō* bunker complex. The report is titled "Iwo Jima Cave Installations." (Original text)

"An integral part of the Japanese defenses on Iwo Jima consisted of an elaborate system of caves and tunnels, most of which were located in the North, Northeast, and Northwest sectors, where the rugged nature of the terrain facilitated their construction and concealment.

While the existence of these caves had been suspected prior to the operation, no information as to extent and location was available until after D-Day. The effectiveness of the cave system was a means of passive defense is evidenced by the extremely light casualties sustained by the Japanese during 70 days of pre-invasion bombings and naval gunfire, and also by the fact that it was finally necessary to clear and close each individual cave during the operation and the mopping-up operations which followed. Interrogations of prisoners of war indicate that the Japanese went underground early in December 1944, abandoning all surface installations except gun positions.

The Japanese employed the caves to house headquarters installations, radio stations, supply and ammunition dumps, hospitals, engineer depots, warehouses and living quarters, many being located in close proximity to surface defense positions. The most elaborate ones were used as Army or Navy headquarters. Establishment of living quarters appeared to be a secondary consideration, as these were inadequate in most instances, even in the most extensive caves.

Construction of the caves varied widely, ranging from small holes to extensive tunnels with no apparent standard plan being followed. The caves and bunkers were created to fit the requirements of the unit that built them. Some bunkers consisted of the enlargement of natural caves, while others were hewn from the soft volcanic rock by hand. Still, others were lined with reinforced concrete. No timber shoring or reinforcing was observed, as the arched construction in solid rock made it unnecessary. Most caves had more than one entrance, and were effectively closed only after several openings had been blasted. In some instances the enemy was able to dig out one entrance while others were being closed.

The interiors of many caves have never been fully investigated, as the presence of belligerent enemy within necessitated their being closed with explosives to avoid casualties. This report describes those caves which were either cleared of the enemy during mopping-up operations by the 147th Infantry or which were closed by blasting and reopened at a later date. Many additional caves were closed after great difficulty, and lie buried under tons of rock and rubble. Airfield and other construction projects have eliminated traces of numerous caves.

Material for this report was gathered from descriptions and diagrams furnished by Battalion S-2s, A&P platoon leaders, demolition teams and patrol leaders.

d. Nampfou [sic] Cave (South Area Air Base Cave) TA 201-R

In Target Area 201-R... Company D, 147th Infantry completed closing an extensive cave on 17 May 1945 after clearing all enemy therefrom. The complexity of the cave involved is indicated by the attached sketch and the description following:

At the beginning of the operation against the cave, 7 May 1945, the numerous entrances were completely closed with one exception. This one opening had been closed previously by patrols but later reopened sufficiently by the enemy to permit an individual to pass through it.

On 7 May 1945, prisoners of war who had recently been captured claimed that they had come from this cave and stated that there were eighty to one hundred persons still living within. In addition one of them drew a diagram of the cave as shown on inset of sketch attached. During interrogations of these prisoners of war, the following information was ascertained:

Name of Cave: Nampfou [sic]. In English the Prisoners-of-War termed it, the "South Area Air Base Cave."

Number of Personnel Housed: Four hundred in the month of March 1945

Units: Naval Aviation, Marines, and Construction Groups.

Identification of Prisoners:

One 2nd Lt in charge – "Zero Pilot"

One 2nd Lt – Communications Officer.

Four 2nd Lts.

One Warrant Officer

Enlisted Naval Personnel

Commanding Officer: Colonel Inoue of the Japanese Marines.

When the cave was cleared of enemies, it was found to be very complex, more so than the POW sketch indicated. The size of the passages varied from four to five feet to thirteen by six and a half feet. They were probably dug out completely by hand since there were no signs of natural caves. The passages had numerous curves and angular turns. Those connecting tunnels were in the form of wide steps.

The sketch lists the various equipment found upon examination of the cave. It should be noted there was a considerable amount of equipment in the burned parts which were entirely destroyed. Twelve Japanese rifles five pistols, two US caliber .30 carbines, and one US Bar, three model 92 Lewis Type machine guns (7.7mm), one model 96 light machine gun (6.5mm), in addition several sabers, and numerous Japanese personal items were found in an excellent condition at the northern part of the cave.

In working this cave, its nature cause several difficulties. It was decided that there were no available means of destroying the cave or killing the Japanese within, from the outside. Therefore attempts were made to remove the enemy personnel by:

1. Smoking them out, but the extensiveness of the cave and the fact that the Japanese could block the passages by use of blankets and canvas prevented the smoke from infiltrating through the cave.

2. To talk them out, but they could not be persuaded. The officer in command, when later captured, stated that he had believed the talks were propaganda.

3. Shooting them out, but the enemy had guards posted at the entrances, who were capable and did fire on anyone entering.

Consequently, it was decided to force the Japanese out by starting a fire within the cave. Seven hundred gallons of salt water were pumped into entrance #3 followed by one hundred ten gallons of gasoline and fifty-five gallons of oil. The fire started set off a large amount of ammunitions and other equipment nearly located in sketch. As a result if the smoke and heat, twenty-nine Japanese were killed or committed suicide, fifty-four were eventually taken into custody after some difficulty. Two of these afterwards committed suicide."

Appendix III: Mopping Up

The US Army's 147th Infantry Regiment conducted ambushes in hopes of catching Japanese who were stealing supplies and causing problems in the rear areas. As example is presented from a US soldier's handwritten letter, presented in here *exactly* as it was written by the veteran, an infantry 2nd Lieutenant, 1st Battalion.[178]

"Combat Patrol Iwo Jima. A typical combat patrol consisted of a reinforced squad or a whole rifle platoon.

In addition, we would have an aidman [sic] and a radioman using a SCR300 portable transceiver.

The squad would be armed with the M-1 rifles, automatic rifle (BAR) and a flamethrower, as needed.

We would also carry hand grenades, concussion grenade, phosphorous grenades, and illuminating grenades.

If we were lucky, we would have a Nisei-American interpreter; at times we would use the Japanese prisoners of war.

The mission and area of responsibility would be given late the day of the action. There would be a briefing of the patrol; ammunition would be issued and rations and water would be supplied.

No later than 700 hours the patrol would leave the command post area. Extreme care had to be taken all during the route for land mines and booby traps. The squad or platoon would advance in a very diverse way. This added to security, but more importantly, we would look for signs of enemy footprints and any potential cave openings.

Movement was slow primarily because of the rocky terrain. All rocks and rocky formations had sharp edges. All around security was paramount.

By dispersal, it was difficult for the Japanese to hit a patrol member. Once alerted we would go into an attack mode. Fire would be brought on the suspected area. If we would discover the cave we would, first, attempt to have the Japanese to surrender with the assistance of the interpreter. We would give them a time limit of approximately 15 minutes. If it didn't work we would attack it first with the use of a combination of first the concussion grenade and then a fragmentation grenade. If we would receive fire from the cave, then a flamethrower would be used.

The most dangerous part of operation was the physical entering of the cave in order to search for ante rooms or additional openings of the cave….On return from the patrol, the patrol leader would make out his report for battalion S-2 and S-3. Usually the patrol was back by 1630 hours."

Appendix IV: Surrender Leaflet

Original 1945 translation of a Japanese language surrender leaflet printed for the stragglers on Iwo Jima. Title - "To Personnel Remaining in the Battle of Iwo Jima[sic]" Body- "Yesterday, all day and all night, American B-29 Flying Fortresses dropped over 1,800 tons of incendiary bombs on Tōkyō's heavy industry installations. Judging by this, one can see that this war, unlike the Russo-Japanese War and the Sino-Japanese War, is not one that can be kept going on Yamato Damashi (Japanese samurai-style fighting spirit) alone. You men are continuing to fight a losing battle of spirit against machine. Instead of clinging to that first lesson of battle, 'One cannot live and bear the humility of being taken prisoner,' your supreme duty is to live and build a new and better Japan. 154 men have realized this and surrendered, and are living at present under the humane treatment of international law. 93 of your wounded comrades have been moved and are being treated in that white hospital ship you see in the waters off the east coast. Therefore, think before you die like a dog. When you hear someone call to you in Japanese, it is safe. Come out, please." (Special thanks to Tom McLeod)

Appendix V: Japanese Military Ranks

WWII Japanese Navy and Army Ranks

Seaman Second Class (Sea 2/c)	Private (Pvt)
Seaman First Class (Sea 1/c)	Private First Class (PFC)
Senior Seaman (Sr Sea)	Senior Private (SrPvt)
Leading Seaman (Ld Sea)	Lance Corporal (LCrp)
Petty Officer Second Class (PO2/c)	Corporal (Corp)
Petty Officer First Class (PO1/c)	Sergeant (Sgt)
Chief Petty Officer (CPO)	Sergeant Major (SgtMaj)
Warrant Officer (WO)	Warrant Officer (WO)
Ensign (Ens)	Second Lieutenant (2nd Lt)
Lieutenant Junior Grade, (Lt(jg))	First Lieutenant (1st Lt)
Lieutenant (Lt)	Captain (Capt)

Lieutenant Commander (LtCdr) Major (Maj)
Commander (Cdr) Lieutenant Colonel (LtCol)
Captain (Capt) Colonel (Col)
Rear Admiral (RAdm) Major General (MajGen)
Vice Admiral (VAdm) Lieutenant General (LtGen)
Admiral (Adm) General (Gen)

About the Author

In the summer of 1981, Dan King first visited Japan as an exchange student with Youth For Understanding (YFU). Following this life-changing experience, he decided to earn a bachelor's degree in Japanese at California State University Los Angeles. He then moved to Japan where he briefly taught English at the YMCA, and then worked for Toyota Motor Corporation, Inc. King was awarded the Japanese Ministry of Education's (*Monbushō*) top-level written/spoken language certification for non-native speakers.

After moving back to the USA, King put his historical knowledge and language skills to use on several movies and documentaries. His first film job was as the Japanese technical/historical consultant on director John Woo's WWII Saipan-based war film *Windtalkers*. His next major film was director Ed Zwick's *The Last Samurai*, where he spent six months in New Zealand working with Tom Cruise and Ken Watanabe.

King conducted historical research for Clint Eastwood's film *Flags of Our Fathers*. He then worked with actors Pat Morita as an on-set consultant for the movie *Only the Brave*, the true story of Japanese-American heroism in WWII. The author traveled to Wake Island to appear in the Emmy-nominated two-hour documentary *Wake Island, Alamo of the Pacific*. King was the Japanese-language consultant and a Voice-Over artist for the HBO series, *The Pacific*. He appears in the documentary, *Peleliu: The Forgotten Battle, War Stories by Oliver North*. King worked as a Japanese technical / historical / language consultant for a series of popular WWII-based video games by EA Games, including *Pacific Assault* and *Rising Sun*. He appeared on-camera with former Marine and television personality R. Lee Ermey in three episodes of the television series *Mail Call*. King later appeared on-camera in the series *Shootout* on the History Channel. He most recently worked with the US National Parks Service as a historical and language consultant for the Pacific War Museum on Guam. He is also a volunteer translator for the National Museum of the Pacific War in Fredericksburg, Texas.

In 2003, King wrote his first book, *Japanese Military Sake Cups 1894–1945*, (Schiffer Publishing). He released his second book, *The Last Zero Fighter* (Pacific Press), in July, 2012.

For the past twenty-five years, Dan King has studied the Pacific War using a three-pronged approach: studying, traveling, and interviewing. As of July 2014, King has interviewed ninety-seven WWII Japanese Army and Navy veterans.

In addition to studying and interviewing, King has visited dozens of battle sites and war museums overseas: Anguar Island (Palau), Australian Army Memorial (Canberra, Australia), Bataan Peninsula, Bridge over the River Kwai (Thailand), Changi War Museum (Singapore), Chichi Jima, Corregidor, Etajima Naval Academy Museum (Hiroshima), Guadalcanal, Guam, Hickam Air Force Base (Oahu), Haha Jima, Ie Shima, Imperial War Museum (London), Iwo Jima, Kanachanaburi POW Museum (Thailand), Kanoya Air Base (Kyūshū, Japan), Kaneohe Marine Corps Base (Oahu), Kaohsiung (former Tainan Kokūtai Air Base in Taiwan), Korean War Museum (Seoul, South Korea), Midway Atoll, Mitsubishi Heavy Industries Air and Space Museum (Nagoya, Japan), Nagasaki Atomic Bomb Peace Museum, Nanking Massacre Memorial Hall (Nanjing, China), National Army Museum (Waiouru, New Zealand), Okinawa Peace Memorial Museum, French Army Museum *Musée de l'Armée* (Paris, France), Naval Station Pearl Harbor, Peleliu, Rabaul (Papua New Guinea), Republic of China Armed Forces Museum (Taipei, Taiwan), Saipan, Tinian A-bomb airfields, Truk Lagoon, Wake Island, Yap Island, Yokaren Peace Memorial Museum (Tsuchiura, Japan) and Yūshūkan Yasukuni War Museum (Tōkyō).

King is the son of the late Virginia King, who was an avid reader and patriot, and Marvin King whose B-29 was shot down by Russian-piloted Mig-15 fighter jets on April 12, 1951. Marvin King spent 2-1/2 years in a North Korean concentration camp. Although tortured by his horrific experiences, the former POW embraced his Christian faith and chose the path of forgiveness.

The author survived his own brush with death when he was diagnosed with stage IV Non-Hodgkins Lymphoma cancer in December 2005. Initially, an oncologist suggested terminal hospice care, but the stubborn patient refused to even consider it. So began a 2-1/2 year struggle that included chemotherapy, radiation,and a stem cell transplant at UCLA. More than once a doctor told him, "God must be watching out for you."

The author is in full remission and enjoys *bonsai*, traveling, and diving on WWII ships and aircraft wrecks. The author and his wife reside with their squad of rescued cats in Southern California.

End Notes

1 Access to this active Japanese military base is strictly regulated.
2 *Task Force 56 Intelligence Report,* 4.
3 *Kantōgun Jōhō Buchō*
4 The lyrics to Japanese Taps, "*Shinpei san kawaiso da ne, mata nete nakuno ka yo.*" (Sad recruit, are you crying yourself to sleep again tonight?)
5 *Shinpei Shushin Sankōshō, Kaigun Shō Kyoiuku Kyoku, (WWII Ministry of the Navy Education Division manual, 1921).*
6 John Miller, Jr., Guadalcanal: The First Offensive (Washington, D.C., U.S. Dept. of the Army, Historical Division, 1949), p 310-311
7 U.S. Office of the Chief of Military History, "The Provost Marshal's Office: Campaign of the Pacific, 1941-1947," chap. 6, mimeographed manuscript, OCMH, file 1 (C), 8-6.
8 Office of the Chief of Military History, "Administrative History, Chief Provost Marshal, United States Army Forces in the Pacific, 6 April 1945 to 31 December 1946" (mimeographed manuscript, OCMH), p. 14, 8-5. 1.
9 Until November 1942, the Japanese Navy had four ranks for enlisted men. From Seaman 4th, 3rd, 2nd and up to Seaman 1st Class. This was changed in November 1942. The ranks were then called (from low to high) Seaman 2nd Class, Seaman 1st Class, Senior Seaman and Leading Seaman. Akikusa began under the old rank system and transitioned to the revised rank system. The petty officer ranks were changed as well. In the original ranks there were PO 3/c, PO 2/c and PO 1/c. It was revised to PO2/c, PO1/c, and Chief Petty Officer.
10 *Futsūka Denshin Gijitsu Rensei or* 第６４期普通科電信技術練生 (64th Cycle, Basic Electronic Technical Communication Trainee)
11 Mutsuai is located about 1 mile from where the author spent his summer as an exchange student in 1981.
12 *Iwo Jima Imada Gyokusai Sezu,* (Iwo Jima has Not Yet Fallen), by Fuyuko Kamisaka, WAC Bunko, 2006. P. 40
13 Tsunezō Wachi's memoir, *Two Remorse Episodes Behind Bars at Sugamo Tōkyō,* June 1977.
14 *Iwo Jima Imada Gyokusai Sezu,* (Iwo Jima has Not Yet Fallen), by Fuyuko Kamisaka, WAC Bunko, Dec 2006, P. 41
15 Personal correspondence with Capt Wachi's daughter, Rosa Ogawa.
16 父島要塞守備隊 (*Chichi Jima Yōsai Shubi Tai*)
17 http://www2u.biglobe.ne.jp/~surplus/tokushu5.htm (Japanese language WWII research website)
18 Rose Ogawa's translation of Wachi's memoir entitled, *The August Virtue of His Imperial Majesty.*
19 *So Sad to Fall in Battle,* Kumiko Kakehashi, p. 29 (The author met Ms. Kakehashi on the island of Iwo Jima in 2009 after the joint US-Japan Reunion of Honor ceremony.)
20 Japanese documentary interview. It is not clear exactly which unit he was serving under. http://www.youtube.com/watch?v=FyBhjQsX3ew

21 *Iōtō Gyokusai Kaigun Gakutōhei Dōkoku no Kiroku*, by Minoru Tada, Asashi Shimbun Publications, 2008, p. 38
22 Ibid., p. 45
23 Ibid., p. 48
24 Ibid., p. 50
25 Japanese documentary interview, http://www.youtube.com/watch?v=FyBhjQsX3ew
26 *The Last Zero Fighter*, by Dan King, Pacific Press, 2012. P. 171
27 USN Overseas Aircraft Loss List June 1944, http://www.aviationarchaeology.com/src/USN/LLJun44.htm. The American losses over Iwo Jima and Chichi Jima include: F6F-3 Hellcat x 10, Sb2C-1c Helldiver x 5, TBF-1C Avenger x 4, TMB-1C Avenger x 2.
28 *Death in the Afternoon*, by Chris Marks, article, September 2012 issue, WWII History magazine.
29 *Shūra no Tsubasa*, by Lt(jg) Kazuo Tsunoda, p. 308-311, NF Bunk Publishing, 2008.
30 Author's direct translation of Ensign Tada's report as it appeared in: *Iōtō Gyokusai Kaigun Gakutōhei Dōkoku no Kiroku*, by Minoru Tada, Asashi Shinbun Publications, 2008, , p. 95
31 Akikusa believes it took two days to reach Kanoya, he recalled spending the night in a newsstand vendor's hut because the men could find nowhere to sleep.
32 http://www.combinedfleet.com/W-27_t.htm (Sokaitei report)
33 From a Japanese language report supplied by the Iwo Jima Association of Japan, "*Rikugun Butai no Sentō Shiryō*" p-85-87
34 *Chūbu Taiheiyō Rikugun Sakusen 2*, by Bōeichō Kenkyūshō Senshi Shitsu, 1966. (Army Strategy in the Central Pacific No.2, Japanese National Institute for Defense Studies, NDIS)
35 *Nihongun Chūsensha*, Ground Power Magazine, April 2004
36 Reference: *The Cobia's Toughest Battle*, Legge, Larry L. *West Virginia Historical Society Quarterly*, Volume XXI, Number 3: July 2007.
37 Shūji Ishii's firsthand accounts come from his Japanese language book, *Iōjima ni Ikiru*, (To Live on Iwo Jima) first published in 1946, then again in 1982 by Kokushō Kankōkai Corp., Ltd. In order to get a clearer picture of the Iwo Jima experience, the author read Ishii's book in the original Japanese text.
38 Genji Hattori wrote a book in Japanese, *Ah, Iwo Jima,* in which he shared his brother's letters from Iwo Jima.
39 Hattori's family believed that he went to Chichi Jima aboard a light cruiser, but Japanese records show that that Major Matsushita's Independent 10th Anti-Tank Battalion was aboard the converted passenger liner *Noto Maru*. Reference: *Chūbu Taiheiyō Rikugun Sakusen 2*, by Bōeichō Kenkyūshō Senshi Shitsu, 1966. (Army Strategy in the Central Pacific No.2, National Institute for Defense Studies (NDIS), published in 1966) *Noto Maru* was later sunk in Oromoc Bay, Phillippines on November 2, 1944. Source: *Nihon Yusen Senji Senshi*, by *Nihon Yusenji Senshi Hensan I'inkai* (Japanese transport Vessels during Wartime, by the Japanese Vessels During Wartime Editing and Compilation Committee, p.20 and pp. 29-30, published

in 1974.)

40   2nd Lt Yasuhiko Murai's statements come from a series of four articles he wrote for the Iwo Jima Association of Japan's Newsletter, *Kaiso no Iwoto*, in March, April, May and July of 1988. Murai's recollections cover 37 pages and span the time he was selected for Iwo Jima until he was returned to Japan after the war. The articles, in Japanese, were supplied to the author by Tom McLeod, author of *Always Ready, the Story of the US 147th Infantry Regiment*. The author translated the articles and used portions to illustrate and support 1st Lt Hattori's experience.

41   *Iwo Jima Yusen Sakusen to Chichi Jima: Dai 4804 Sendan no Muko Jima oki hogekisen wo megutte*, (Examining the Naval artillery against Transport Convoy No. 4804 at Muko Jima Island, and Iwo Jima transport plans) by Akihiko Kamishino, Tokyo Metropolitan University Institutional Repository. May 2011, p. 37 http://www.repository.lib.tmu.ac.jp/dspace/bitstream/10748/4215/1/20002-34-004.pdf

42   Cpl Torao Miyazaki's son Makoto assembled his father's letters sent from Iwo Jima into a book called *Inochi wa doko ni arimasuka?* (Where is Life?), Bungeisha Publishing, March 2014.

43   The author and GySgt Quay Terry met Colonel David Severance in his home to hear of his firsthand accounts.

44   http://scc.lexum.org/en/1941/1941scr0-230/1941scr0-230.html Website accessed Oct 16, 2012.

45   *Wartime Log of the 11th Raisentai commander, December 1, 1943 thru May 31, 1945*. Japan Center for Historical Asian Records, National Archives of Japan. Reference code:C08030127100 (Japanese language)

46   *Imperial General Navy Headquarters, Combined Fleet (6)*, by Asagumo Shinbunsha, 1971. Page 67, pages 378-379. Army Strategy in the Central Pacific No.2, National Institute for Defense Studies (NDIS),

47   *Wartime history of 4th destroyer Fleet July 1 – July 31, 1944*. JACAR, Ref. C08030145900 (Japanese language)

48   *Ogasawara Retto Iō Jima no Rekishi to Genjō*, by Tatsuya Akano, pdf accessed 10/18/2012 (The history of The Ogasawara Islands and Iwo Jima)

49   *Official Chronology of the US Navy WWII*, by Robert Cressman

50   *Wartime Report of the Chichi Jima Special Base Defense Force*. 父島方面特別根拠地隊戦闘詳報

51   Excerpt from letter from Rosa Ogawa (Wachi's daughter) to Charles Tatum. http://www.marineswwii.com/pdfs/captain_watchi.pdf

52   *Iwo Jima Mada Gyokusai Sezu*, by Fuyuko Kamisaka, p. 49

53   Documentary video, "Return to Iwo Jima" (Homevision Studio released June, 2000)

54   Pacificwrecks.com, American Missions Against Iwo Jima, accessed Oct 27, 2012, July 4, 1944 - February 27, 1945

55   Much of the information on Ichimaru were gathered from the Japanese language reference "Iwo Jima to Baron Nishi," Bijinesusha publishing, 2006, Japan.

56   第３期航空術学生　*Dai Sanki Kōkūjitsu Gakusei* (Third Cycle, Air Technical Trainee)

57   1) *Nanpō Shotō Naval Air Group was a non-flying Otsu (B type) Kōkutai unit*

charged with air base management for Iwo Jima, Chichi Jima and Marcus Island. This Naval Ground Defense unit (Keibitai) was a ground force that manned machine guns, Anti-Aircraft guns, infantry guns and large casemated naval guns.

2) Kantō Naval Air Group (Kisarazu Air Base), a non-flying Otsu (B type) Kōkutai tasked with air base defense in the home islands.

3) 131st Air Group (Katori Air Base), 1 Nakajima C6N "Myrt" Reconn Squadron and 2 Nakajima J1N "Irving" Night Fighter Squarons. In November 1944 the Reconn Squadron was reassigned to the 752nd Bomber Group and both Night fighter squadrons reassigned to the Hokuto Naval Air Group, a non-flying Otsu (B type) unit in Hokkaido.

4) 801st Air Group (Oita Air Base), 2 Squadrons of Type-1 "Betty" Bombers, and 2 Squadrons of Kawanishi Type-2 "Emily" Flying Boats for night reconn missions.

5) 252nd Air Group (Iwo Jima), 3 Squadrons of Zero Fighters dispatched from Atsugi Air Base to Iwo Jima June 1944 for operation A-Go, better known as "The Mariana Turkey Shoot." The survivors including aces such as Saburō Sakai, Kaneyoshi Muto and Isamu Miyazaki were reorganized for use in the Philippines.

6) 752nd Air Group (Iwo Jima, then Kisarazu). 1 Squadron of Type 1 "Betty" Bombers, 1 Squadron of "Irving" and Yokosuka D4Y "Comet" Night fighters, 1 Squadron of Yokosuka P1Y "Frances" attack bombers, and 2 Squadrons of "Myrt" recon aircraft. They were sent to Iwo Jima in June 1944 and decimated in the Mariana Turkey Shoot.

 58 This is a quote from another interview he did for the book, *Eiyu Naki: Iwo Jima Sen Ikinokori Moto Kaigun Chui no Shōgen* by Shinobu Hisayama, Sankei Shinbun, 2008. King's interview with Ōmagari precedes this book by 2 years. Part of King's 2006 interview with Ōmagari seems to have been given to Hisayama by a Japanese film crewman that had taped King's interview.

 59 *Eiyū Naki: Iwo Jima Sen Ikinokori Moto Kaigun Chui no Shogen* by Shinobu Hisayama, Sankei Shinbun, 2008. P. 54-56

 60 Chapter 3 and 4 of *The Last Zero Fighter*, (Pacific Press 2012), by Dan King.

 61 *Shūra no Tsubasa*, by Kazuo Tsunoda, NF Bunko, p. 336 (2008)

 62 *Eiyū Naki: Iwo Jima Sen Ikinokori Moto Kaigun Chui no Shogen* by Satoru Ōmagari and Shinobu Hisayama, Sankei Shinbun, 2008. P. 56-57

 63 Ibid P. 25-56

 64 Major Yoshitaka Horie also refers to contentious nature of such meetings in *The Memoirs of Fighting Spirit, Major Yoshitaka Horie and the Battle of Iwo Jima*, edited and annotated by Robert D. Eldridge and Charles W. Tatum, printed by Naval Institute Press, 2011

 65 *So Sad to Fall in Battle,* by Kumiko Kakehashi, p. 62

 66 *Iwo Jima,* by Richard Newcomb, p. 307

 67 *So Sad to Fall in Battle,* by Kumiko Kakehashi p. 50-60. The author met Ms. Kakehashi on the island of Iwo Jima in 2010. She presented him with a signed copy of her book.

 68 Diary of Ensign Tamotsu Yoshino, 13th Naval Reserve, 1023rd Naval Air Group is referenced several times in *Iōtō Gyokusai Kaigun Gakutōhei Dōkoku no Kiroku*, by Minoru Tada, Asashi Shinbun Publications, 2008, p. 175

 69 Color of the bombs confirmed on p. 39 of report, *Headquarters, Expeditionary*

Troops, Task Force 56, G-2 Report of Intelligence, Iwo Jima Operation, 1 April 1945.

70   From video interview of Teruo Sasamine, NHK *Senso Shogen* (Testimony to War) series.
http://cgi2.nhk.or.jp/shogenarchives/shogen/movie.cgi?das_id=D0001100621_00000

71   Toshio Koshimura's firsthand account, *Iwo Jima no Heitai*, (The Soldiers of Iwo Jima) edited by his daughter Professor Kiyomi Yoshikawa, Published by Asahi Shimbunsha, Dec 2006. Originally published in 1973 as *Iō Jima Shubitai* (Iwo Jima Defense Force) by Gendaishi Shuppan Kaisha.

72   Earthquakes on December 7, 1944, and January 13, 1945, killed 200 civilians in Handa City. From a report, *Damage from December 7 1944 Tokai Earthquake*, by Aichi Prefecture Bosai Kaigi.

73   This was also stated by Seiji Ozawa in *Iwo Jima Haisenki* (The loss of the battle of Iwo Jima), that appeared in the 102 issue of Asakaze.

74   Original Japanese language obtained on April 12, 2013 from Japan Policy Institute Website http://www.seisaku-center.net/modules/wordpress/index.php?p=390

75   Kuribayashi's original "Oath of Combat" in Japanese:
一、我等は全力を奮って本島を守り抜かん。
一、我等は爆薬を擁きて敵の戦車にぶつかりこれを粉砕せん。
一、我等は挺身敵中に斬込み敵を鏖殺せん。
一、我等は一発必中の射撃に依って敵を撃ち斃さん。
一、我等は各自敵十人をたおさざれば死すとも死せず。
一、我等は最後の一人となるも「ゲリラ」によって敵を悩まさん。

76   Information from Mr. Takizawa's website. http://www3.plala.or.jp/takihome/artillery.htm

77   Iwao Yamada was interviewed for a docu-drama about this event called "*Iwo Jima Senjo no Yubin Haitatsu*" 硫黄島〜戦場の郵便配達. It first aired in Japan in December 2006.

78   *The Last Zero Fighter*, by Dan King (Pacific Press, 2012)

79   The shipment of green bamboo poles was confirmed in the separate interview with Iwao Yamada.

80   http://home.earthlink.net/~atdouble/~318thFighterGroup.Saipan.html. Accessed August 12, 2013.

81   All correspondence from PFC Eric Ojerholm provided courtesy of his younger brother David who clearly remembered the day that "the dreaded telegram" arrived to inform the family of Eric's death. Eric and David's father, Eric Ojerholm Sr. was a Marine Corps Major who was recalled during WWII. Twelve years after Eric's death on Iwo Jima, his younger brother David Ojerholm enlisted in the Marines and served as a First Lieutenant from 1958-1961. Ironically, Eric's battalion commander on Iwo Jima, Major John Antonelli, would become David's brigade commander while David was serving at Marine Air Station Kanehoe Bay, Ohau.

82   US Air Force Museum, Dayton Ohio.

83   *Nihon Kaigun no Sensuikan*, (Submarines of the Japanese Navy) by Tatsuya Katsume, Dainippon Kaiga Press, 2010, isbn 978-4-499-23033-9

84   *Iwo Jima Recon The US Navy at War, February 17, 1945* by Dick Camp, The At War Series, 2007.

85   *Iwo Jima Recon The US Navy at War, February 17, 1945* by Dick Camp, The At War Series, p. 109, 2007

86   According to Col Dick Camp's book, *Iwo Jima Recon: The U.S. Navy at War, February 17, 1945*, these UDT frogmen used grease to insulate themselves against the cold.

87   *Iwo Jima Recon The US Navy at War, February 17, 1945* by Dick Camp, The At War Series, p. 74

88   Morrson. Chapter 2, Preliminary Poundings. http://www.ibiblio.org/hyperwar/USN/USN-Ops-XIV/USN-XIV-2.html

89   *Medal of Honor Recipients*, US Army Center of Military History, http://www.history.army.mil/moh/index.html

90   Footage of the spraying of DDT can be seen in the documentary by Scott Freund called, "Iwo Jima."

91   *Iwo Jima Recon The US Navy at War, February 17, 1945* by Dick Camp, The At War Series, 2007

92   *Eiyū Naki Shima* by Satoru Ōmagari and Shinobu Hisayama 2008, Sankei Shinbun Publishing, p. 68 - 69

93   Ibid p. 82-83

94   The author accompanied John McKenzie, and his son Jon, to Iwo Jima in March 2014.

95   *Iwo Jima Legacy of Valor*, by Bill Ross, Vintage Books Random House NY, 1986, p.72

96   *Closing In: Marines in the Seizure of Iwo Jima*, by Colonel Joseph H. Alexander

97   *Ah, Iwo Jima.* The story of Genichi Hattori edited and compiled by his younger brother Genji Hattori, pp.104-110

98   Lawrence Snowden rose to the rank of Lieutenant General. He served in WWII, Korea, Vietnam, and then as Chief of Staff in Japan, and Chief of Staff at Marine Corps Headquarters. He also served in the American business community in Japan. He received awards and commendations from the Government of Japan and even one from the Emperor; the Sacred Treasure 2nd Class. His US military awards and decorations are too many to list here.

99   From the author's conversations with LtGen Lawrence Snowden on Guam and Iwo Jima in March 2010, 2011, 2012, 2013 and 2014.

100   http://www.pbs.org/memorialdayconcert/features/iwo_jima.html#danny

101   Article, *Legend of the Unstoppable Marine Danny Thomas*, by Chris Farlakas, Times Herald Record, May 31, 2004.

102   Corporal Abe's daughter Yoshiko, and PFC Dunn's daughter Kathy Dunn-Painton met for the first time in March 2013 on Iwo Jima during the annual US-Japan Reunion of Honor ceremony. Kathy was wearing the locket her father gave her before he went off to war. They met again on Iwo Jima in March 2014.

103   At one time, the author and Hershel Willams lived in the neighboring counties of Putnam and Cabel, WVa.

104   A record of the event was written by Ensign Masayoshi Nemoto.

105   From Ensign Masayoshi Nemoto's written account.

http://www.aramant.com/chuukou/page04_04.html#anchor

106 *The Japanese Submarine Force and World War II*, by Carl Boyd and Akihito Yoshida, Naval Institute Press, 1995, p. 171-172

107 The author met MajGen Fred Haynes during the 2009 visit to Iwo Jima. Fred Haynes and James Warren co-authored, *The Lions of Iwo Jima*, Henry Holt and Company LLC, 2008.

108 Capt. J.W. Thomason, III, USMCR, "The Fourth Division at Iwo Jima," a manuscript, 21Aug45; 4th MarDiv D-2 Periodic Rpts; 4th MarDiv Preliminary POW Interrogation Rpt No. 5, 27Feb45. These defenses, prepared by the 2nd Mixed Brigade Engineers, were reported by POW's to be the most extensive and powerful on the island.

109 USMC Historical Monograph, Iwo Jima Amphibious Epic, Lt.Col. Whitman S. Bartley, p. 172

110 http://www.ibiblio.org/hyperwar/USMC/USMC-M-IwoJima/USMC-M-IwoJima-8.html

111 Lt(jg) Satoru Ōmagari's experiences first appeared in a Japanese language book, *Iwo Jima Kessen* written by Iwo Jima survivor Army 1st Lt. Kikuzo Musashino, Shigekisha Press, 1952. 1stLt. Musashino was the commander of the 109th Division's 2nd Combat Engineer Company. Musashino drew on firsthand accounts from many of his fellow Iwo Jima POWs including 1stLt Ichiro Kouda and Senior Private Yasuo Kato.

112 Video interview. http://www.youtube.com/watch?v=-BkJmmlOUes

113 Keith Wheeler, *THE ROAD TO TOKYO*, Time-Life Books, 1979, Alexandria, Virginia, p.50

114 Satoru Ōmagari referred to him only as "Naval Pilot, Wing Commander T." In the author's interview with Akikusa, he refused to state Tachikawa's name claiming it would be bad if Tachikawa's family ever read the negative comments about him. After extensive research, the author confirmed through other sources that Tachikawa had been the un-named man referred to as "Naval Pilot, Wing Commander T." It should be noted that Commander Tachikawa doesn't appear to have survived the battle so is unable to present his side of the story regarding the final months of the battle.

115 *Kaigun Kōkutai Shimatsuki, 343Ku Saigō no Yusen*, by Minoru Genda. Bungei Shinju Ltd., Dec 1996 p.313-315. (Written Testament of the Naval Air Groups, The Last Brave Fight of the 343 Air Group)

116 Information gathered from article written by Yasuo Suzuki former Japanese Naval Reconn pilot who was a member of LtCdr Tachikawa's 4th Teisatsu Squadron. It appeared in the Feb. 1977 edition of the *Naniwa Newsletter*. A monthly printed newsletter for former WWII veterans to share their experiences. Discovered on website http://www5f.biglobe.ne.jp/~ma480/senki-1-teisatudai4hikoutai-suzuki1.html

117 Riichi Koyatsu's account of the pilot leaving the bunker to steel a US aircraft, and that of others seeking to make a raft to get off the island dovetail with Akikusa's accounts. They appear in Richard Newcomb's book *Iwo Jima*. The account dovetails with PO3/c Koyatsu account as gathered in an interview with Fred Saito for Newcomb's book in 1964.

118 In the author's 2006 interview with Satoru Ōmagari, the veteran didn't

mention putting the dead man's intestines into a rip in his own pant leg, just his own jacket. The account of the ripped pant leg appears in his 2008 book *Eiyu Naki Shima*. Ōmagari co-authored it with Shinobu Hisayama.

119 Records from the late Lt James Short's daughter Vicki Hawkins who still has her father's sea trunk that is painted with all of his duty stations including: Quanitico Va., Dunedin FL, Camp Elliot Ca., Camp Pendleton Ca., Camp Tarawa T.H. (Territory of Hawaii), Guam, Saipan, Tinian, Kwajalein, Enewitok and Iwo Jima.

120 From an article written by Satoru Ōmagari in 1994 entitled *Watashi no Senjō Taikenki* (My Experiences in Battle) http://www.geocities.jp/sato1922jp/naiti2.htm#taikenki

121 *Iwo Jima Senki*, by Shoichi Kawai, NF Bunko Publishing, Japan 2012, p. 72-74

122 The original message in Japanese: 国の為　重きつとめを　果たし得で　矢弾尽き果て　散るぞ悲しき。仇討たで　野辺には朽ちじ　吾は又　七度生まれて　矛を執らんぞ。醜草の　島に蔓延る　その時に　皇国の行手　一途に思ふ。栗林中将　以上

123 From a report dated March 22, 1945, *Nin Rikugun Taisho, Rikugun Chujo Kuribayashi Tadamichi*, (Acting General, LtGeneral Tadamichi Kuribayashi) by General Hajime Sugiyama and General Kuniaki Koiso. Japan Center for Historical Asian Records, National Archives of Japan. Code Reference A03023553200

124 http://www.jacklummus.com/Files/Files_A/awarding_the_congressional_medal_of_honor.htm

125 http://www.ibiblio.org/hyperwar/USMC/USMC-M-IwoJima/USMC-M-IwoJima-II.html

126 Naval History & Herirage Comamand, 9th Naval Construction Brigade, Historical Information, pdf accessed August 28, 2013. http://www.history.navy.mil/museums/seabee/UnitListPages/Brigades-WWII/09%20NCBr.pdf

127 This story was not told to the author in 2006, but appears in a 2008 interview done for Shinobu Hisayama's book, *Eiyu Naki no Shima*, (An Island Without Honor) p. 153

128 Japanese TV documentary about Iwo Jima that is available on youtube. http://www.youtube.com/watch?v=2VQKN_6DEXc&feature=endscreen&NR=1

129 Documentary video, "Return to Iwo Jima" (Homevision Studio released June, 2000)

130 The phrase "Duty is heavier than a mountain, Life is lighter than a feather" has a deeper meaning in the original. The word "mountain" actually refers to "Taizan" or Mount Tai in China. It is foremost of China's "Great Five Sacred Mountains." It is associated with sunrise, birth, and renewal. Mount Tai has been a place of worship for at least 3,000 years and served as one of the most important ceremonial centers of China during large portions of this period. The actual expression of duty is heavier than Mt. Taizan comes from a Chinese philosopher known in Japan as "Shibasen." His name in Chinese is Sima Qian (ca. 145 or 135 BC – 86 BC).

131 Documentary video, *Return to Iwo Jima* (Homevision Studio released June, 2000)

132 *Prayers for Iwo Jima,* Army physician 1st Lieutenant Kazuyoshi Morimoto,

1966 (Japanese Language)

133 Japanese language website, http://dolphy.jugem.jp/?month=201208

134 Iwao Yamada's combat record for March 25, 1945.

135 http://www.aramant.com/chuukou/page04_04.html

136 *Iwo Jima*, by Eric Hammel, p235.

137 *Blacks in the Marine Corps*, by Henry I. Shaw Jr and Ralph W. Donnelly. History and Museums Division, US Marine Corps, 1975.

138 Video interview from Japanese documentary on Iwo Jima survivors, "Senso Iyada." (Youtube)

139 *Victory in the Pacific 1945*, Samuel Eliot Morison, p.70

140 The author visited Iwo Jima with Jerry Yellin and his two sons in March 2010.

141 Phone conversation April 22, 2013. The author and Mr. Jerry Yellin first met on Guam in March 2010, during the annual visit to Iwo Jima.

142 *Iōjima ni Ikiru*, (To Live on Iwo Jima) by Shūji Ishii, published in 1982 by Kokushō Kankōkai Corp., Ltd., p. 59-62

143 imbd., p.68-70

144 Author's conversations with Edward Mervich from March 17-20, 2014, while visiting the islands of Guam and Iwo Jima.

145 Some of the details of Ōmagari's activities in April and May came from other interviews he had with Japanese authors, and from his appearance in Japanese documentaries.

146 Personal correspondence from Ivan Prall, August 2013.

147 Japanese TV documentary. http://www.youtube.com/watch?v=znYfjYF_4cs&feature=relmfu

148 Japanese TV documentary. http://www.youtube.com/watch?v=znYfjYF_4cs&feature=relmfu

149 Japanese NHK (PBS) documentary about Iwo Jima, "Sensō Iyada" (I Hate War).

150 Interview on Japanese televesion that can be seen on Youtube. http://www.youtube.com/watch?v=2VQKN_6DEXc&feature=endscreen&NR=1

151 Haruji Mita wrote of his experiences in the Japanese language book, 悲惨な攻防戦硫黄島-死から生への回帰道 *Hisan na Kōbōsen Iwōtō – Shi Kara Sei e no Kaikimichi* (*The Road Back from Death to Life, the Disastrous Defensive Battle of Iwo Jima*), 2008, Bungeisha Publishing.

152 On-line video interview recorded by "Japan Veterans Video Archive Project." http://www.jvvap.jp/mita_haruji_v.html

153 Japanese Documentary interview, http://www.youtube.com/watch?v=FyBhjQsX3ew

154 *Iwo Jima*, Newcomb, p. 259

155 According to James C. Naughton's, *Nisei Linguists*, the MIS Japanese language school students included Nisei volunteers and Americans of European Ancestry (AEA).

156 In his biography, *Chronicles of My Life, An American in the Heart of Japan*, (Columbia University Press New York, pp 42-47) Donald Keene states he and Lt Otis

Carey both worked in Hawaii as US Navy interrogators, but it seems that Keene didn't meet Satoru Ōmagari at that time because Keene was at sea from April –July, 1945, in support of the Okinawa invasion. Keene later became a professor at Columbia University, penned dozens of books about Japan, and took recently took on Japanese citizenship. He resides in Tokyo.

157 "William R. Gorham (1888–1949) and Japanese Industry," by Kawakami, Kenjiro (2002). *International Conference on Business & Technology Transfer*. ALSO see *Nihonjinn ni natta Americajin Gishi* (The American Engineer who Became a Japanese Citizen) *A Biography of William Gorham*, by Yoji Katsuragi, published in 1993 by Guranpuri Shuppan, Japan.

158 *Iōjima ni Ikiru*, (To Live on Iwo Jima) by Shūji Ishii, published in 1982 by Kokushō Kankōkai Corp., Ltd., p. 98-99

159 Report of Inspection, Japanese Prisoner of War Camp, Angel Island, by the International Committee of the Red Cross, and the Special War Problems Division, Department of State, September 16, 1944, R.G. 389, Modern Military Branch of the National Archivces, (MMB-NA)

160 Dave Smith & John Bland & Lee Schaeffer, http://www.schaeffersite.com/michaux/

161 US Army War College website, http://www.carlisle.army.mil/banner/article.cfm?id=683

162 *Iōjima ni Ikiru* (To Live on Iwo Jima), by Shūji Ishii, first published in 1946, then again in 1982 by Kokushō Kankōkai Corp., Ltd. The Pennsylvania POW camp experiences are outlined in p. 119- 126.

163 It is possible that some of Mr. Akikusa's memories have blurred since 1945. Some of his recollections from Pinegrove Furnace POW Camp (where there was only 1 Italian POW) and Fort Eustis POW Camp (where there were many Italian POWs). There might be some blurred edges and unintended crossover points. The author has used Akikusa's own POW record from 1945, his written and oral statements and background research to untangle disjointed memories.

164 *Iōjima ni Ikiru* (To Live on Iwo Jima), by Shūji Ishii, first published in 1946, then again in 1982 by Kokushō Kankōkai Corp., Ltd. p. 76-77

165 http://www.downloaddailymotion.com/video/0-the-capture-of-the-tachibana-maru.html

166 *Senso: The Japanese Remember the Pacific War: Letters to the Editor of Asahi Shimbun*, edited by Frank Gary and M.E. Sharpe, 1995 and 2007. Published by Pacific Basin Institute. P. 140

167 Corporal Toshiharu Takahashi's handwritten memoirs were posted by his grandson, Takahiro Fujiwara. http://www5f.biglobe.ne.jp/~iwojima/page4.html

168 Ōmagari thinks it might have been Pinegrove Furnace POW Camp.

169 *360,000 POWs the Hope of Germany*, by US Army Captain Robert Lowe Kunzig, is an article that appeared in "The American Magazine," 1946.

170 Since the Americans lacked both the personnel and the rear-area facilities to detain POWs in the Pacific area, the US War Department reached an agreement in September 1942 that nearly all POWs from the Pacific-except for those whose potential military intelligence value that necessitated their shipment to the United

States were to be handed over to Australia and New Zealand for detention. In return, the US helped shoulder the load of POW maintenance costs through lend-lease aid, and was responsible for repatriating POWs at the end of the war.

171 *360,000 POWs the Hope of Germany*, by US Army Captain Robert Lowe Kunzig, is an article that appeared in "The American Magazine," 1946. p. 89

172 *Iōjima ni Ikiru* (To Live on Iwo Jima), by Shūji Ishii, first published in 1946, then again in 1982 by Kokushō Kankōkai Corp., Ltd. p. 162-163

173 The very number of the Japanese POWs held in the US is in question according to official sources. The figures range from 569 (George G. Lewis and John Mewha, "History of Prisoner of War Utilization by the United States Army, 1776-1945," U.S. Dept. of the Army Pamphlet No. 20-213 [Washington, D.C., June 1955], to 3,260 POWs ("Investigations of the National War Effort," H. Rep. 728, 79 Cong., 1 sess., [June 12, 1945], 6). A detailed examination of the Records of the Provost Marshal General's Office (Record Group 389), at the Modern Military Branch of the National Archives, Washington, D.C. (MMB-NA), resulted in 5,424 Japanese POWs. Source: Japanese Prisoners of War by Arnold Krammer, Professor of History, Texas A & M University. Pacific Historical Review, Vol. 52, No. 1 (Feb. 1983), pp. 67-91

174 Japanese documentary interview, http://www.youtube.com/watch?v=FyBhjQsX3ew

175 Takeshi Shimono, 145th Infantry as interviewed by NHK regarding his experiences on Iwo Jima and what it was like to come back to Japan after being a Prisoner of War.
http://cgi2.nhk.or.jp/shogenarchives/shogen/movie.cgi?das_id=D0001100622_00000

176 The author has a photocopy of the original letter from Wachi to LtCol R.W. Hayward dated 11/10/1945.

177 Copies of report provided by Tom McLeod, author of *Always Ready, The Story of the United State's 147th Infantry Regiment. (1999)*

178 Provided by author and 147th Infantry historian, Tom McLeod.

Made in the USA
San Bernardino, CA
02 November 2014